55th Annual Meeting of the Association for Computational Linguistics (ACL 2017)

Student Research Workshop

Vancouver, Canada
30 July – 4 August 2017

ISBN: 978-1-5108-4569-5

ACL 2017

The 55th Annual Meeting of the
Association for Computational Linguistics

Proceedings of the Student Research Workshop

July 30 - August 4, 2017
Vancouver, Canada

Introduction

Welcome to the ACL 2017 Student Research Workshop!

The ACL 2017 Student Research Workshop (SRW) is a forum for student researchers in computational linguistics and natural language processing. The workshop provides a unique opportunity for student participants to present their work and receive valuable feedback from the international research community as well as from selected mentors.

Following the tradition of the previous years' student research workshops, we have two tracks: research papers and research proposals. The research paper track is a venue for Ph.D. students, Masters students, and advanced undergraduates to describe completed work or work-in-progress along with preliminary results. The research proposal track is offered for advanced Masters and Ph.D. students who have decided on a thesis topic and are interested in feedback on their proposal and ideas about future directions for their work.

We received in total 58 submissions: 16 research proposals and 42 research papers. We accepted 6 research proposals and 17 research papers, giving an acceptance rate of 40% overall. This year, all of the accepted papers will be presented as posters in an evening poster session during the main conference.

Mentoring is at the heart of the SRW. In keeping with previous years, students had the opportunity to participate in a pre-submission mentoring program prior to the submission deadline. This program offered students a chance to receive comments from an experienced researcher, in order to improve the quality of the writing and presentation before making their submission. Twenty-two authors participated in the pre-submission mentoring. In addition, authors of accepted SRW papers are matched with mentors who will meet with the students in person during the workshop. Each mentor prepares in-depth comments and questions prior to the student's presentation, and provides discussion and feedback during the workshop.

We are grateful for the support of the Don and Betty Walker Scholarship Fund and the National Science Foundation under award No. 1714855, which help support the travel expenses of workshop participants.

We would also like to thank our program committee members for their careful reviews of each paper, and all of our mentors for donating their time to provide feedback to our student authors. Thank you to our faculty advisors Cecilia Ovesdotter Alm, Marine Carpuat, and Mark Dredze for their essential advice and guidance, and to members of the ACL 2017 organizing committee, including Chris Callison-Burch, Min-Yen Kan, Regina Barzilay, Charley Chan, Christian Federmann and Priscilla Rasmussen, for their helpful support. Finally, thank you to our student participants!

Organizers:

Allyson Ettinger, University of Maryland
Spandana Gella, University of Edinburgh
Matthieu Labeau, University Paris-Saclay

Faculty Advisors:

Cecilia Ovesdotter Alm, Rochester Institute of Technology
Marine Carpuat, University of Maryland
Mark Dredze, Johns Hopkins University

Program Committee:

Alexandre Allauzen, University Paris-Saclay
Hadi Amiri, University of Maryland
Antonios Anastasopoulos, University of Notre Dame
Bharat Ram Ambati, Apple Inc.
Lauriane Aufrant, University Paris-Saclay
Timothy Baldwin, The University of Melbourne
Kalika Bali, Microsoft Research, India
Rachel Bawden, University Paris-Saclay
Julian Brooke, The University of Melbourne
John Carroll, University of Sussex
Danqi Chen, Stanford University
Wanxiang Che, Harbin Institute of Technology
David Chiang, University of Notre Dame
Kyunghyun Cho, New York University
Tejaswini Deoskar, University of Amsterdam
Long Duong, Voicebox Technologies
Lea Frermann, University of Edinburgh
Kevin Gimpel, Toyota Technological Institute at Chicago
Ralph Grishman, New York University
Alvin Grissom, University of Colorado
Jiang Guo, Harbin Institute of Technology
Xiaodong He, Microsoft Research, USA
Eduard Hovy, Carnegie Mellon University
Mohit Iyyer, University of Maryland
Kristiina Jokinen, University of Cambridge
Daisuke Kawahara, Kyoto University
Eric Laporte, University Paris-Est Marne-la-Vallée
Haizhou Li, A*STAR Institute for Infocomm Research
Junyi Jessy Li, University of Pennsylvania
Zhenghua Li, Soochow University
Annie Louis, University of Essex
Julie Medero, Harvey Mudd College
Mitchell Marcus, University of Pennsylvania
Prashant Mathur, Ebay Research
Diana McCarthy, University of Cambridge
Saif Mohammad, National Research Council Canada

Taesun Moon, IBM Research
Maria Nadejde, University of Edinburgh
Karthik Narasimhan, Massachusetts Institute of Technology
Shashi Narayanan, University of Edinburgh
Graham Neubig, Carnegie Mellon University
Yannick Parmentier, University of Orléans
Gerald Penn, University of Toronto
Emily Pitler, Google Research, USA
Massimo Poesio, University of Essex
Emily Prud'hommeaux, Rochester Institute of Technology
Avinesh PVS, Technishe Universität Darmstadt
Siva Reddy, University of Edinburgh
Brian Roark, Google Research, USA
Michael Roth, University of Illinois Urbana-Champaign
Markus Saers, Hong Kong University of Science and Technology
David Schlangen, Bielefeld University
Carina Silberer, Saarland University
Ekaterina Shutova, University of Cambridge
Sunayana Sitaram, Microsoft Research, India
Kevin Small, Amazon
Richard Sproat, Google Research, USA
Christoph Teichmann, University of Potsdam
Sowmya Vajjala, Iowa State University
Marlies van der Wees, University of Amsterdam
William Yang Wang, Carnegie Mellon University
Bonnie Webber, University of Edinburgh
Alessandra Zarcone, Saarland University
Meishan Zhang, Singapore University of Technology and Design
Yuan Zhang, Massachusetts Institute of Technology
Yue Zhang, Singapore University of Technology and Design

Table of Contents

Computational Characterization of Mental States: A Natural Language Processing Approach
Facundo Carrillo 1

Improving Distributed Representations of Tweets - Present and Future
Ganesh Jawahar 4

Bilingual Word Embeddings with Bucketed CNN for Parallel Sentence Extraction
Jeenu Grover and Pabitra Mitra 11

nQuery - A Natural Language Statement to SQL Query Generator
Nandan Sukthankar, Sanket Maharnawar, Pranay Deshmukh, Yashodhara Haribhakta and Vibhavari
Kamble 17

V for Vocab: An Intelligent Flashcard Application
Nihal V. Nayak, Tanmay Chinchore, Aishwarya Hanumanth Rao, Shane Michael Martin, Sagar
Nagaraj Simha, G. M. Lingaraju and H. S. Jamadagni 24

Are You Asking the Right Questions? Teaching Machines to Ask Clarification Questions
Sudha Rao 30

Building a Non-Trivial Paraphrase Corpus Using Multiple Machine Translation Systems
Yui Suzuki, Tomoyuki Kajiwara and Mamoru Komachi 36

Segmentation Guided Attention Networks for Visual Question Answering
Vasu Sharma, Ankita Bishnu and Labhesh Patel 43

*Text-based Speaker Identification on Multiparty Dialogues Using Multi-document Convolutional Neural
Networks*
Kaixin Ma, Catherine Xiao and Jinho D. Choi 49

Variation Autoencoder Based Network Representation Learning for Classification
Hang Li, Haozheng Wang, Zhenglu Yang and Masato Odagaki 56

Blind Phoneme Segmentation With Temporal Prediction Errors
Paul Michel, Okko Räsänen, Roland Thiolliere and Emmanuel Dupoux 62

Automatic Generation of Jokes in Hindi
Srishti Aggarwal and Radhika Mamidi 69

Word Embedding for Response-To-Text Assessment of Evidence
Haoran Zhang and Diane Litman 75

Domain Specific Automatic Question Generation from Text
Katira Soleymanzadeh 82

SoccEval: An Annotation Schema for Rating Soccer Players
Jose Ramirez, Matthew Garber and Xinhao Wang 89

Accent Adaptation for the Air Traffic Control Domain
Matthew Garber, Meital Singer and Christopher Ward 95

Generating Steganographic Text with LSTMs
Tina Fang, Martin Jaggi and Katerina Argyraki 100

Predicting Depression for Japanese Blog Text
    Misato Hiraga 107

Fast Forward Through Opportunistic Incremental Meaning Representation Construction
    Petr Babkin and Sergei Nirenburg 114

Modeling Situations in Neural Chat Bots
    Shoetsu Sato, Naoki Yoshinaga, Masashi Toyoda and Masaru Kitsuregawa 120

An Empirical Study on End-to-End Sentence Modelling
    Kurt Junshean Espinosa 128

Varying Linguistic Purposes of Emoji in (Twitter) Context
    Noa Naaman, Hannah Provenza and Orion Montoya 136

Negotiation of Antibiotic Treatment in Medical Consultations: A Corpus Based Study
    Nan Wang 142

Conference Program

Monday July 31 - Evening poster session

Computational Characterization of Mental States: A Natural Language Processing Approach
Facundo Carrillo

Improving Distributed Representations of Tweets - Present and Future
Ganesh Jawahar

Bilingual Word Embeddings with Bucketed CNN for Parallel Sentence Extraction
Jeenu Grover and Pabitra Mitra

nQuery - A Natural Language Statement to SQL Query Generator
Nandan Sukthankar, Sanket Maharnawar, Pranay Deshmukh, Yashodhara Haribhakta and Vibhavari Kamble

V for Vocab: An Intelligent Flashcard Application
Nihal V. Nayak, Tanmay Chinchore, Aishwarya Hanumanth Rao, Shane Michael Martin, Sagar Nagaraj Simha, G. M. Lingaraju and H. S. Jamadagni

Are You Asking the Right Questions? Teaching Machines to Ask Clarification Questions
Sudha Rao

Building a Non-Trivial Paraphrase Corpus Using Multiple Machine Translation Systems
Yui Suzuki, Tomoyuki Kajiwara and Mamoru Komachi

Segmentation Guided Attention Networks for Visual Question Answering
Vasu Sharma, Ankita Bishnu and Labhesh Patel

Text-based Speaker Identification on Multiparty Dialogues Using Multi-document Convolutional Neural Networks
Kaixin Ma, Catherine Xiao and Jinho D. Choi

Variation Autoencoder Based Network Representation Learning for Classification
Hang Li, Haozheng Wang, Zhenglu Yang and Masato Odagaki

Blind Phoneme Segmentation With Temporal Prediction Errors
Paul Michel, Okko Räsänen, Roland Thiolliere and Emmanuel Dupoux

Automatic Generation of Jokes in Hindi
Srishti Aggarwal and Radhika Mamidi

Word Embedding for Response-To-Text Assessment of Evidence
Haoran Zhang and Diane Litman

Domain Specific Automatic Question Generation from Text
Katira Soleymanzadeh

SoccEval: An Annotation Schema for Rating Soccer Players
Jose Ramirez, Matthew Garber and Xinhao Wang

Accent Adaptation for the Air Traffic Control Domain
Matthew Garber, Meital Singer and Christopher Ward

Generating Steganographic Text with LSTMs
Tina Fang, Martin Jaggi and Katerina Argyraki

Predicting Depression for Japanese Blog Text
Misato Hiraga

Fast Forward Through Opportunistic Incremental Meaning Representation Construction
Petr Babkin and Sergei Nirenburg

Modeling Situations in Neural Chat Bots
Shoetsu Sato, Naoki Yoshinaga, Masashi Toyoda and Masaru Kitsuregawa

An Empirical Study on End-to-End Sentence Modelling
Kurt Junshean Espinosa

Varying Linguistic Purposes of Emoji in (Twitter) Context
Noa Naaman, Hannah Provenza and Orion Montoya

Negotiation of Antibiotic Treatment in Medical Consultations: A Corpus Based Study
Nan Wang

Computational characterization of mental states: A natural language processing approach

Facundo Carrillo
Computer Science Dept, School of Science,
Buenos Aires University
fcarrillo@dc.uba.ar

Abstract

Psychiatry is an area of medicine that strongly bases its diagnoses on the psychiatrists subjective appreciation. The task of diagnosis loosely resembles the common pipelines used in supervised learning schema. Therefore, we propose to augment the psychiatrists diagnosis toolbox with an artificial intelligence system based on natural language processing and machine learning algorithms. This approach has been validated in many works in which the performance of the diagnosis has been increased with the use of automatic classification.

1 Introduction

Psychiatry is an area of medicine that strongly bases its diagnoses on the psychiatrists subjective appreciation. More precisely, speech is used almost exclusively as a window to the patients mind. Few other cues are available to objectively justify a diagnostic, unlike what happens in other disciplines which count on laboratory tests or imaging procedures, such as X-rays. Daily practice is based on the use of semi-structured interviews and standardized tests to build the diagnoses, heavily relying on her personal experience. This methodology has a big problem: diagnoses are commonly validated a posteriori in function of how the pharmacological treatment works. This validation cannot be done until months after the start of the treatment and, if the patient condition does not improve, the psychiatrist often changes the diagnosis and along with the pharmacological treatment. This delay prolongs the patient's suffering until the correct diagnosis is found. According to NIMH, more than 1% and 2 % of US population is affected by Schizophrenia and Bipolar Disorder,

respectively. Moreover, the WHO reported that the global cost of mental illness reached \$2.5T in 2010 (Mathers et al., 2008) .

The task of diagnosis, largely simplified, mainly consists of understanding the mind state through the extraction of patterns from the patient's speech and finding the best matching pathology in the standard diagnostic literature. This pipeline, consisting of extracting patterns and then classifying them, loosely resembles the common pipelines used in supervised learning schema. Therefore, we propose to augment the psychiatrists diagnosis toolbox with an artificial intelligence system based on natural language processing and machine learning algorithms. The proposed system would assist in the diagnostic using a patients speech as input. The understanding and insights obtained from customizing these systems to specific pathologies is likely to be more broadly applicable to other NLP tasks, therefore we expect to make contributions not only for psychiatry but also within the computer science community. We intend to develop these ideas and evaluate them beyond the lab setting. Our end goal is to make it possible for a practitioner to integrate our tools into her daily practice with minimal effort.

2 Methodology

In order to complement the manual diagnosis it is necessary to have samples from real patients. To collect these samples, we have ongoing collaborations with different psychiatric institutions from many countries: United States, Colombia, Brazil and Argentina. These centers provide us with access to the relevant patient data and we jointly collaborate testing different protocols in a variety languages. We have already started studies with two pathologies: Schizophrenia and Bipolar Disorder.

Regarding our technical setup, we are using and

Proceedings of the 55th Annual Meeting of the Association for Computational Linguistics- Student Research Workshop, pages 1–3
Vancouver, Canada, July 30 - August 4, 2017. ©2017 Association for Computational Linguistics
https://doi.org/10.18653/v1/P17-3001

developing tools to capture different characteristics of the speech. In all cases, we work with high-quality transcriptions of speech. Our experiments are focused on analyzing different aspects of the speech: 1) Grammatical-morphological changes based on topology of Speech Graphs. 2) Coherence Algorithm: Semantic coherence using proximity in semantic embeddings. 3) Changes in Emotional language and other semantic categories

3 Preliminary Results

Many groups have already validated this paradigm (Roark et al., 2011; Fraser et al., 2014; Resnik et al., 2013; Lehr et al., 2012; Fraser et al., 2016; Mitchell et al., 2015). First, Speech Graphs has been used in different pathologies (schizophrenic and bipolar), results are published in (Carrillo et al., 2014; Mota et al., 2014, 2012). In (Carrillo et al., 2014), the autors can automatically diagnose based on the graphs with an accuracy greater than 85%. This approach consists in modeling the language, or a transformation of it (for example the part of speech symbols of a text), as a graph. With this new representation the authors use graph topology features (average grade of nodes, number of loops, centrality, etc) as features of patient speech. Regarding coherence analysis, some researchers has developed an algorithm that quantifies the semantic divergence of the speech. To do that, they used semantic embeddings (like Latent Semantic Analysis(Landauer and Dumais, 1997), Word2vec(Mikolov et al., 2013), or Twitter Semantic Similarity(Carrillo et al., 2015)) to measure when consecutive sentences of spontaneous speech differ too much. The authors used this algorithm, combined with machine learning classifiers, to predict which high-risk subjects would have their first psychotic episode within 2 years (with 100% accuracy) (Bedi et al., 2015). The latter result was very relevant because it presented evidence that this automatic diagnostic methodology could not only perform at levels comparable to experts but also, under some conditions, even outperform experts (classical medical tests achieved 40% of accuracy). Dr. Insel, former director of National Institute of Mental Health cited this work in his blog on his post: Look who is getting into mental health research as one.

Regarding Emotional language, some researchers presented evidence of how some endocrine regulations change the language. This methods are based on quantifying different emotional levels. This methodology has been used to diagnose depression and postpartum depression by Eric Horvitz (De Choudhury et al., 2013). Others researchers also have used this method to diagnose patients with Parkinsons disease(García et al., 2016).

4 Current Work

Currently, we are working on the coherence algorithm (Bedi et al., 2015), understanding some properties and its potential applications, such as automatic composition of text and feature extraction for bot detection. Meanwhile, we are receiving new speech samples from 3 different mental health hospitals in Argentina provided by patients with new pathologies like frontotemporal dementia and anxiety. We are also building methods to detect depression in young patients using the change of emotions in time.

5 Future work

The tasks for the following 2/3 years are: 1) Improve implementations of developed algorithms and make them open source. 2) Integrate the different pipelines of features extraction and classification to generate a generic classifier for several pathologies. 3) Build a mobile application for medical use (for this aim, Google has awarded our project with the Google Research Awards for Latin America 2016: Prognosis in a Box: Computational Characterization of Mental State). At the moment the data is recorded and then transcribed by an external doctor. We want a full automatic procedure, from the moment when the doctor performs the interview to the moment when she receives the results. 4) Write the PhD thesis.

References

Gillinder Bedi, Facundo Carrillo, Guillermo A Cecchi, Diego Fernández Slezak, Mariano Sigman, Natália B Mota, Sidarta Ribeiro, Daniel C Javitt, Mauro Copelli, and Cheryl M Corcoran. 2015. Automated analysis of free speech predicts psychosis onset in high-risk youths. *npj Schizophrenia* 1:15030.

Facundo Carrillo, Guillermo A Cecchi, Mariano Sigman, and Diego Fernández Slezak. 2015. Fast distributed dynamics of semantic networks via social media. *Computational intelligence and neuroscience* 2015:50.

Facundo Carrillo, Natalia Mota, Mauro Copelli, Sidarta Ribeiro, Mariano Sigman, Guillermo Cecchi, and Diego Fernandez Slezak. 2014. Automated speech analysis for psychosis evaluation. In *International Workshop on Machine Learning and Interpretation in Neuroimaging*. Springer, pages 31–39.

Munmun De Choudhury, Michael Gamon, Scott Counts, and Eric Horvitz. 2013. Predicting depression via social media. In *ICWSM*. page 2.

Kathleen C Fraser, Jed A Meltzer, Naida L Graham, Carol Leonard, Graeme Hirst, Sandra E Black, and Elizabeth Rochon. 2014. Automated classification of primary progressive aphasia subtypes from narrative speech transcripts. *Cortex* 55:43–60.

Kathleen C Fraser, Jed A Meltzer, and Frank Rudzicz. 2016. Linguistic features identify alzheimers disease in narrative speech. *Journal of Alzheimer's Disease* 49(2):407–422.

Adolfo M García, Facundo Carrillo, Juan Rafael Orozco-Arroyave, Natalia Trujillo, Jesús F Vargas Bonilla, Sol Fittipaldi, Federico Adolfi, Elmar Nöth, Mariano Sigman, Diego Fernández Slezak, et al. 2016. How language flows when movements dont: An automated analysis of spontaneous discourse in parkinsons disease. *Brain and Language* 162:19–28.

Thomas K Landauer and Susan T Dumais. 1997. A solution to plato's problem: The latent semantic analysis theory of acquisition, induction, and representation of knowledge. *Psychological review* 104(2):211.

Maider Lehr, Emily Prud'hommeaux, Izhak Shafran, and Brian Roark. 2012. Fully automated neuropsychological assessment for detecting mild cognitive impairment. In *Thirteenth Annual Conference of the International Speech Communication Association*.

C Mathers, T Boerma, and D Ma Fat. 2008. The global burden of disease: 2004 update: World health organisation .

Tomas Mikolov, Ilya Sutskever, Kai Chen, Greg S Corrado, and Jeff Dean. 2013. Distributed representations of words and phrases and their compositionality. In *Advances in neural information processing systems*. pages 3111–3119.

Margaret Mitchell, Kristy Hollingshead, and Glen Coppersmith. 2015. Quantifying the language of schizophrenia in social media. In *Proceedings of the 2015 Annual Conference of the North American Chapter of the Association for Computational Linguistics: Human Language Technologies (NAACL HLT)*. page 11.

Natália B Mota, Raimundo Furtado, Pedro PC Maia, Mauro Copelli, and Sidarta Ribeiro. 2014. Graph analysis of dream reports is especially informative about psychosis. *Scientific reports* 4:3691.

Natalia B Mota, Nivaldo AP Vasconcelos, Nathalia Lemos, Ana C Pieretti, Osame Kinouchi, Guillermo A Cecchi, Mauro Copelli, and Sidarta Ribeiro. 2012. Speech graphs provide a quantitative measure of thought disorder in psychosis. *PloS one* 7(4):e34928.

Philip Resnik, Anderson Garron, and Rebecca Resnik. 2013. Using topic modeling to improve prediction of neuroticism and depression. In *Proceedings of the 2013 Conference on Empirical Methods in Natural*. Association for Computational Linguistics, pages 1348–1353.

Brian Roark, Margaret Mitchell, John-Paul Hosom, Kristy Hollingshead, and Jeffrey Kaye. 2011. Spoken language derived measures for detecting mild cognitive impairment. *IEEE transactions on audio, speech, and language processing* 19(7):2081–2090.

Improving Distributed Representations of Tweets - Present and Future

Ganesh Jawahar
Information Retrieval and Extraction Laboratory
IIIT Hyderabad
Telangana, India
ganesh.j@research.iiit.ac.in

Abstract

Unsupervised representation learning for tweets is an important research field which helps in solving several business applications such as sentiment analysis, hashtag prediction, paraphrase detection and microblog ranking. A good tweet representation learning model must handle the idiosyncratic nature of tweets which poses several challenges such as short length, informal words, unusual grammar and misspellings. However, there is a lack of prior work which surveys the representation learning models with a focus on tweets. In this work, we organize the models based on its objective function which aids the understanding of the literature. We also provide interesting future directions, which we believe are fruitful in advancing this field by building high-quality tweet representation learning models.

1   Introduction

Twitter is a widely used microblogging platform, where users post and interact with messages, "tweets". Understanding the semantic representation of tweets can benefit a plethora of applications such as sentiment analysis (Ren et al., 2016; Giachanou and Crestani, 2016), hashtag prediction (Dhingra et al., 2016), paraphrase detection (Vosoughi et al., 2016) and microblog ranking (Huang et al., 2013; Shen et al., 2014). However, tweets are difficult to model as they pose several challenges such as short length, informal words, unusual grammar and misspellings. Recently, researchers are focusing on leveraging unsupervised representation learning methods based on neural networks to solve this problem. Once these representations are learned, we can use off-

the-shelf predictors taking the representation as input to solve the downstream task (Bengio, 2013a; Bengio et al., 2013b). These methods enjoy several advantages: (1) they are cheaper to train, as they work with unlabelled data, (2) they reduce the dependence on domain level experts, and (3) they are highly effective across multiple applications, in practice.

Despite this, there is a lack of prior work which surveys the tweet-specific unsupervised representation learning models. In this work, we attempt to fill this gap by investigating the models in an organized fashion. Specifically, we group the models based on the objective function it optimizes. We believe this work can aid the understanding of the existing literature. We conclude the paper by presenting interesting future research directions, which we believe are fruitful in advancing this field by building high-quality tweet representation learning models.

2   Unsupervised Tweet Representation Models

There are various models spanning across different model architectures and objective functions in the literature to compute tweet representation in an unsupervised fashion. These models work in a semi-supervised way - the representations generated by the model is fed to an off-the-shelf predictor like Support Vector Machines (SVM) to solve a particular downstream task. These models span across a wide variety of neural network based architectures including average of word vectors, convolutional-based, recurrent-based and so on. We believe that the performance of these models is highly dependent on the objective function it optimizes – predicting adjacent word (within-tweet relationships), adjacent tweet (inter-tweet relationships), the tweet itself (autoencoder), mod-

4

Proceedings of the 55th Annual Meeting of the Association for Computational Linguistics- Student Research Workshop, pages 4–10
Vancouver, Canada, July 30 - August 4, 2017. ©2017 Association for Computational Linguistics
https://doi.org/10.18653/v1/P17-3002

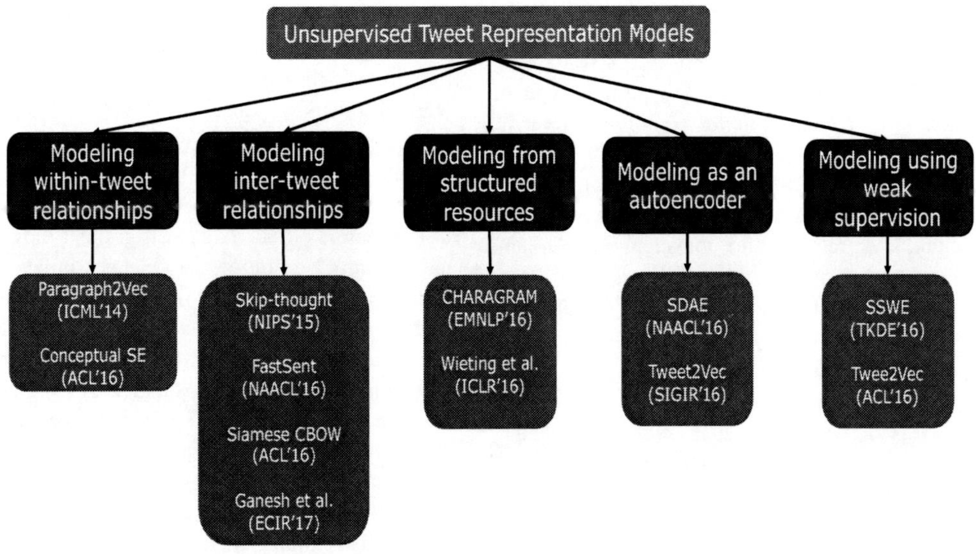

Figure 1: Unsupervised Tweet Representation Models Hierarchy based on Optimized Objective Function

eling from structured resources like paraphrase databases and weak supervision. In this section, we provide the first of its kind survey of the recent tweet-specific unsupervised models in an organized fashion to understand the literature. Specifically, we categorize each model based on the optimized objective function as shown in Figure 1. Next, we study each category one by one.

2.1 Modeling within-tweet relationships

Motivation: Every tweet is assumed to have a latent topic vector, which influences the distribution of the words in the tweet. For example, though the appearance of the phrase *catch the ball* is frequent in the corpus, if we know that the topic of a tweet is about "technology", we can expect words such as *bug* or *exception* after the word *catch* (ignoring *the*) instead of the word *ball* since *catch the bug/exception* is more plausible under the topic "technology". On the other hand, if the topic of the tweet is about "sports", then we can expect *ball* after *catch*. These intuitions indicate that the prediction of neighboring words for a given word strongly relies on the tweet also.

Models: (Le and Mikolov, 2014)'s work is the first to exploit this idea to compute distributed document representations that are good at predicting words in the document. They propose two models: PV-DM and PV-DBOW, that are extensions of Continuous Bag Of Words (CBOW) and Skip-

gram model variants of the popular Word2Vec model (Mikolov et al., 2013) respectively – PV-DM inserts an additional document token (which can be thought of as another word) which is shared across all contexts generated from the same document; PV-DBOW attempts to predict the sampled words from the document given the document representation. Although originally employed for paragraphs and documents, these models work better than the traditional models: BOW (Harris, 1954) and LDA (Blei et al., 2003) for tweet classification and microblog retrieval tasks (Wang et al., 2016). The authors in (Wang et al., 2016) make the PV-DM and PV-DBOW models *concept-aware* (a rich semantic signal from a tweet) by augmenting two features: attention over contextual words and conceptual tweet embedding, which jointly exploit concept-level senses of tweets to compute better representations. Both the discussed works have the following characteristics: (1) they use a shallow architecture, which enables fast training, (2) computing representations for test tweets requires computing gradients, which is time-consuming for real-time Twitter applications, and (3) most importantly, they fail to exploit textual information from related tweets that can bear salient semantic signals.

2.2 Modeling inter-tweet relationships

Motivation: To capture rich tweet semantics, researchers are attempting to exploit a type of *sentence-level Distributional Hypothesis* (Harris, 1954; Polajnar et al., 2015). The idea is to infer the tweet representation from the content of adjacent tweets in a related stream like users' Twitter timeline, topical, retweet and conversational stream. This approach significantly alleviates the context insufficiency problem caused due to the ambiguous and short nature of tweets (Ren et al., 2016; Ganesh et al., 2017).

Models: Skip-thought vectors (Kiros et al., 2015) (STV) is a widely popular sentence encoder, which is trained to predict adjacent sentences in the book corpus (Zhu et al., 2015). Although the testing is cheap as it involves a cheap forward propagation of the test sentence, STV is very slow to train thanks to its complicated model architecture. To combat this computational inefficiency, FastSent (Hill et al., 2016) propose a simple additive (log-linear) sentence model, which predicts adjacent sentences (represented as BOW) taking the BOW representation of some sentence in context. This model can exploit the same signal, but at a much lower computational expense. Parallel to this work, Siamase CBOW (Kenter et al., 2016) develop a model which directly compares the BOW representation of two sentence to bring the embeddings of a sentence closer to its adjacent sentence, away from a randomly occurring sentence in the corpus. For FastSent and Siamese CBOW, the test sentence representation is a simple average of word vectors obtained after training. Both of these models are general purpose sentence representation models trained on book corpus, yet give a competitive performance over previous models on the tweet semantic similarity computation task. (Ganesh et al., 2017)'s model attempt to exploit these signals directly from Twitter. With the help of attention technique and learned user representation, this log-linear model is able to capture salient semantic information from chronologically adjacent tweets of a target tweet in users' Twitter timeline.

2.3 Modeling from structured resources

Motivation: In recent times, building representation models based on supervision from richly structured resources such as Paraphrase Database (PPDB) (Ganitkevitch et al., 2013) (containing noisy phrase pairs) has yielded high quality sentence representations. These methods work by maximizing the similarity of the sentences in the learned semantic space.

Models: *CHARAGRAM* (Wieting et al., 2016a) embeds textual sequences by learning a character-based compositional model that involves addition of the vectors of its character n-grams followed by an elementwise nonlinearity. This simpler architecture trained on PPDB is able to beat models with complex architectures like CNN, LSTM on SemEval 2015 Twitter textual similarity task by a large margin. This result emphasizes the importance of character-level models that address differences due to spelling variation and word choice. The authors in their subsequent work (Wieting et al., 2016b) conduct a comprehensive analysis of models spanning the range of complexity from word averaging to LSTMs for its ability to do transfer and supervised learning after optimizing a margin based loss on PPDB. For transfer learning, they find models based on word averaging perform well on both the in-domain and out-of-domain textual similarity tasks, beating LSTM model by a large margin. On the other hand, the word averaging models perform well for both sentence similarity and textual entailment tasks, outperforming the LSTM. However, for sentiment classification task, they find LSTM (trained on PPDB) to beat the averaging models to establish a new state of the art. The above results suggest that structured resources play a vital role in computing general-purpose embeddings useful in downstream applications.

2.4 Modeling as an autoencoder

Motivation: The *autoencoder* based approach learns latent (or compressed) representation by reconstructing its own input. Since textual data like tweets contain discrete input signals, *sequence-to-sequence models* (Sutskever et al., 2014) like STV can be used to build the solution. The encoder model which encodes the input tweet can typically be a CNN (Kim, 2014), recurrent models like RNN, GRU, LSTM (Karpathy et al., 2015) or memory networks (Sukhbaatar et al., 2015). The decoder model which generates the output tweet can typically be a recurrent model that predicts a output token at every time step.

Models: Sequential Denoising Autoencoders (SDAE) (Hill et al., 2016) is a LSTM-based sequence-to-sequence model, which is trained to recover the original data from the corrupted version. SDAE produces robust representations by learning to represent the data in terms of features that explain its important factors of variation. Tweet2Vec (Vosoughi et al., 2016) is a recent model which uses a character-level CNN-LSTM encoder-decoder architecture trained to construct the input tweet directly. This model outperforms competitive models that work on word-level like PV-DM, PV-DBOW on semantic similarity computation and sentiment classification tasks, thereby showing that the character-level nature of Tweet2Vec is best-suited to deal with the noise and idiosyncrasies of tweets. Tweet2Vec controls the generalization error by using a data augmentation technique, wherein tweets are replicated and some of the words in the replicated tweets are replaced with their synonyms. Both SDAE and Tweet2Vec has the advantage that they don't need a coherent inter-sentence narrative (like STV), which is hard to obtain in Twitter.

2.5 Modeling using weak supervision

Motivation: In a weakly supervised setup, we create labels for a tweet automatically and predict them to learn potentially sophisticated models than those obtained by unsupervised learning alone. Examples of labels include sentiment of the overall tweet, words like hashtag present in the tweet and so on. This technique can create a *huge* labeled dataset especially for building data-hungry, sophisticated deep learning models.

Models: (Tang et al., 2016) learns sentiment-specific word embedding (SSWE), which encodes the polarity information in the word representations so that words with contrasting polarities and similar syntactic context (like *good* and *bad*) are pushed away from each other in the semantic space that it learns. SSWE utilizes the massive distant-supervised tweets collected by positive and negative emoticons to build a powerful tweet representation, which are shown to be useful in tasks such as sentiment classification and word similarity computation in sentiment lexicon. (Dhingra et al., 2016) observes that *hashtags* in tweets can be considered as topics and hence tweets with similar hashtags must come closer to each other. Their model predicts the hashtags by using a Bi-GRU layer to embed the tweets from its characters. Due to subword modeling, such character-level models can approximate the representations for rare words and new words (words not seen during training) in the test tweets really well. This model outperforms the word-level baselines for hashtag prediction task, thereby concluding that exploring character-level models for tweets is a worthy research direction to pursue. Both these works fail to study the model's generality (Weston et al., 2014), i.e., the ability of the model to transfer the learned representations to diverse tasks.

3 Future Directions

In this section we present the future research directions which we believe can be worth pursuing to generate high quality tweet embeddings.

- (Ren et al., 2016) propose a supervised neural network utilizing contextualized features from conversation, author and topic based context about a target tweet to perform well in classification of tweet. Apart from (Ganesh et al., 2017)'s work which utilizes author context, there is no other work which builds unsupervised tweet representation model on Twitter-specific contexts such as conversation and topical streams. We believe such a solution directly exploits semantic signals (or nuances) from Twitter, unlike STV or Siamese CBOW which are trained on books corpus.

- (dos Santos and Gatti, 2014) propose a supervised, hybrid model exploiting both the character and word level information for Twitter sentiment analysis task. Since the settings when the character level model beats the word level model is not well understood yet, we believe it would be interesting to explore such a hybrid compositional model to build unsupervised tweet representations.

- Twitter provides a platform for the users to interact with other users. To the best of our knowledge, there is no related work that computes unsupervised tweet representation by exploiting the user profile attributes like profile picture, user biography and set of followers, and social interactions like retweet context (set of surrounding tweets in a users retweet stream) and favorite context (set of surrounding tweets in a users favorite tweet stream).

- DSSM (Huang et al., 2013; Shen et al., 2014) propose a family of deep models that are trained to maximize the relevance of clicked documents given a query. Such a ranking loss function helps the model cater to a wide variety of applications[1] such as web search ranking, ad selection/relevance, question answering, knowledge inference and machine translation. We observe such a loss function has not been explored for building unsupervised tweet representations. We believe employing a ranking loss directly on tweets using a large scale microblog dataset[2] can result in representations which can be useful to Twitter applications beyond those studied in the tweet representation learning literature.

- Linguists assume that language is best understood as a hierarchical tree of phrases, rather than a flat sequence of words or characters. It's difficult to get the syntactic trees for tweets as most of them are not grammatically correct. The average of word vectors model has the most simplest compositional architecture with no additional parameters, yet displays a strong performance outperforming complex architectures such as CNN, LSTM and so on for several downstream applications (Wieting et al., 2016a,b). We believe a theoretical understanding of why word averaging models perform well can help in embracing these models by linguists.

- Models in (Wieting et al., 2016a,b) learn from noisy phrase pairs of PPDB. Note that the source of the underlying texts is completely different from Twitter. It can be interesting to see the effectiveness of such models when directly trained on structural resources from Twitter like Twitter Paraphrase Corpus (Xu et al., 2014). The main challenge with this approach is the small size of the annotated Twitter resources, which can encourage models like (Arora et al., 2017) that work well even when the training data is scarce or nonexistent.

- Tweets mostly have an accompanying image which sometimes has visual correspondence with its textual content (Chen et al., 2013; Wang et al., 2014) ('visual' tweet). To the best of our knowledge, there is no work which explores the following question: *can we build multimodal representations for tweets accompanying correlated visual content and compare with traditional benchmarks?*. We can leverage insights from multimodal skip-gram model (Lazaridou et al., 2015) which builds multimodally-enhanced word vectors that perform well in the traditional semantic benchmarks. However, it's hard to detect visual tweets and learning from a non-visual tweet can degrade its tweet representation. It would be interesting to see if a dispersion metric (Kiela et al., 2014) for tweets can be explored to overcome this problem of building a nondegradable, improved tweet representation.

- Interpreting the tweet representations to unearth the encoded features responsible for its performance on a downstream task is an important, but a less studied research area. (Ganesh et al., 2016)'s work is the first to open the blackbox of vector embeddings for tweets. They propose elementary property prediction tasks which predicts the accuracy to which a given tweet representation encodes the elementary property (like slang words, hashtags, mentions, etc). The main drawback of the work is that they fail to correlate their study with downstream applications. We believe performing such a correlation study can clearly highlight the set of elementary features behind the performance of a particular representation model over other for a given downstream task.

4 Conclusion

In this work we study the problem of learning unsupervised tweet representations. We believe our survey of the existing works based on the objective function can give vital perspectives to researchers and aid their understanding of the field. We also believe the future research directions studied in this work can help in breaking the barriers in building high quality, general purpose tweet representation models.

---

[1] https://www.microsoft.com/en-us/research/project/dssm/

[2] http://trec.nist.gov/

References

Sanjeev Arora, Yingyu Liang, and Tengyu Ma. 2017. A simple but tough-to-beat baseline for sentence embeddings. *CoRR* .

Yoshua Bengio. 2013a. Deep Learning of Representations: Looking Forward. In *Proc. of the 1st Intl. Conf. on Statistical Language and Speech Processing.* pages 1–37.

Yoshua Bengio, Aaron C. Courville, and Pascal Vincent. 2013b. Representation Learning: A Review and New Perspectives. *IEEE Transactions on Pattern Analysis and Machine Intelligence* 35(8):1798–1828.

David M. Blei, Andrew Y. Ng, and Michael I. Jordan. 2003. Latent Dirichlet Allocation. *Journal of Machine Learning Research* 3:993–1022.

Tao Chen, Dongyuan Lu, Min-Yen Kan, and Peng Cui. 2013. Understanding and classifying image tweets. In *ACM Multimedia Conference, MM '13.* pages 781–784.

Bhuwan Dhingra, Zhong Zhou, Dylan Fitzpatrick, Michael Muehl, and William W. Cohen. 2016. Tweet2Vec: Character-Based Distributed Representations for Social Media. In *Proc. of the 54th Annual Meeting of the Association for Computational Linguistics.*

Cícero Nogueira dos Santos and Maira Gatti. 2014. Deep convolutional neural networks for sentiment analysis of short texts. In 25th *Intl. Conf. on Computational Linguistics.* pages 69–78.

J Ganesh, Manish Gupta, and Vasudeva Varma. 2016. Interpreting the syntactic and social elements of the tweet representations via elementary property prediction tasks. *CoRR* abs/1611.04887.

J Ganesh, Manish Gupta, and Vasudeva Varma. 2017. Improving tweet representations using temporal and user context. In *Advances in Information Retrieval - 39th European Conference on IR Research, ECIR.* pages 575–581.

Juri Ganitkevitch, Benjamin Van Durme, and Chris Callison-Burch. 2013. PPDB: the paraphrase database. In *Proc. of conf. of the North American Chapter of the Association of Computational Linguistics.* pages 758–764.

Anastasia Giachanou and Fabio Crestani. 2016. Like it or not: A Survey of Twitter Sentiment Analysis Methods. *ACM Computing Surveys (CSUR)* 49(2):28.

Zellig S Harris. 1954. Distributional Structure. *Word* 10(2-3):146–162.

Felix Hill, Kyunghyun Cho, and Anna Korhonen. 2016. Learning Distributed Representations of Sentences from Unlabelled Data. In *Proc. of the Conf. of the North American Chapter of the Association for Computational Linguistics: Human Language Technologies.* pages 1367–1377.

Po-Sen Huang, Xiaodong He, Jianfeng Gao, Li Deng, Alex Acero, and Larry P. Heck. 2013. Learning Deep Structured Semantic Models for Web Search using Clickthrough Data. In *Proc. of the 22nd ACM Intl. Conf. on Information and Knowledge Management.* pages 2333–2338.

Andrej Karpathy, Justin Johnson, and Fei-Fei Li. 2015. Visualizing and understanding recurrent networks. *CoRR* abs/1506.02078.

Tom Kenter, Alexey Borisov, and Maarten de Rijke. 2016. Siamese CBOW: Optimizing Word Embeddings for Sentence Representations. In *Proc. of the 54th Annual Meeting of the Association for Computational Linguistics.*

Douwe Kiela, Felix Hill, Anna Korhonen, and Stephen Clark. 2014. Improving multi-modal representations using image dispersion: Why less is sometimes more. In *Proc. of the 52nd Annual Meeting of the Association for Computational Linguistics.* pages 835–841.

Yoon Kim. 2014. Convolutional Neural Networks for Sentence Classification. In *Proc. of the 2014 Conf. on Empirical Methods in Natural Language Processing.* pages 1746–1751.

Ryan Kiros, Yukun Zhu, Ruslan Salakhutdinov, Richard S. Zemel, Raquel Urtasun, Antonio Torralba, and Sanja Fidler. 2015. Skip-Thought Vectors. In *Proc. of the 2015 Intl. Conf. on Advances in Neural Information Processing Systems.* pages 3294–3302.

Angeliki Lazaridou, Nghia The Pham, and Marco Baroni. 2015. Combining language and vision with a multimodal skip-gram model. In *Proc. of conf. of the North American Chapter of the Association of Computational Linguistics.* pages 153–163.

Quoc V. Le and Tomas Mikolov. 2014. Distributed Representations of Sentences and Documents. In *Proc. of the 31st Intl. Conf. on Machine Learning.* pages 1188–1196.

Tomas Mikolov, Ilya Sutskever, Kai Chen, Greg Corrado, and Jeffrey Dean. 2013. Distributed Representations of Words and Phrases and Their Compositionality. In *Proc. of the 26th Intl. Conf. on Neural Information Processing Systems.* pages 3111–3119.

Tamara Polajnar, Laura Rimell, and Stephen Clark. 2015. An exploration of discourse-based sentence spaces for compositional distributional semantics. In *Workshop on Linking Models of Lexical, Sentential and Discourse-level Semantics (LSDSem).* page 1.

Yafeng Ren, Yue Zhang, Meishan Zhang, and Donghong Ji. 2016. Context-sensitive twitter sentiment classification using neural network. In *Proc. of the 13th AAAI Conference on Artificial Intelligence.* pages 215–221.

Yelong Shen, Xiaodong He, Jianfeng Gao, Li Deng, and Grégoire Mesnil. 2014. A Latent Semantic Model with Convolutional-Pooling Structure for Information Retrieval. In *Proc. of the 23rd ACM Intl. Conf. on Conference on Information and Knowledge Management.* pages 101–110.

Sainbayar Sukhbaatar, Arthur Szlam, Jason Weston, and Rob Fergus. 2015. End-to-end memory networks. In *NIPS.* pages 2440–2448.

Ilya Sutskever, Oriol Vinyals, and Quoc V. Le. 2014. Sequence to sequence learning with neural networks. In *NIPS.* pages 3104–3112.

Duyu Tang, Furu Wei, Bing Qin, Nan Yang, Ting Liu, and Ming Zhou. 2016. Sentiment Embeddings with Applications to Sentiment Analysis. *IEEE Transactions on Knowledge and Data Engineering* 28(2):496–509.

Soroush Vosoughi, Prashanth Vijayaraghavan, and Deb Roy. 2016. Tweet2Vec: Learning Tweet Embeddings Using Character-level CNN-LSTM Encoder-Decoder. In *Proc. of the 39th Intl. ACM SIGIR Conf. on Research and Development in Information Retrieval.* pages 1041–1044.

Yashen Wang, Heyan Huang, Chong Feng, Qiang Zhou, Jiahui Gu, and Xiong Gao. 2016. CSE: conceptual sentence embeddings based on attention model. In *Proc. of the 54th Annual Meeting of the Association for Computational Linguistics.*

Zhiyu Wang, Peng Cui, Lexing Xie, Wenwu Zhu, Yong Rui, and Shiqiang Yang. 2014. Bilateral correspondence model for words-and-pictures association in multimedia-rich microblogs. *TOMCCAP* 10(4):34:1–34:21.

Jason Weston, Sumit Chopra, and Keith Adams. 2014. #tagspace: Semantic embeddings from hashtags. In *Proc. of the 2014 Conf. on Empirical Methods in Natural Language Processing.* pages 1822–1827.

John Wieting, Mohit Bansal, Kevin Gimpel, and Karen Livescu. 2016a. Charagram: Embedding words and sentences via character n-grams. In *Proc. of the 2016 Conference on Empirical Methods in Natural Language Processing, EMNLP.* pages 1504–1515.

John Wieting, Mohit Bansal, Kevin Gimpel, and Karen Livescu. 2016b. Towards universal paraphrastic sentence embeddings. *CoRR* abs/1511.08198.

Wei Xu, Alan Ritter, Chris Callison-Burch, William B. Dolan, and Yangfeng Ji. 2014. Extracting lexically divergent paraphrases from twitter. *TACL* 2:435–448.

Yukun Zhu, Ryan Kiros, Richard S. Zemel, Ruslan Salakhutdinov, Raquel Urtasun, Antonio Torralba, and Sanja Fidler. 2015. Aligning books and movies: Towards story-like visual explanations by watching movies and reading books. In *IEEE Intl. Conf. on Computer Vision, ICCV.* pages 19–27.

Bilingual Word Embeddings with Bucketed CNN for Parallel Sentence Extraction

Jeenu Grover
IIT Kharagpur
India - 721302
groverjeenu@gmail.com

Pabitra Mitra
IIT Kharagpur
India - 721302
pabitra@cse.iitkgp.ernet.in

Abstract

We propose a novel model which can be used to align the sentences of two different languages using neural architectures. First, we train our model to get the bilingual word embeddings and then, we create a similarity matrix between the words of the two sentences. Because of different lengths of the sentences involved, we get a matrix of varying dimension. We dynamically pool the similarity matrix into a matrix of fixed dimension and use Convolutional Neural Network (CNN) to classify the sentences as aligned or not. To further improve upon this technique, we bucket the sentence pairs to be classified into different groups and train CNN's separately. Our approach not only solves sentence alignment problem but our model can be regarded as a generic bag-of-words similarity measure for monolingual or bilingual corpora.

1 Introduction

Parallel bilingual corpora are very crucial for building natural language processing systems, including machine translation, word disambiguation, and cross-language information retrieval. Machine translation tasks need a lot of parallel data for training purposes (Brown et al., 1993). Sentence alignment between two parallel monolingual corpora is used for getting the parallel data. But the present sentence alignment algorithms rely mainly on surface based properties of the sentence pairs and lexicon-based approaches (Varga et al., 2007; Moore, 2002; Gale and Church, 1993). A little work has been done using the neural network models for sentence alignment. We propose a novel approach based on neural networks for sentence alignment which performs exceedingly well as compared to standard alignment techniques which can not capture the semantics being conveyed by the text. Our model uses distributed word-embeddings which have been behind the success of many NLP applications in recent years. We then leverage upon the use of CNNs (Zou et al., 2013; Kusner et al., 2015; Norouzi et al., 2013) for capturing the word-overlapping and word-ordering features in similarity matrix for classification.

2 Model

The different aspects of our model are presented below.

2.1 Bilingual word embeddings

Bilingual Word embeddings (Bengio and Corrado, 2015; Luong et al., 2015) are a representation of the words of two languages in the same semantic space. The three ways of getting the bilingual word representations as mentioned by Luong et al. are: bilingual mapping (Mikolov et al., 2013a), monolingual adaptation (Zou et al., 2013) and bilingual training (AP et al., 2014; Pham et al., 2015).

The semantic relatedness of two words across different languages have been compared by using translation dictionaries for the purpose of sentence alignment tasks. But, this method of telling if the two words across languages are synonyms or not, is very discrete, because a word would be called a synonym only if it is present in list of top k synonyms of the other word. Words having a little similarity with each other would be totally ignored. Our approach intends to mitigate this difference by using bilingual word embeddings. Our method is not discrete, because even if the word is not present in the list of top synonyms for the

Proceedings of the 55th Annual Meeting of the Association for Computational Linguistics- Student Research Workshop, pages 11–16
Vancouver, Canada, July 30 - August 4, 2017. ©2017 Association for Computational Linguistics
https://doi.org/10.18653/v1/P17-3003

other, we would still get their similarity (albeit low) using the bilingual embeddings.

In our paper, we would be using bilingual training for getting word representations as proposed by (Luong et al., 2015). Bilingual training does not depend on independently trained word representation on monolingual corpora of either language. Instead, we learn monolingual and bilingual representations jointly on a parallel corpora.

2.2 Similarity Matrix

Two semantically similar sentences in same or different languages would use same or similar words albeit with a change of order introduced by various factors like language grammar, change of narrative, change of tense or even paraphrasing. We assume that if a sentence pair has high word-overlap, then it might be conveying the same semantics. Here, we are ignoring the cases in which same set of words may convey different semantics because parallel corpora contains a few such instances. Handling such instances would lead to minor changes in precision or recall due to fewer instances and is beyond the scope of this paper. Moreover, none of the existing approaches to sentence alignment deal with such cases.

To capture word-overlap, some alignment techniques use measures like TF-IDF similarity (Fung and Cheung, 2004) or even the basic Jaccard similarity along with translation dictionaries. In our approach, we generate a similarity matrix for each sentence pair, where entries in rows are corresponding to the words of the sentence of one language in their order of occurrence. Same way, columns denote the entries for the words of sentence of second language. The entry $S(i, j)$ of S denotes a similarity measure between the words w_i of s_1 and w_j' of s_2. If we find a word in the sentence which is not present in the corresponding vocabulary, we simply omit it. The different similarity measures that we used include cosine similarity and euclidean distance between the embeddings.

2.3 Bucketing and Dynamic Poling

Last step gave us the similarity matrix for the sentences s_1 and s_2, but the size of the matrix is variable owing to different sentence lengths. We would pool this similarity matrix dynamically to convert it into a matrix of fixed dimension. But we were a bit skeptical of this step as even sentences with very short and very long lengths would be pooled to the same dimension. To overcome it, we bucketed the sentences into different sentence length ranges. Bucketing is done on the basis of mean length of the two sentences in the pair to be classified.

Thus, we trained different classifiers for each range of the buckets. The main limitation of this method is that the effective training data reduces for each of the classifiers. This may degrade the performance of the model as compared to a single classifier which has all the data available for training. If parallel annotated data is available in abundance, then this method would work better than a single classifier.

To convert matrix to a fixed size representation, we pool it dynamically to a matrix of fixed dimension as mentioned in Socher et al. We divide each dimension of 2D matrix into dim chunks of $\lfloor \frac{len}{dim} \rfloor$ size, where dim is the bucket size and len is the length of dimension. If the length len of any dimension is lesser than dim, we duplicate the matrix entries along that dimension till len becomes greater than or equal to dim. If there are l leftover entries where $l = len - dim * \lfloor \frac{len}{dim} \rfloor$, we distribute them to the last l chunks. We do it for both the dimensions.

Now, for a particular chunk, we can pool the entries in it using methods like average, minimum and maximum pooling. When we take cosine similarity between words as the matrix entries, we take max-pooling and with euclidean distance, we take min-pooling. This is because we do not want to fade the effect of two words with high similarity entries in the same chunk and the mentioned pooling methods for each similarity measure, take care of it.

2.4 Convolution Neural Network

CNN's have been found to be performing well where we need to capture the spatial properties of the input in the neural network (Krizhevsky et al., 2012; Kim, 2014). The intention behind using CNN's on matrix rather than training a simple neural classifier on input of flattened data is that the similarity matrices not only contain the similarity scores between words but they also capture the word-order. Thus a matching phrase would appear as a high intensity diagonal streak in the similarity matrix (Refer figure 4). A single 1D vector would loose such visual word-ordering features of the similarity matrix. We also report the performance of a multilayer perceptron classifier as compared to CNN's, justifying our choice.

3 Experiments

3.1 Data

We performed our experiment on the sentence alignment dataset (Zweigenbaum et al., 2016) provided by shared task of 10th BUCC workshop[1]. We performed experiments on the English-German (en-de) dataset. The dataset consists of 399,337 sentences of monolingual English Corpora and 413,869 sentences of monolingual German corpora. The gold alignment has been provided with the data. The gold alignment between the two languages consists of 9580 matching sentence pairs.

3.2 Sampling

As described above, the sizes of monolingual corpora are large as compared to actual aligned sentences. The total possible sentence pairs are 165 billion which contains just 9580 positive sentence pairs, creating a huge class imbalance. It would be difficult to train or even store 165 billion sentence pairs. Moreover, large presence of negative data in the corpora would also make the classifiers less sensitive towards positive data. To overcome these difficulties, we sampled negative examples from the data. Table 1 gives the sizes of datasets after sampling.

3.3 Training of Word Embeddings

We used the English German word embeddings as mentioned in the paper by Luong et al.[2] The dimension of all embeddings used in our experiments is 128. The embeddings are trained on parallel Europarl v7 corpus between German (de) and English (en) (Koehn, 2005), which consists of 1.9M parallel sentences. The training settings as described in Mikolov et al. and Luong et al. were used. The hyper-parameter α is 1 and β is 4 in our experiments as described in Luong et al. The vocabulary size for en is 40,054 and for de is 95,195.

3.4 Similarity Matrix and Bucketing

We split the sentence pairs in data into training, validation and testing set having a ratio of 6:1:3

B size	Train	Valid	Test	Par	Ratio
[0,5]	0	0	0	4431	0
(5,8]	76	15	43	10281	7.392
(8,10]	1024	189	469	15681	65.302
(10,12]	3561	630	1829	22281	159.822
(12, 15]	8585	1630	4409	34431	249.339
(15,18]	4862	867	2602	49281	98.659
(18,20]	452	78	222	60681	7.449
(20,25]	4	2	7	94431	0.0424
Total	18654	3411	9581	34431	**541.779**

Table 1: Table showing bucket-ranges and the number of sentence pairs in train, validation and test set. Number of parameters (Par) and Ratio of Training data to Parameter size ($Ratio = Train \div Par$, in 10^{-3} units) are shown for each bucket

respectively, giving data splits of size 18654, 3411 and 9581 respectively. The bucketed data ranges for each data split are shown in Table 1. There were no sentence pairs in our dataset with mean length of pair below 5 or above 25. More over, the splits for range (5,8] and (20,25] do not contain enough data for training, so we exclude them from the experiments. Thus, out of total 8 buckets in Table 1, we ran the experiments for only 5 buckets as well as all non-bucketed data. We report our results using cosine similarity, as it performed better than using euclidean distance as similarity measure.

3.5 Model Parameters

The neural network architecture is described below:

- Convolution Layer 1 with Relu Activation: We used a 3D convolution volume of area 3×3 and depth 12 on input of size $dim \times dim \times 1$ where dim is the bucket size. The strides of 1 unit were used in each direction. The zero padding was done to keep output height and width same as input. The convolution layer was followed by a layer of Rectified Linear Units (Relu) to introduce the non-linearity in the model

- Max-Pooling Layer 1: We used max pooling on the output of the previous layer to reduce its size by half. This was done using strides of 2 units for both height and width.

- Convolution Layer 2 with Relu : It uses a 3D volume of area 3×3 and depth 16. Rest all properties are same as Convolution Layer 1.

- Max-Pooling Layer 2: It again reduces the

---

[1] https://comparable.limsi.fr/bucc2017/bucc2017-task.html

[2] The code and pre-trained embeddings can be downloaded from http://stanford.edu/~lmthang/bivec

size of input by half using strides of 2 units in both directions. The output of this layer is flattened from 3D to 1D to pass it to next layer as input.

- Fully Connected Layer 1 (FC1) with Relu: This layer maps the flattened input to a hidden layer with 200 units. Relu Activation was used here on the output of hidden units.

- Dropout Layer: We used a layer with dropout probability of 0.2 to prevent over-fitting in the model.

- Full Connected layer 2: This layer maps the output of previous layer with 200 hidden units into a single output, which is further passed to sigmoid activation unit. The value of the sigmoid unit is the predicted output.

The model was trained using 20 epochs with batch-size of 5. The loss function is the mean squared error between actual and predicted output. The Adam optimizer (Kingma and Ba, 2014) was used for stochastic optimization for backpropagation. The learning rate parameter (eta) is 0.0005. The motivation behind using Relu as activation function is to overcome gradient decays, which hinder the training of the neural networks. All the hyper-parameters were tuned by random search in hyper-parameter space and testing on the validation dataset. The total number of parameters to be trained in the model are $150 \times dim^2 + 681$, where dim is the bucket size. This gives us number of parameters ranging from 15,681 for lowest size bucket with $dim = 10$ and 60,681 for largest bucket with $dim = 20$.

4   Results and Analysis

To evaluate, we ran our algorithm on the *en-de Test set* mentioned beforehand. Our algorithm assigns a score to each sentence pair, denoting the probability of two sentences conveying same semantics. If the score is greater than a certain threshold th, we take it as a positive. Table 2 shows results for $th = 0.5$. When we performed experiments for all data (Total in Table 2), without bucketing, we chose $dim = 15$ as highest number of data entries fall in that bucket. We expected that bucketing data would yield better results compared to non-bucketing as each sentence pair would be pooled to a matrix of the dimension comparable to its

T Data	TP	FP	FN	P	R	F1
(8,10]	128	2	3	.9846	.9771	.9808
(10,12]	472	6	34	.9874	.9328	.9593
(12, 15]	1207	63	13	.9504	**.9893**	.9695
(15,18]	904	4	22	.9956	.9762	.9858
(18,20]	67	0	6	**1.0000**	.9178	.9571
Total*	2825	18	49	.9937	.9830	**.9883**
Macro	-	-	-	.9836	.9586	.9710
Micro	2778	75	78	.9737	.9726	.9731
Baseline	2221	92	653	.9603	.7728	.8564

Table 2: Table showing *Test dataset type (T Data), True Positives (TP), False Positives (FP), False Negatives (FN), Precision (P), Recall (R), and F1-score (F1). *Includes all non-bucketed data*

actual length. But as seen in Table 2, the non-bucketed approach performs very well and in some cases, even better than a few buckets. This happens because the training data available for non-bucketed approach (18654 pairs) is atleast double of any of the buckets. *Ratio* column in Table 1 shows the ratio of Training data to number of parameters in the model, which is highest for non-bucketed data with $dim = 15$. If we had more training data in each bucket, then all the buckets might have achieved better performance than non-bucketed approach. *Macro* and *Micro* in Table 2 denote the Macro-average and Micro-average respectively for all the 5 buckets taken for experiment.

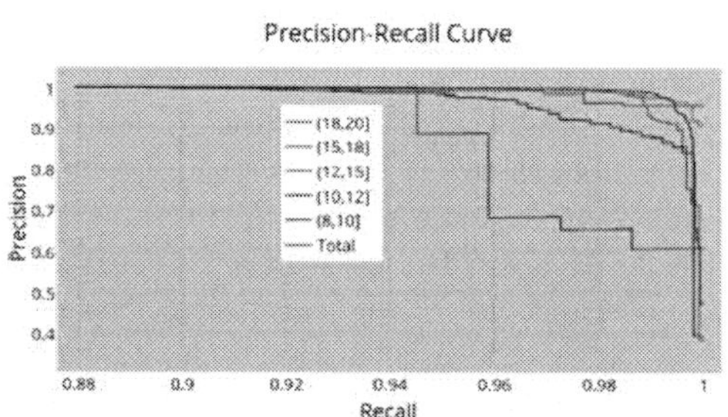

Figure 1: Precision-Recall Curve for all the buckets as well as total data. The different dimensions have been zoomed appropriately to show relevant parts of the plot.

We also used a multilayer perceptron classifier on non-bucketed data with flattened matrices as input (*Baseline* in Table 2), but that performed poorly with F1 score of 0.8564. Figure 2 and 3 depict the similarity matrices for True Positives and True Negatives. We can clearly observe some visual features of the similarity matrices, such as the presence of high intensity streaks along diagonal, which denote high similarity between the entries in close vicinity in one sentence to the entries in close vicinity in the other. This justifies our hypothesis that, unlike multilayer perceptron, CNN is able to capture the relations between word similarity and their ordering, which is represented by the matrices. Our method also performs much better than other baseline methods such as a classifier using sentence length features.

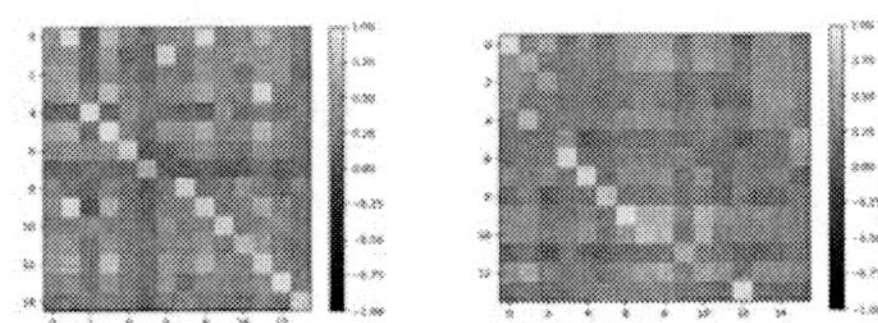

Figure 2: True Positive examples. Left image shows a sentence pair with high overlap and right image shows a sentence pair with low overlap.

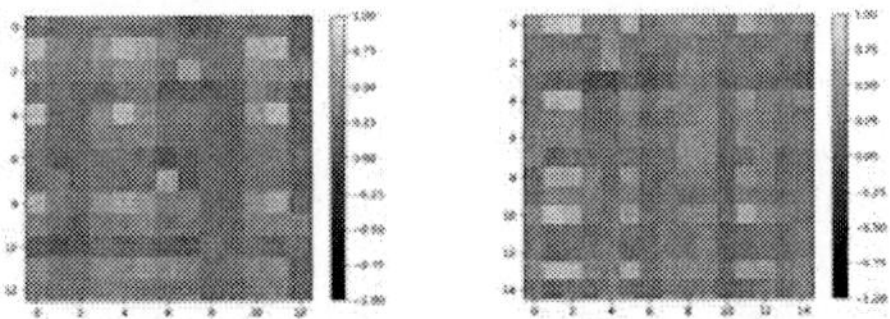

Figure 3: True Negative examples. Both the images are visually different from True Positives.

As an abstraction, our model can be viewed as a neural equivalent of bag-of-words similarity measures such as TF-IDF similarity or Jaccard similarity as this approach covers the word-overlap between two documents (sentences here). Moreover, rather just capturing the overlap, it also captures the order in which the words match in two documents. So, it can be dubbed as neural-bag-of-words like model which remembers matching order.

5 Future Work

We have used the dynamically pooled similarity matrices with CNN for the purpose of sentence alignment. But as already mentioned, our approach specifies a general way of obtaining the similarity between two texts whether they belong to same or different languages. The sentences belonging to the same language can be handled in

the same way, but only monolingual word embeddings would suffice for that purpose.

A unique feature of our similarity measure is that we get the similarity between two texts without mapping them to their respective vectors in the vector space. We can interpret it like a kernel function which gives dot product $\phi(x).\phi(y)$ between two entities without actually transforming x or y to $\phi(x)$ or $\phi(y)$ respectively. Also, unlike TF-IDF, where each vector is of the size of the vocabulary, our similarity approach takes only dim^2 space per sentence pair, which is much lesser than the former.

Our current approach assumes that the two texts are of comparable length, because that is generally the case for aligned sentences and that's why we took the dynamically pooled matrices with both dimensions of same size. But, if we want to use our approach for information retrieval purposes, then the size of document D would be much larger than size of the query q. In that case, we would have to take rectangular dynamically pooled matrices with appropriate dimensions. We would like to study the efficacy of our approach in all such scenarios.

Also, since our approach can tell the parts of the document it is matching, unlike TF-IDF, we can use it to assign different scores for matching phrases in different parts of the document. For example, to search for a query on a webpage which has an article and comments from the readers (just like a blog), our approach can be trained to give more importance to the matches in the article as compared to the reader comments, thus leading to a better information retrieval approach. In the future, we would also like to study how different properties like time and space complexity of our approach scale for large dataset. We would also like to explore the applications of our approach for tasks like cross-lingual as well as monolingual information retrieval, query expansion, cross-lingual recommender systems etc.

6 Conclusion

The novelty of our approach lies in using neural word embeddings in bilingual semantic space along with CNN to capture the sentence similarity and we have achieved very good results over the dataset by BUCC. Our model provides a new equivalent of bag-of-words similarity measures which is also aware of the matching order. The architecture proposed by our algorithm is not just for this specific task but can be used for a number of other tasks like Information Retrieval in monolingual as well as bilingual corpora, query expansion for cross-lingual search etc. We would like to study the different properties and explore the applications of our approach in future.

7 Acknowledgements

We would like to thank all the anonymous reviewers for their valuable feedback.

References

Sarath Chandar AP, Stanislas Lauly, Hugo Larochelle, Mitesh Khapra, Balaraman Ravindran, Vikas C Raykar, and Amrita Saha. 2014. An autoencoder approach to learning bilingual word representations. In *Advances in Neural Information Processing Systems*. pages 1853–1861.

Yoshua Bengio and Greg Corrado. 2015. Bilbowa: Fast bilingual distributed representations without word alignments .

Peter F Brown, Vincent J Della Pietra, Stephen A Della Pietra, and Robert L Mercer. 1993. The mathematics of statistical machine translation: Parameter estimation. *Computational linguistics* 19(2):263–311.

Pascale Fung and Percy Cheung. 2004. Mining very-non-parallel corpora: Parallel sentence and lexicon extraction via bootstrapping and e. In *EMNLP*. Citeseer, pages 57–63.

William A Gale and Kenneth W Church. 1993. A program for aligning sentences in bilingual corpora. *Computational linguistics* 19(1):75–102.

Yoon Kim. 2014. Convolutional neural networks for sentence classification. *arXiv preprint arXiv:1408.5882* .

Diederik Kingma and Jimmy Ba. 2014. Adam: A method for stochastic optimization. *arXiv preprint arXiv:1412.6980* .

Philipp Koehn. 2005. Europarl: A parallel corpus for statistical machine translation. In *MT summit*. volume 5, pages 79–86.

Alex Krizhevsky, Ilya Sutskever, and Geoffrey E Hinton. 2012. Imagenet classification with deep convolutional neural networks. In *Advances in neural information processing systems*. pages 1097–1105.

Matt J Kusner, Yu Sun, Nicholas I Kolkin, Kilian Q Weinberger, et al. 2015. From word embeddings to document distances. In *ICML*. volume 15, pages 957–966.

Thang Luong, Hieu Pham, and Christopher D Manning. 2015. Bilingual word representations with monolingual quality in mind. In *Proceedings of the 1st Workshop on Vector Space Modeling for Natural Language Processing*. pages 151–159.

Tomas Mikolov, Quoc V Le, and Ilya Sutskever. 2013a. Exploiting similarities among languages for machine translation. *arXiv preprint arXiv:1309.4168* .

Tomas Mikolov, Ilya Sutskever, Kai Chen, Greg S Corrado, and Jeff Dean. 2013b. Distributed representations of words and phrases and their compositionality. In *Advances in neural information processing systems*. pages 3111–3119.

Robert C Moore. 2002. Fast and accurate sentence alignment of bilingual corpora. In *Conference of the Association for Machine Translation in the Americas*. Springer, pages 135–144.

Mohammad Norouzi, Tomas Mikolov, Samy Bengio, Yoram Singer, Jonathon Shlens, Andrea Frome, Greg S Corrado, and Jeffrey Dean. 2013. Zero-shot learning by convex combination of semantic embeddings. *arXiv preprint arXiv:1312.5650* .

Hieu Pham, Minh-Thang Luong, and Christopher D Manning. 2015. Learning distributed representations for multilingual text sequences. In *Proceedings of NAACL-HLT*. pages 88–94.

Richard Socher, Eric H Huang, Jeffrey Pennington, Andrew Y Ng, and Christopher D Manning. 2011. Dynamic pooling and unfolding recursive autoencoders for paraphrase detection. In *NIPS*. volume 24, pages 801–809.

Dániel Varga, Péter Halácsy, András Kornai, Viktor Nagy, László Németh, and Viktor Trón. 2007. Parallel corpora for medium density languages. *AMSTERDAM STUDIES IN THE THEORY AND HISTORY OF LINGUISTIC SCIENCE SERIES 4* 292:247.

Will Y Zou, Richard Socher, Daniel M Cer, and Christopher D Manning. 2013. Bilingual word embeddings for phrase-based machine translation. In *EMNLP*. pages 1393–1398.

Pierre Zweigenbaum, Serge Sharoff, and Reinhard Rapp. 2016. Towards preparation of the second bucc shared task: Detecting parallel sentences in comparable corpora. In *Ninth Workshop on Building and Using Comparable Corpora*. page 38.

nQuery - A Natural Language Statement to SQL Query Generator

Nandan Sukthankar, Sanket Maharnawar, Pranay Deshmukh
Yashodhara Haribhakta, Vibhavari Kamble
Department of Computer Engineering and Information Technology
College of Engineering Pune
Wellesley Road, Shivajinagar, Pune, Maharashtra, India
http://www.coep.org.in
{nandans16, sanketmaharnawar, pranay.s.deshmukh}@gmail.com
{ybl.comp, vvk.comp}@coep.ac.in

Abstract

In this research, an intelligent system is designed between the user and the database system which accepts natural language input and then converts it into an SQL query. The research focuses on incorporating complex queries along with simple queries irrespective of the database. The system accommodates aggregate functions, multiple conditions in WHERE clause, advanced clauses like ORDER BY, GROUP BY and HAVING. The system handles single sentence natural language inputs, which are with respect to selected database. The research currently concentrates on MySQL database system. The natural language statement goes through various stages of Natural Language Processing like morphological, lexical, syntactic and semantic analysis resulting in SQL query formation.

1 Introduction

Today, virtually every relational database management system (RDBMS) uses Structured Query Language (SQL) for querying and maintaining the database. Users accessing relational databases need to learn SQL and build queries in the right syntax for retrieving the data. It becomes a big hurdle for all those who are not technically knowledgeable in this domain to write the queries in SQL. It would be very convenient if the relational database system can be queried using natural language like English.

Natural language processing (NLP) is the ability of a computer program to understand human speech as it is spoken. While natural language may be easy for people to learn and use, it has been proved to be hard for a computer to master. Despite such challenges, natural language processing is regarded as a promising and important endeavor in the field of computer research.

nQuery will translate natural language queries into SQL before retrieving data from database. It will deal with single sentence inputs given by the user using a particular database. The system mainly focuses on data retrieval but also provides the facility to convert DML natural language statements to SQL. However, the system will output queries which can be used for querying the MySQL database system only. The aim of the system is to reduce the complexity of database querying. The approach our system uses, extracts certain keywords from the natural language statement and goes through various steps of Natural Language Processing. This system focuses on table mapping, attribute mapping and clause tagging to generate the resultant query.

2 Related Work

Over the years, certain systems which focus only on a particular database have been built to serve a particular purpose. (Woods, 1973) developed a system called LUNAR, that answered questions about rock samples brought back from the moon. LIFER/LADDER designed by (Hendrix, 1978) was designed as a natural language interface to a database of information about US Navy ships. The system could only support simple one-table queries on a specific database.

Some of the recent developments try to build a complete system which can generate various types of queries. An expert system was proposed by (Siasar et al., May 2008) using the concepts of syntactic and semantic knowledge. They have also suggested a selection algorithm to select most appropriate query from the suggested possi-

17

Proceedings of the 55th Annual Meeting of the Association for Computational Linguistics- Student Research Workshop, pages 17–23
Vancouver, Canada, July 30 - August 4, 2017. ©2017 Association for Computational Linguistics
https://doi.org/10.18653/v1/P17-3004

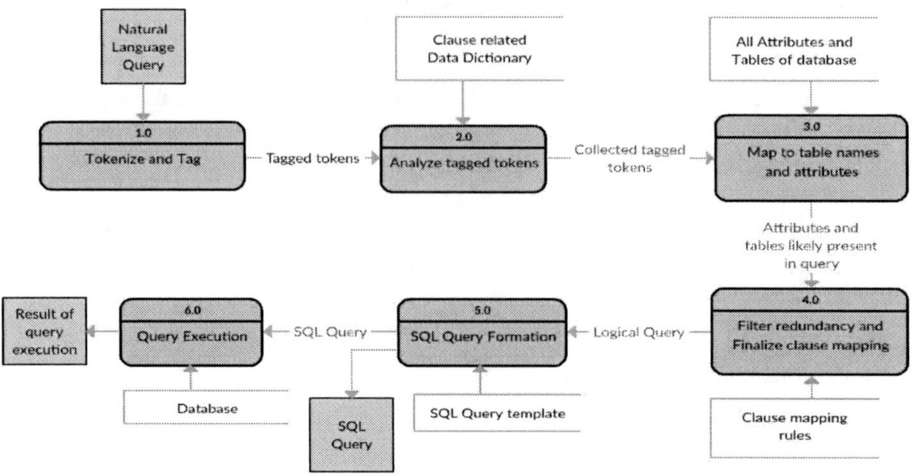

Figure 1: nQuery - Data Flow Diagram

ble query. (Rao et al., 2010) have put forth a system in which simple queries along with basic implicit queries are covered. (Chaudhari, November 2013) implemented a system which handled simple queries and aggregate functions using a prototype approach. Both the above methods have not handled multiple tables and advanced clauses. . (Ghosh et al., 2014) built on the development done by (Chaudhari, November 2013) and developed an automatic query generator which took natural language input in the form of text or speech. It provided support for simple nested queries and aggregate functions. The system handled sentences which explicitly mention the attribute names as they are in the Database. Our system handles the problem by a specific substring algorithm we have developed. We have looked to do the tasks which the above systems do in a more efficient way by building a different type of algorithm relying on conditional substring matching to map the words to attributes and tables. We also go beyond by including various different types of queries.

A different type of approach was used by (Reinaldha and Widagdo, 2014) in which the different kinds of questions which can be asked when a database is to be queried were analyzed. They have made use of semantic rules to find out dependencies among the words present in the question asked. (Palakurthi et al., 2015) provides information about the types of attributes and classification features. They describe how different kinds of attributes are handled differently when they occur in sentences. We handle explicit attributes and certain types of implicit attributes in sentences. (Ghosal et al., March 2016) proposed a system which worked well on simple queries involving multiple tables. But the data dictionaries used for the system are limited and the grammar is hard coded. (Kaur and J, Jan 2016) emphasized on simple queries and basic JOIN operations. However, the system does not accommodate advance clauses like aggregate functions, GROUP BY and HAVING Clauses. Our system incorporates advanced clauses along with all the simple queries and generalizes well on different databases. (Singh and Solanki, 2016) proposed an algorithm to convert natural language sentence to SQL queries. They used verb lists, noun lists and rules to map attributes and tables to the words in the sentence. The system also handled ambiguity among the inputs. We have tried to use concepts discussed in this algorithm like noun and verb lists in order to develop our algorithm.

From the above literature survey, we were able to get a fair idea of the work carried out in this field of research. The shortcomings of the referred papers and applications along with the future work mentioned motivated us to take up this research. The increasing importance of Natural Language Processing lured us towards learning these concepts. The system we propose looks to go beyond the accomplished work.

3 System Design

As we have seen from the literature survey, every system had limitations. We propose a system which looks to overcome the shortcomings of the existing systems. Our system gets a natural language sentence as an input, which is then passed through various phases of NLP to form the final SQL query. Refer Fig 1 for the data flow diagram and Fig 2 for the running example.

3.1 Tokenize and Tag

The input natural language query gets split into different tokens with the help of the tokenizer from 'NLTK' package. The tokenized array of words is tagged according to the part-of-speech tagger. All processes following this step use these tagged tokens for processing.

3.2 Analyze tagged tokens

Based on the tagged tokens of earlier step, the noun map and verb list is prepared through one iteration over the tokens. The tokens corresponding to aggregate functions are also mapped with their respective nouns. The decision whether the natural language statement represents a data retrieval query (SELECT) or a DML query (INSERT, UPDATE, DELETE) is taken at this stage with the help of certain 'data arrays' for denoting type of query. For example, when words like 'insert' and its certain synonyms appear in the input, the type of query is 'INSERT' and so on. In any type of query, the tentative tags 'S' (SELECT), 'W' (WHERE), 'O' (ORDER BY) are mapped to the nouns indicating the clauses to which they belong. For this, we have designed 'data dictionaries' for different clauses. These data dictionaries consist of the token-clause term pair, for e.g. aggregate clause data dictionary is "number": "COUNT", "count": "COUNT", "total": "SUM", "sum": "SUM", "average": "AVG", "mean": "AVG". Thus, if any of these tokens is encountered, it is likely to have aggregate clause and accordingly the nouns are tagged with the clause tag.

3.3 Map to table names and attributes

Using the noun map and verb list, the table set is prepared, which will hold the tables that are needed in the query to be formed. This is based on the fact that the table names are either nouns or verbs. The noun map is used to find the attributes which are needed in the final query. The

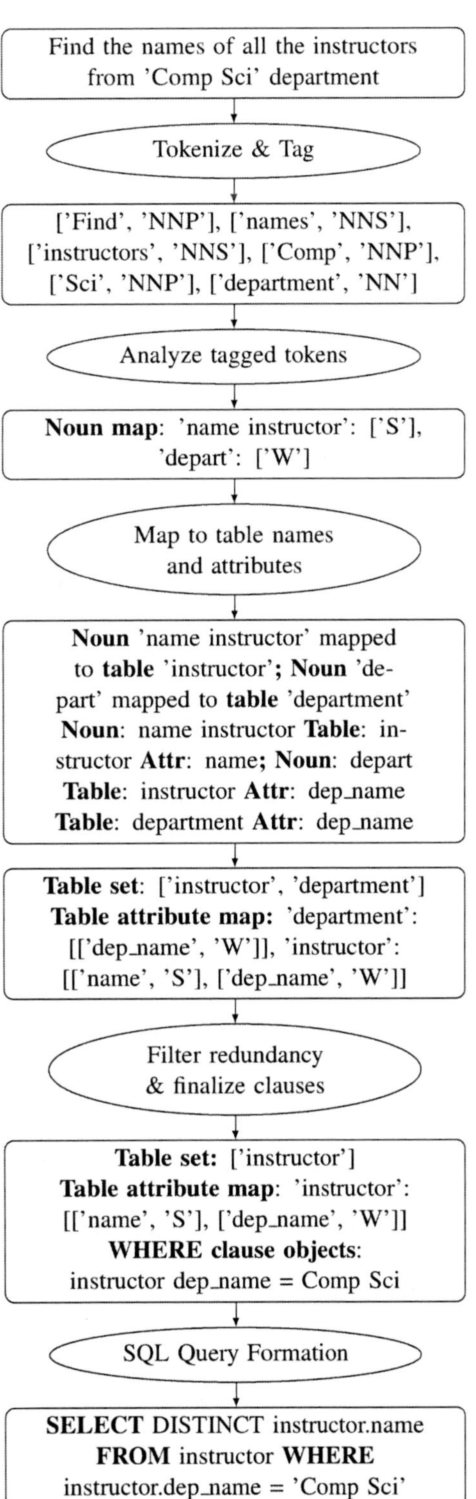

Figure 2: Algorithm with example

attributes, the table associated with the attribute and the clause tag are stored in an attribute-table map which is used in the final stage of query formation. This is done using the string matching algorithm that we have implemented in our system. The words in the input sentence need not exactly be as they are in the database. The stemmer and lemmatiser are applied on the words before they are matched using our string matching algorithm. The data obtained during this step i.e. table set and attribute-table map, is most likely to be in the final query, however, it might be refined later.

3.4 Filter redundancy and finalize clauses of the query

Using the various data dictionaries defined, the system has already decided which clauses are likely to exist in the final query and has mapped the data to the clauses. But, some of the data has to be finalized at this stage. The data related to GROUP BY and HAVING clause is collected using the previous data and the basic rules of SQL. For example, if aggregate function is compared to a constant, i.e. 'MAX(salary) > 40000', then 'HAVING' clause has to be used instead of 'WHERE' clause.

As mentioned in the earlier step, the refinement of data must be done. Here, the redundant tables and attributes are removed using some filter algorithms. For example, one of the algorithm filters the table and their corresponding attributes which are a subset of some other table in table set. i.e. if table set has [table1, table2] and table1 has attributes [a1, a2] and table2 has [a1, a2, a3] after the previous steps, then table2 is enough to represent all the attributes required and hence table1 is removed. There are various other algorithms applied in order to filter the results and finalize the table set and table-attribute map.

3.5 Form the final query and execute

Currently, as our system handles only MySQL queries, the templates used for the query formation will be according to the MySQL syntax. According to the type of query selected in the second stage of the process (Analyze tagged tokens), the appropriate template is chosen.
The template is selected from the following:

1. For data retrieval queries (SELECT):

   - SELECT <select clause>
     FROM <tables>

   WHERE <where clause>
   ORDER BY <order by clause >
   GROUP BY <group by clause>
   HAVING <having clause>
   LIMIT <limit clause>.

2. For data manipulation queries (INSERT, UPDATE, DELETE):

   - INSERT INTO <insert clause>
     VALUES <values clause>
   - UPDATE <update clause>
     SET <set clause>
     WHERE <where clause>
   - DELETE FROM <delete clause>
     WHERE <where clause>

Based on the data about various clauses collected from earlier steps and the information about attributes and tables stored in the attribute-table map, the final query is formed by filling in the information into the appropriate template. Depending on the clause data collected from earlier steps, corresponding <> are filled.
Depending on the relation between multiple tables, the decision of INNER JOIN or NATURAL JOIN is taken. For example, if there are two tables. If these two tables have one common attribute and is named the same in both, then there is NATURAL JOIN between the tables. But if the common attribute is named differently in the two tables, then there is INNER JOIN between the tables. The final query is as shown in Fig 2.

4 Results and Analysis

The corpus that can be used to test our system is not readily available and is dependent on a database. Hence, we have tested our system on a synthesized corpus of natural language statements related to a bank and a university database. The university and bank database consists of 11 and 6 tables respectively. However, system can work on any complex database. The natural language statement has to be a single sentence. The system has been evaluated on a corpus of around 75 natural language statements of university database and around 50 related to bank database. The accuracy of the system is found out to be around 86%. The system gives the same SQL query as the output when the same natural language statement is represented in different ways. If the system fails to generate SQL query corresponding to any natural language statement, an error message is displayed. These are a few results given by the system on the university corpus:

1. Find the student name where instructor name is 'Crick'.

   - SELECT DISTINCT student.stud_name
     FROM instructor
     INNER JOIN advisor
     ON instructor.ID = advisor.inst_ID
     INNER JOIN student
     ON student.ID = advisor.stud_ID
     WHERE instructor.name = 'Crick'

   In this database, the tables 'student' and 'instructor' are linked through the table 'advisor'. So, we can see that this query deals with multiple tables which are joined by INNER JOIN.

2. Find all student name whose credits are between 90 and 100 and department name is 'Finance' or 'Biology'.

   - SELECT DISTINCT student.stud_name
     FROM student
     WHERE (student.tot_cred
     BETWEEN '90' AND '100') AND (
     student.dep_name = 'Finance' OR
     student.dep_name = 'Biology')

   The above query showcases multiple conditions within the WHERE clause. This query also involves use of BETWEEN clause and logical clauses like AND, OR.

3. List all student names whose credits are 50 in decreasing order of credits.

   - SELECT DISTINCT student.stud_name
     FROM student
     WHERE student.tot_cred = '50'
     ORDER BY student.tot_cred DESC

   Another type of query is the one involving sorting its result based on some attribute. For this purpose, the query uses the ORDER BY clause to sort the results in decreasing order.

4. Give the department name where maximum salary of instructor is greater than 50000.

   - SELECT DISTINCT
     instructor.dep_name
     FROM instructor

GROUP BY instructor.dep_name
HAVING
MAX(instructor.salary) >'50000'

In SQL, when an aggregate function is compared to constant, like in this case maximum of salary is compared to 50000, then the query involves use of HAVING clause instead of a WHERE clause. Also, whenever HAVING is used, the results are supposed to be grouped by the attributes in the SELECT clause.

5. Give the department name where salary of instructor is greater than average of salary.

   - SELECT DISTINCT
     instructor.dep_name
     FROM instructor
     WHERE instructor.salary >
     (SELECT AVG(instructor.salary)
     FROM instructor)

This query showcases a special case of nested queries. Whenever an attribute is compared to the result of an aggregate function, i.e. in this case salary greater than average of salary, we have to use nested query.

6. Find the course taught by Crick.

   - SELECT DISTINCT teaches.course_id
     FROM teaches NATURAL JOIN instructor
     WHERE instructor.name = 'Crick'

Till now, we have seen cases in which an attribute associated to the value is mentioned in the natural language statement. In this case, we handle cases where attribute is not mentioned. We find out the most appropriate attribute for the given value.

7. (a) Publish in alphabetic order the names of all instructors.
   (b) Give names of all the instructors in alphabetic order.
   (c) Give instructors names in ascending order.

   - SELECT DISTINCT instructor.name
     FROM instructor
     ORDER BY instructor.name ASC

As seen in this example, there can be multiple ways of representing the same natural language statement.The system gives the same

SQL query as the output when the same natural language statement is represented in different ways.

8. Insert a student whose id is 5, name is Josh, department name is Physics and credits are 150.

   - INSERT INTO student
     (student.ID, student.stud_name,
     student.dep_name, student.tot_cred)
     VALUES
     ('5' , 'Josh' , 'Physics' , '150')

In addition to the data retrieval queries, our system also provides a natural language interface to insert data into the database. Other DML queries such as UPDATE and DELETE are also provided by the system.

5   Limitations

The following are some of the types of inputs that are not presently handled by our system.

1. Find the capacity of the classroom number 3128 in building Taylor

   - SELECT *
     FROM classroom
     WHERE classroom.capacity = '3128'
     AND classroom.building = 'Taylor'

   In this particular example, the system fails to decide whether to take 'capacity of classroom' or 'classroom number' as an n-gram. Hence, the mapping fails.

2. Who teaches Physics?

   - SELECT *
     FROM department
     WHERE
     department.dep_name = 'Physics'

   In this example, the implicit query module of our system is able to map Physics to 'department name' attribute from table 'department'. But it fails to identify that 'who' refers to a person (an instructor).

6   Comparison and Conclusion

Similar existing systems:

1. Complex Queries are not handled very well.

2. Only a few types of aggregate functions have been taken care of.

3. No system has incorporated HAVING, GROUP BY and other clauses.

4. Many systems were specific use systems which were limited to a certain database.

5. No system till date incorporates such a wide range of queries.

Our System:

- The system is currently capable of generating

   1. Simple queries.
   2. Complex queries involving natural and inner joins.
   3. Aggregate functions in queries.
   4. Advanced 'WHERE' clauses.
   5. ORDER BY, GROUP BY, HAVING and LIMIT clauses.
   6. Basic implicit queries.
   7. DML Queries like INSERT, UPDATE and DELETE.

- The system works irrespective of the selected MySQL database.

- No system till date incorporates such a wide range of queries.

7   Future Work

The following points are not yet incorporated in the system and are hence left as future work. The development on the points mentioned in future work is in progress.

1. It is possible that a natural language statement can result in multiple SQL queries. Machine learning can be incorporated to choose the most efficient query.

2. This system only considers MySQL database system. It can be expanded to work for any other database system or unstructured databases.

3. More efficient algorithm to handle implicit queries can be developed.

4. Only single sentence natural language input is handled. Multiple sentences which result in a single query can be incorporated.

5. Neural methods can be used to solve the problem of indecisiveness of n-grams.

References

Pranali P. Chaudhari. November 2013. Natural language statement to sql query translator. *International Journal of Computer Applications (0975-8887)* 82(5).

Prof. Debarati Ghosal, Tejas Waghmare, Vivek Satam, and Chinmay Hajirnis. March 2016. Sql query formation using natural language processing (nlp). *International Journal of Advanced Research in Computer and Communication Engineering* 5(3).

Prasun Kanti Ghosh, Saparja Dey, and Subhabrata Sengupta. 2014. Automatic sql query formation from natural language query. *International Journal of Computer Applications (0975-8887), International Conference on Microelectronics, Circuits and Systems (MICRO-2014)* .

Hendrix. 1978. Lifer / ladder .

Prabhdeep Kaur and Shruthi J. Jan 2016. Conversion of natural language query to sql. *International Journal of Engineering Sciences and Emerging Technologies* .

Ashish Palakurthi, Ruthu S. M., Arjun R. Akula, and Radhika Mamidi. 2015. Classification of attributes in a natural language query into different sql clauses. *IBM Research, Bangalore, India* .

Gauri Rao, Chanchal Agarwal, Snehal Chaudhry, Nikita Kulkarni, and Dr. S.H. Patil. 2010. Natural language query processing using semantic grammar. *International Journal on Computer Science and Engineering* 2(2):219–223.

Filbert Reinaldha and Tricya E. Widagdo. 2014. Natural language interfaces to database (nlidb): Question handling and unit conversion. *IEEE* .

F. Siasar, M. Norouzifard, S. H. Davarpanah, and M. H. Shenassa. May 2008. Using natural language processing in order to create sql queries. *Proceedings of the International Conference on Computer and Communication Engineering 2008* .

Garima Singh and Arun Solanki. 2016. An algorithm to transform natural language into sql queries for relational databases. *Selforganizology* 3(3):100–116.

W. A. Woods. 1973. Progress in natural language understanding-an application to lunar geology. *National Computer Conference* pages 451–460.

V for Vocab: An Intelligent Flashcard Application

Nihal V. Nayak[1], Tanmay Chinchore[1], Aishwarya Hanumanth Rao[1]
Shane Michael Martin[1], Sagar Nagaraj Simha[2], G.M. Lingaraju[1] and H.S. Jamadagni[2]
[1]M S Ramaiah Institute of Technology, Department of Information Science and Engineering
[2]Indian Institute of Science, Department of Electronic Systems Engineering
`{nihalnayak,tanmayrc,aishwarya.hrao,shanemartin1995}@gmail.com`

Abstract

Students choose to use flashcard applications available on the Internet to help memorize word-meaning pairs. This is helpful for tests such as GRE, TOEFL or IELTS, which emphasize on verbal skills. However, monotonous nature of flashcard applications can be diminished with the help of Cognitive Science through Testing Effect. Experimental evidences have shown that memory tests are an important tool for long term retention (Roediger and Karpicke, 2006). Based on these evidences, we developed a novel flashcard application called "V for Vocab" that implements short answer based tests for learning new words. Furthermore, we aid this by implementing our short answer grading algorithm which automatically scores the user's answer. The algorithm makes use of an alternate thesaurus instead of traditional Wordnet and delivers state-of-the-art performance on popular word similarity datasets. We also look to lay the foundation for analysis based on implicit data collected from our application.

1 Introduction

In recent times, we have seen how Internet has revolutionized the field of education through Massive Open Online Courses (MOOCs). Universities are incorporating MOOCs as a part of their regular coursework. Since most of these courses are in English, the students are expected to know the language before they are admitted to the university. In order to provide proof of English proficiency, students take up exams such as TOEFL (Test Of English as a Foreign Language), IELTS (International English Language Testing System),etc. In addition, students are required to take up GRE (Graduate Record Examination) in some universities. All these tests require the students to expand their vocabulary.

Students use several materials and applications in order to prepare for these tests. Amongst several techniques that have known to be effective for acquiring vocabulary, flashcard applications are the most popular. We believe the benefits of flashcard applications can be further amplified by incorporating techniques from Cognitive Science. One such technique that has been supported by experimental results is the Testing Effect, also referred to as Test Enhanced Learning. This phenomenon suggests that taking a memory test not only assesses what one knows, but also enhances later retention (Roediger and Karpicke, 2006).

In this paper, we start by briefly discussing Testing Effect and other key works that influenced the development of the automatic short answer grading algorithm, implemented in V for Vocab[1] for acquiring vocabulary. Next, we have an overview of the application along with the methodology we use to collect data. In the later section, we describe our automatic short answer grading algorithm and present the evaluation results for variants of this algorithm on popular word similarity datasets such as RG65, WS353, SimLex-999 and SimVerb 3500. To conclude, we present a discussion that provides fodder for future work in this application.

2 Background

We have seen that flashcards have gained a lot of popularity among language learners. Students extensively use electronic flashcards while preparing for tests such as TOEFL, GRE and IELTS. Wissman et al. (2012) surveyed the use of flashcards among students and established that they are mostly used for memorization. To understand the

---

[1]https://goo.gl/1BBWN4

Proceedings of the 55th Annual Meeting of the Association for Computational Linguistics- Student Research Workshop, pages 24–29
Vancouver, Canada, July 30 - August 4, 2017. ©2017 Association for Computational Linguistics
https://doi.org/10.18653/v1/P17-3005

(a) Front Flip (b) Back Flip (c) Score Card

Figure 1: a) Front of the card showing a textbox b) Back of the card giving feedback to the user c) Session Scorecard

decay of memory in humans, we delve into the concept of forgetting curve. Hermann Ebbinghaus was the first to investigate this concept way back in the 19th century. Since then, researchers have studied the benefits of several strategies which improve long term memory retention in an attempt to combat the forgetting curve. One such strategy is Testing Effect.

Our application is an amalgamation of the regular flashcard concept and Testing Effect. Roediger and Karpicke (2006) showed that repeated testing facilitates long term retention when compared to repeated studying. Further investigation revealed that short answer based tests are more effective in comparison to multiple choice question tests (Larsen and Butler, 2013). Experimental evidence also suggested that providing feedback to test takers improved their performance (Mcdaniel and Fisher, 1991; Pashler et al., 2005). This motivated us to incorporate short answer based tests with feedback in V for Vocab. To automate the process of scoring these tests, we developed a grading algorithm.

Since production tests allow the users to be more expressive, we had to develop an algorithm to grade answers that range from a single word to several words. The task of grading anywhere between a fill-in-the-gap and an essay is known as Automatic Short Answer Grading (ASAG) (Burrows et al., 2015). Thomas (2003) used a boolean pattern matching system to score answers which makes use of a thesauri and uses a boolean function OR to check with alternate options. FreeText Author (Jordan and Mitchell, 2009) provides an interface for teachers to give templates for the answer along with mandatory keywords. Different permutations for these templates are generated using synonyms obtained from thesauri. On similar lines, we developed an algorithm which employs an online thesaurus as a knowledge base.

3 Our Application

V for Vocab is an electronic version of the flashcard concept for learning new words. On these flashcards, we populate words from a popular wordlist[2] supplemented with sentences from an online dictionary[3]. These words have been divided into 25 groups and are saved in a database. The word, meaning and sentence combinations present in the data were verified by a qualified person. The interface we provide for our users is an Android Application. The application is designed to be simple and intuitive and is modelled based on other popular flashcard softwares.

On signing up, the user is prompted with a survey. The survey asks basic profile questions such as Name, Gender, Date of Birth, Occupation and

---

[2]https://quizlet.com/6876275/barrons-800-high-frequency-gre-word-list-flash-cards/

[3]http://sentence.yourdictionary.com

Number of Words	Raw Answers(%)	Bag of words of answers(%)
1	58.507	67.408
2	18.128	23.298
3	10.994	5.562
4 to N	12.369	2.356

Table 1: Statistical information regarding the data collected from our application where users had typed a meaning. The first column indicates the number of tokens or words in user's answers. N refers to the highest number of words typed by the user. The second column represents the percentage of raw answers or unprocessed responses, N = 16. The third column represents the percentage of answers after processing its bag of words, N = 8. However, after computing bag of words we saw of loss of 1.37% where the user's meaning was reduced to 0 words. In that case, the user's answer would not be graded.

Place of Origin. Apart from this, we ask whether the user is a voracious reader, whether the user is preparing for GRE and the background of the user. This background has been described by Educational Testing Service (ETS) [4], the organization that conducts tests such as TOEFL and GRE.

As mentioned earlier, the user can study from any of the 25 groups. Flashcards from the selected group are shown to the user one at a time in random order. On the front of the card, we provide a text field where the user may type his/her understanding of the word (Refer to Figure 1a). Regardless of whether the user submits an answer, the back of the card shows the word, its part-of-speech, dictionary meaning and a sample sentence (Refer to Figure 1b). This serves as feedback to the user as they review the meaning of the word. Before going to the next flashcard, we send implicit data to the server. If the user has submitted an answer, our algorithm scores it and returns back a score. On quitting, the user is prompted with a learning summary (Refer to Figure 1c).

3.1 Data Collection

During each flip of the card, V for Vocab collects implicit data from the phone in order to facilitate future analysis. The following data points are collected -

- Time spent on the front of the card in milliseconds

- Time spent on the back of the card in milliseconds

- Ambient Sensor value data in SI lux units

The ambient sensor value data is calculated by tapping into the mobile phone's light sensor.

[4]www.ets.org/s/gre/pdf/snapshot_test_taker_data_2014.pdf

These values are found to be dependent on the manufacturer of the light sensor. They are only retrieved when there is a change in the sensor value data and stored in an array.

4 Short Answer Grading Algorithm

Algorithm 1: Grading Algorithm

Input: B1 & B2, the sets of Bag of Words for Text1 & Text2

Output: Similarity Score between Text1 & Text2

1   $score, match\_count, total\_count \leftarrow 0$
2   **for** w_i in B_1 **do**
3     $total\_count \leftarrow total\_count + 1$
4   **for** w_j in B_2 **do**
5       $flag \leftarrow 0$
6   **for** s_i in $synonym(w_i)$ **do**
7   **for** s_j in $synonym(w_j)$ **do**
8   **if** $lemma(s_i) == lemma(s_j)$ **then**
9             $match\_count \leftarrow match\_count + 1$
10             $flag \leftarrow 1$
11   break
12   shortend
13   **if** $flag == 1$ **then**
14   break
15   **if** $flag == 1$ **then**
16   break
17   $score \leftarrow match\_count/total\_count$
18   **return** $score$

In order to build a grading algorithm that suited V for Vocab, we first needed to understand the variation in the answers provided by our users. For

Dataset	S.L.	W.L.
RG65	0.632 / 0.617	**0.752 / 0.727**
WS353	0.286 / 0.313	**0.316 / 0.346**
Simlex-999	0.443 / 0.440	**0.523 / 0.521**
SimVerb-3500	0.278 / 0.276	**0.369 / 0.367**

Table 2: Pearson and Spearman rank correlation coefficients (separated by /; first one is Pearson correlation) computed between the human-annotated similarity score and the score given by our algorithm for a given pair of words from each dataset (S.L : Spacy Lemmatizer and W.L. : Wordnet Lemmatizer)

our analysis, we used 3027 data points collected over 2 months from different users. We found that in 1528 data points users had typed an answer. Based on statistical evidence, we observed that 58.507% of the answers were one word response. After performing bag of words computation on these answers, 67.408% of them were reduced to one word (See Table 1). This meant that our algorithm had to be tailored to grade one word answers, yet be versatile enough so as to grade answers which contained more words.

The answers from the users included a mix of synonyms for the main word or a paraphrase for the definition of the word. Therefore, in order to grade, we first compute the textual similarity of the answer with the word itself and then with the meaning from our database. These are considered as answer templates against which we compare the user's answers to compute the score. Our grader resembles the algorithm described in (Pilehvar et al., 2013) with minuscule changes in similarity measure, which is defined by the ratio of the total number of synonym overlap between word pairs in the answer templates and the user's answers to the total number of words in the answer template (See Algorithm 1). It should be noted that the bag of words is passed to the algorithm for computing the score. The algorithm scores the answers and returns a decimal score in the range [0,1] with a score of 1 being the highest.

Traditionally, people have used Wordnet (Miller, 1995) as a thesauri to find synonyms for a given word. Majority of the words in our wordlist being adjectives, Wordnet posed a disadvantage as it does not work well with adjectives. We also looked into word2vec (Mikolov et al., 2013), but we decided to not go with that approach as we

got a high similarity score between a word and its antonym. Therefore, we preferred to retrieve the synonyms using a python module called PyDictionary [5]. This web scrapes synonyms from 21st Century Roget's Thesaurus [6].

We preprocess the user's answers with the help of a lemmatizer and stopwords list in order to compute the bag of words. The resulting bag of words is passed to the algorithm and it computes the strict synonym overlap between the user's answers and answer templates to calculate the score. Table 3 shows an example of the scores generated by our algorithm [7].

We developed this algorithm using lemmatizers from two popular NLP libraries - NLTK and Spacy, independently. Table 2 shows our evaluation results on popular datasets. We noticed that the algorithm produced higher correlation with NLTK's Wordnet lemmatizer, even though no explicit POS information was passed to the lemmatizer.

In case of an error caused due to absence of synonyms while web scraping, our algorithm returned a score of 0 which we have included during evaluation with the datasets.

User's Answers	Score
Trustworthy	0
Providing	0.33
Providing for the future	0.67
Frugal	1

Table 3: The table shows the evaluation of user's short answer for the word - provident, with the meaning - providing for future needs; frugal. Multiple meanings are separated by a ;(semicolon).

5   Discussion and Future Work

With trends showing that many applications curate their business model around data, we believe that the data collected from our application is valuable. We have the unique opportunity of performing analytics on an individual user and on all users as a whole. By analyzing the individual's data, we can personalize the application to each user. One way would be to observe the user's scores on the words studied and subsequently categorize them

---

[5]https://pypi.python.org/pypi/PyDictionary/1.5.2
[6]http://www.thesaurus.com
[7]The answers in Table 3 are compiled from the actual data we have collected from our users

into easy, medium and hard. We also have the potential to carry out exploratory analysis and bring out interesting patterns from our data. For example, we are hoping to discover an optimal duration to study words in a day so that the user can study effectively. Similarly, light sensor values could be used to understand how a user's learning would vary in a well lit environment versus a darker environment.

Spacing Effect is the robust phenomenon which states that spacing the learning events results in long term retention (Kornell, 2009). Anki, a popular flashcard application incorporates a scheduling algorithm in order to implement spacing effect. More recently we have seen Duolingo, a language learning application implement a machine learning based spacing effect called Half-Life-Regression (Settles and Meeder, 2016). With Testing Effect in place, it would be beneficial to incorporate spacing effect as it has shown great promise in practical applications . A thorough juxtaposition of Testing Effect versus the combination of Testing Effect with Spacing Effect, in terms of data, will help us better evaluate these memory techniques.

We can further improve the system through a mechanical turk. The turk could be any linguist or a person well versed with the language. The mechanical turk compares the answer templates with the user's answer and provides a score that represents how close the two are according to the turk's intuition. With labelled data, we can apply supervised learning and improve the algorithm.

When learning a new language, people often try to remember a word and its translation in a language they already know. For example, a person well versed in English who is trying to learn German will try to recollect word-translation pairs. With a bit of content curation for German-English word pairs, our grading algorithm will work seamlessly, as our algorithm is tailored to grade short answers in English. We believe that in future, V for Vocab can be ported to other languages as well.

Therefore, with the help of this application we are able to improve upon existing flashcard applications and lay groundwork for intelligent flashcard systems.

Acknowledgments

We thank the anonymous reviewers for their insightful comments. We also thank Dr. Vijaya Kumar B P, Professor at M S Ramaiah Institute of Technology, Bangalore for his valuable suggestions. This research was supported by Department of Electronic Systems Engineering (formerly CEDT), Indian Institute of Science.

References

Steven Burrows, Iryna Gurevych, and Benno Stein. 2015. The eras and trends of automatic short answer grading. *International Journal of Artificial Intelligence in Education* 25(1):60–117. https://doi.org/10.1007/s40593-014-0026-8.

Sally Jordan and Tom Mitchell. 2009. e-assessment for learning? the potential of short-answer free-text questions with tailored feedback. *British Journal of Educational Technology* 40(2):371–385. http://oro.open.ac.uk/15270/.

Nate Kornell. 2009. Optimising learning using flashcards: Spacing is more effective than cramming. *Applied Cognitive Psychology* 23(9):1297–1317. https://doi.org/10.1002/acp.1537.

Douglas P. Larsen and Andrew C. Butler. 2013. Test-enhanced learning. *Oxford Textbook of Medical Education* pages 443–452.

Mark A. Mcdaniel and Ronald P. Fisher. 1991. Tests and test feedback as learning sources. *Contemporary Educational Psychology* 16(2):192–201. https://doi.org/10.1016/0361-476x(91)90037-l.

Tomas Mikolov, Ilya Sutskever, Kai Chen, Greg S Corrado, and Jeff Dean. 2013. Distributed representations of words and phrases and their compositionality. In C. J. C. Burges, L. Bottou, M. Welling, Z. Ghahramani, and K. Q. Weinberger, editors, *Advances in Neural Information Processing Systems 26*, Curran Associates, Inc., pages 3111–3119. http://papers.nips.cc/paper/5021-distributed-representations-of-words-and-phrases-and-their-compositionality.pdf.

George A. Miller. 1995. Wordnet: A lexical database for english. *Commun. ACM* 38(11):39–41. https://doi.org/10.1145/219717.219748.

Harold Pashler, Nicholas J. Cepeda, John T. Wixted, and Doug Rohrer. 2005. When does feedback facilitate learning of words? *Journal of Experimental Psychology: Learning, Memory, and Cognition* 31(1):3–8. https://doi.org/10.1037/0278-7393.31.1.3.

Mohammad Taher Pilehvar, David Jurgens, and Roberto Navigli. 2013. Align, disambiguate and walk: A unified approach for measuring semantic similarity. In *Proceedings of the 51st Annual Meeting of the Association for Computational Linguistics (Volume 1: Long Papers)*. Association for Computational Linguistics, Sofia, Bulgaria, pages 1341–1351. http://www.aclweb.org/anthology/P13-1132.

Henry L. Roediger and Jeffrey D. Karpicke. 2006. Test-enhanced learning. *Psychological Science* 17(3):249–255. https://doi.org/10.1111/j.1467-9280.2006.01693.x.

Burr Settles and Brendan Meeder. 2016. A trainable spaced repetition model for language learning. In *Proceedings of the 54th Annual Meeting of the Association for Computational Linguistics (Volume 1: Long Papers)*. Association for Computational Linguistics, Berlin, Germany, pages 1848–1858. http://www.aclweb.org/anthology/P16-1174.

Pete Thomas. 2003. The evaluation of electronic marking of examinations. *SIGCSE Bull.* 35(3):50–54. https://doi.org/10.1145/961290.961528.

Kathryn T. Wissman, Katherine A. Rawson, and Mary A. Pyc. 2012. How and when do students use flashcards? *Memory* 20(6):568–579. https://doi.org/10.1080/09658211.2012.687052.

Are you asking the right questions?
Teaching Machines to Ask Clarification Questions

Sudha Rao
Department of Computer Science
University Of Maryland, College Park
raosudha@cs.umd.edu

Abstract

Inquiry is fundamental to communication, and machines cannot effectively collaborate with humans unless they can ask questions. In this thesis work, we explore how can we teach machines to ask clarification questions when faced with uncertainty, a goal of increasing importance in today's automated society. We do a preliminary study using data from StackExchange, a plentiful online resource where people routinely ask clarifying questions to posts so that they can better offer assistance to the original poster. We build neural network models inspired by the idea of the expected value of perfect information: a good question is one whose expected answer is going to be most useful. To build generalizable systems, we propose two future research directions: a template-based model and a sequence-to-sequence based neural generative model.

1 Introduction

A main goal of asking questions is to fill information gaps, typically through clarification questions, which naturally occur in conversations (Purver, 2004; Ginzburg, 2012). A good question is one whose *likely answer* is going to be the most useful. Consider the exchange in Figure 1, in which an initial poster (who we'll call "Terry") asks for help configuring environment variables. This question is underspecified and a responder ("Parker") asks a clarifying question "(a) What version of Ubuntu do you have?" Parker could alternatively have asked one of:

(b) Is the moon waxing or waning?

(c) Are you running Ubuntu 14.10 kernel 4.4.0-59-generic on an x86_64 architecture?

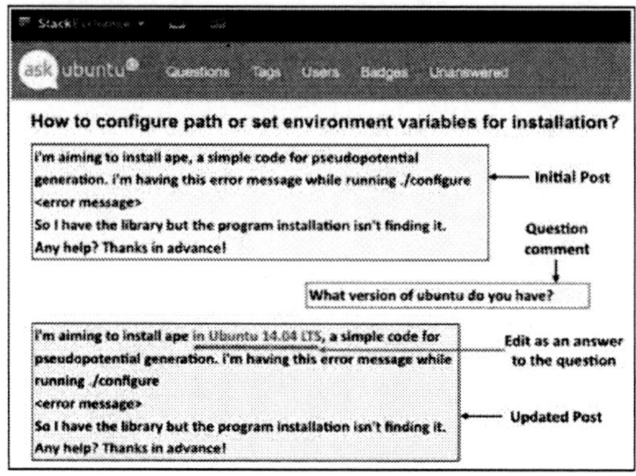

Figure 1: A post on an online Q & A forum "askubuntu.com" is updated to fill the missing information pointed out by the question comment

Parker should not ask (b) because it's not useful; they should not ask (c) because it's too specific and an answer of "No" gives little help. Parker's question (a) is optimal: it is both likely to be useful, and is plausibly answerable by Terry. Our goal in this work is to automate Parker. Specifically, after Terry writes their initial post, we aim to generate a clarification question so that Terry can immediately amend their post in hopes of getting faster and better replies.

Our work has two main contributions:

1. A novel neural-network model for addressing this task that integrates the notion of expected value of perfect information (§2).

2. A novel dataset, derived from StackExchange, that enables us to learn a model to ask clarifying questions by looking at the types of questions people ask (§4.1).[1]

To develop our model we take inspiration from the decision theoretic framework of the Expected

---

[1] We use data from StackExchange; per license cc-by-sa 3.0, the data is "intended to be shared and remixed" (with attribution). We will release all of the data we extract.

Proceedings of the 55th Annual Meeting of the Association for Computational Linguistics- Student Research Workshop, pages 30–35
Vancouver, Canada, July 30 - August 4, 2017. ©2017 Association for Computational Linguistics
https://doi.org/10.18653/v1/P17-3006

Value of Perfect Information (EVPI) (Avriel and Williams, 1970), a measure of the value of gathering additional information. In our setting, we use EVPI to calculate which question is most likely to elicit an answer that would make the post more informative. Formally, for an input post p, we want to choose a question q that maximizes $\mathbb{E}_{a \sim p,q}[\mathbb{U}(p+a)]$, where a is a hypothetical answer and U is a utility function measuring the *completeness* of post p if a were to be added to it. To achieve this, we construct two models: (1) an answer model, which estimates $\mathbb{P}[a \mid p, q]$, the likelihood of receiving answer a if one were to ask question q on post p; (2) a completeness model, $\mathbb{U}(p)$, which measures how complete a post is. Given these two models, at prediction time we search over a shortlist of possible questions for that which maximizes the EVPI.

We are able to train these models jointly based on (p, q, a) triples that we extract automatically from StackExchange. Figure 1 depicts how we do this using StackExchange's edit history. In the figure, the initial post fails to state what version of Ubuntu is being run. In response to Parker's question in the comments section, Terry, the author of the post, edits the post to answer Parker's clarification question. We extract the initial post as p, question posted in the comments section as q, and edit to the original post as answer a to form our (p, q, a) triples.

Our results show significant improvements from using the EVPI formalism over both standard feedforward network architectures and bag-of-ngrams baselines, even when our system builds on strong information retrieval scaffolding. In comparison, without this scaffolding, the bag-of-ngrams model outperforms the feedforward network. We additionally analyze the difficulty of this task for non-expert humans.

2 Related Work

The problem of question generation has received sparse attention from the natural language processing community. Most prior work focuses on generating reading comprehension questions: given text, write questions that one might find on a standardized test (Vanderwende, 2008; Heilman, 2011; Rus et al., 2011). Comprehension questions, by definition, are answerable from the provided text. Clarification questions are not. Outside reading comprehension questions, Labu-

tov et al. (2015) studied the problem of generating question templates via crowdsourcing, Liu et al. (2010) use template-based question generation to help authors write better related work sections, Mostafazadeh et al. (2016) consider question generation from images, and Artzi and Zettlemoyer (2011) use human-generated clarification questions to drive a semantic parser.

3 Model Description

In order to choose what question to ask, we build a neural network model inspired by the theory of expected value of perfect information (EVPI). EVPI is a measurement of: if I were to acquire information X, how useful would that be to me? However, because we haven't acquired X yet, we have to take this quantity in expectation over all possible X, weighted by each X's likelihood. In the question generation setting, for any given question q that we can ask, there is set A of possible answers that could be given. For each possible answer $a \in A$, there is some probability of getting that answer, and some utility if that were the answer we got. The value of this question q is the expected utility, over all possible answers. The theory of EVPI then states that we want to choose the question q that maximizes:

$$\arg\max_{q \in Q} \sum_{a \in A} \mathbb{P}[a|p, q]\mathbb{U}(p + a) \qquad (1)$$

In Eq 1, p is the post, q is a potential question from a set of candidate questions Q (§3.1) and a is a potential answer from a set of candidate answers A (§3.1). $\mathbb{P}[a|p, q]$ (§3.2) measures the probability of getting an answer a given an initial post p and a clarifying question q. $\mathbb{U}(p + a)$ (§3.3) measures how useful it would be if p were augmented with answer a. Finally, using these pieces, we build a joint neural network that we can optimize end-to-end over our data (§3.4). Figure 2 describes the behavior of our model during test time.

3.1 Question & Answer Candidate Generator

Given a post, our first step is to generate a set of candidate questions and answers. Our model learns to ask questions by looking at questions asked in previous similar situations. We first identify 10 posts similar to the given post in our dataset using Lucene[2] (a software extensively used in information retrieval) and then consider the ques-

---

[2]`https://lucene.apache.org/`

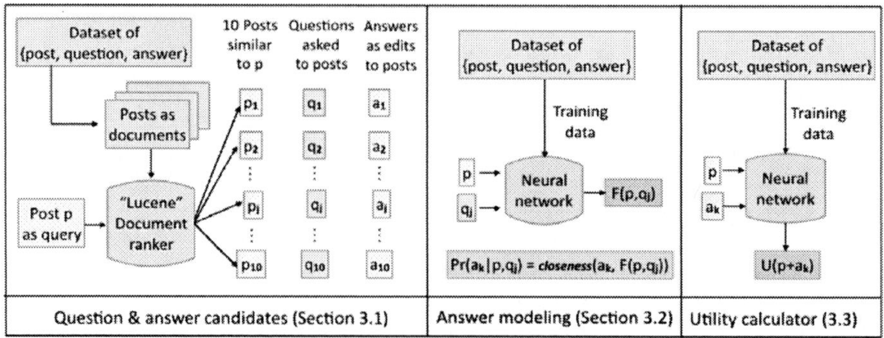

Figure 2: The behavior of our model during test time. Given a post p, we retrieve 10 posts similar to p using Lucene and consider the questions asked to those as question candidates and the edits made to the posts in response to the questions as answer candidates. Our answer model generates an answer representation $F_{ans}(p, q_j)$ for each question candidate q_j and calculates how close is an answer candidate a_k to $F_{ans}(p, q_j)$. Our utility calculator calculates the utility of the post if it were updated with the answer a_k. We select the question q_j that maximizes the expected utility of the post p (Equation 1).

tions asked to these posts as our set of question candidates and the edits made to the posts in response to the questions as our set of answer candidates.

3.2 Answer Modeling

Given a post p and a question candidate q_i, our second step is to calculate how likely is this question to be answered using one of our answer candidates a_k. To calculate this probability, we first generate an answer representation $F_{ans}(p, q_i)$ and then measure how close is the answer candidate a_k to our answer representation using the equation:

$$\mathbb{P}[a_k | p, q_i] = \frac{1}{Z} \exp\left[-\lambda ||a_k - F_{ans}(p, q_i)||^2\right]$$

$$(2)$$

where λ is a tunable parameter that controls the variance of the distribution.

We train our answer generator using the following intuition: a question can be asked in several different ways. For e.g. in Figure 1, the question "What version of Ubuntu do you have?" can be asked in other ways like "What version of operating system are you using?", "Version of OS?", etc. Additionally, a question can generate several different answers. For instance, "Ubuntu 14.04 LTS", "Ubuntu 12.0", "Ubuntu 9.0", are all valid answers. To capture these generalizations, we define the following loss function:

$$\text{loss}_{ans}(\bar{p}, \bar{q}, \bar{a}, Q) = ||F_{ans}(\bar{p}, \bar{q}) - \bar{a}||^2 \quad (3)$$
$$+ \sum_{j \in Q} \left(||F_{ans}(\bar{p}, \bar{q}) - \bar{a_j}||^2 (1 - \tanh(||\bar{q} - \bar{q_j}||^2)) \right)$$

In equation 3, the first term forces the answer representation $F_{ans}(\bar{p}_i, \bar{q}_i)$ to be as close as possible to the correct answer a_i and the second term forces it to be close to the answer a_j corresponding to a question q_j very similar to q_i (i.e. $||\bar{q}_i - \bar{q}_j||$ is near zero).

3.3 Utility Calculator

Given a post p and an answer candidate a_k, our third step is to calculate the utility of the updated post i.e. $\mathbb{U}(p + a_k)$ which measures how useful it would be if a given post p were augmented with an answer a_k. We use the intuition that a post p_i, when updated with the answer a_i that it is paired with in our dataset, would be more complete than if it is updated with some other answer a_j. Therefore we label all the (p_i, a_i) pairs from our dataset as positive ($y = 1$) and label p_i paired with other nine answer candidates generated using Lucene (§3.1) as negative ($y = 0$). The utility of the updated post is then defined as $\mathbb{U}(p + a) = \sigma(F_{utility}(\bar{p}, \bar{a}))$ where $F_{utility}$ is a feedforward neural network. We want this utility to be close to one for all the positively labelled (p, a) pairs and close to zero for all the negatively labelled (p, a) pairs. We therefore define our loss using the binary cross-entropy formulation below:

$$\text{loss}_{util}(y, \bar{p}, \bar{a}) = y \log(\sigma(F_{utility}(\bar{p}, \bar{a}))) \quad (4)$$

3.4 Our joint neural network model

Our fundamental representation is based on recurrent neural network, specifically long short-term memory architecture (LSTM) (Hochreiter and Schmidhuber, 1997) over word embeddings

Models	Lucene negative candidates				Random negative candidates			
	Acc	MRR	R@3	R@5	Acc	MRR	R@3	R@5
Random	10.0	29.3	30.0	50.0	10.0	29.3	30.0	50.0
Bag-of-ngrams	11.6	31.3	32.5	54.6	54.9	70.5	83.1	92.0
Feed-forward	17.4	37.8	43.2	63.9	49.0	66.8	81.3	92.8
EVPI	**23.3**	**43.4**	**51.0**	**70.3**	**61.1**	**75.5**	**87.9**	**95.8**

Table 1: Results of two setups 'Lucene negative candidates' and 'Random negative candidates' on askubuntu when trained on a combination of three domains: askubuntu, unix and superuser. We report four metrics: accuracy (percent of time the top ranked question was correct), mean reciprocal rank (the reciprocal of the ranked position of the correct question in the top 10 list), recall at 3 (percent of time the correct answer is in the top three) and recall at 5.

obtained using a GloVe (Pennington et al., 2014) model trained on the entire datadump of StackExchange. We define three LSTMs corresponding to p, q and a and two feedforward neural networks corresponding to our answer model $F_{ans}(\bar{p}, \bar{q})$ and our utility calculator $F_{utility}(\bar{p}, \bar{a})$. We jointly train the parameters of all our neural network models to minimize the sum of the loss of our answer model (Eq 3) and our utility calculator (Eq 4):

$$\sum_i \text{loss}_{\text{ans}}(\bar{p}_i, \bar{q}_i, \bar{a}_i, Q_i) + \text{loss}_{\text{util}}(y_i, \bar{p}_i, \bar{a}_i) \quad (5)$$

Given such an estimate $\mathbb{P}[a|p, q]$ of an answer and a utility $\mathbb{U}(p + a)$ of the updated post, predictions can be done by choosing that "q" that maximizes Eq 1.

4 Experiments and Results

4.1 Dataset

StackExchange is a network of online question answering websites containing timestamped information about the posts, comments on the post and the history of the revisions made to the post. Using this, we create our dataset of {*post, question, answer*} triples: where *post* is the initial unedited post, *question* is the comment containing a question and *answer* is the edit made to the post that matches the question comment [3]. We extract a total of 37K triples from the following three domains of StackExchange: askubuntu, unix and superuser.

4.2 Experimental Setups

We define our task as given a post and 10 question candidates, select the correct question candidate. For every post p in our dataset of (p, q, a) triples, the question q paired with p is our positive question candidate. We define two approaches to generate negative question candidates:
Lucene Negative Candidates: We retrieve nine

question candidates using Lucene (§3.1) and
Random Negative Candidates: We randomly sample nine other questions from our dataset.

4.3 Primary Research Questions

Our primary research questions that we evaluate experimentally are:
a. Does a neural architecture improve upon a simple bag-of-ngrams baseline?
b. Does the EVPI formalism provide leverage over a similarly expressive feed-forward network?
c. How much harder is the task when the negative candidate questions come from Lucene rather than selected randomly?

4.4 Baseline Methods

Random: Randomly permute the set of 10 candidate questions uniformly.
Bag-of-ngrams: Construct a bag-of-ngrams representation for the post, the question and the answer and train a classifier to minimize hinge loss on misclassification loss.
Feed-forward neural: Concatenate the post LSTM representation, the question LSTM representation and the answer LSTM representation and feed it through a feed forward neural network of two fully-connected hidden layers.

4.5 Results

We describe results on a test split of askubuntu when our models are trained on the union of all data, summarized in Table 1. The left half of this table shows results when the candidate sets is from Lucene—the "hard" setting and the right half of this table shows the same results when the candidate set is chosen randomly—the "easy" setting. Here, we see that for all the evaluation metrics, EVPI outperforms all the baselines by at least a few percentage points. A final performance of 51% recall at 3 in the "hard" setting is encouraging, though clearly there is a long way to go for a perfect system.

---

[3] We measure the cosine similarity between the averaged word embeddings of the question and the edit.

5   How good are humans at this task?

In this section we address two natural questions: (a) How does the performance of our system compare to a human solving the same task? (b) Just because the system selects a question that is not the exact gold standard question, is it certainly wrong? To answer these questions, we had 14 computer science graduate students perform the task on 50 examples. Most of these graduate students are *not* experts in unix or ubuntu, but are knowledgable. Given a post and a randomized list of ten possible questions, they were instructed to select what they thought was the *single* best question to ask, and additionally mark as "valid" any additional questions that they thought would also be okay to ask. We also asked them to rate their confidence in $\{0, 1, 2, 3\}$. Most found this task quite challenging because many of the questions are about subtle nuances of operating system behavior.

These annotator's accuracy on the "hard" task of Lucene-selected questions, was only 36%, significantly better than our best system (23%), but still far from perfect. If we limited to those examples on which they were more confident (confidence of 2 or 3), their accuracy raised to 42%, but never surpassed that. A major problem for the human annotators is the amount of background knowledge required to solve this problem. On an easier domain, or with annotators who are truly experts, we might expect these numbers to be higher.

6   Proposed Research Directions

In our preliminary work, we focus on the question selection problem i.e. select the right clarification question from a set of prior questions. To enable our system to generalize well to new context, we propose two future research directions:

6.1   Template Based Question Generation

Consider a template like "What version of ___ are you running?". This template can generate thousands of specific variants found in the data like "What version of Ubuntu are you running?", "What version of apt-get are you running?", etc. We propose the following four step approach to our template-based question generation method:

1. Cluster questions based on their lexical and semantic similarity.
2. Generate a template for each cluster by removing topic specific words from questions.

3. Given a post, select a question template from a set of candidate question templates using a model similar to our preliminary work.
4. Finally, fill in the blanks in the template using topic specific words retrieved from the post.

6.2   Neural Network Generative Model

Sequence-to-sequence neural network models have proven to be effective for several language generation tasks like machine translation (Sutskever et al., 2014), dialog generation (Serban et al., 2016), etc. These models are based on an encoder-decoder framework where the encoder takes in a sequence of words and generates a vector representation which is then taken in by a decoder to generate the output sequence of words.

On similar lines, we propose a model for generating the clarification question one word at a time, given the words of a post. A recent neural generative question answering model (Yin et al., 2016) built an answer language model which decides, at each time step, whether to generate a common vocabulary word or an answer word retrieved from a knowledge base. Inspired from this work, we propose to build a question generation model which will decide, at each time step, whether to generate a common vocabulary word or a topic specific word retrieved from the current post, thus incorporating the template-based method into a more general neural network framework.

7   Conclusion

In our work, we introduce a novel dataset for clarification question generation, and build a model that integrates neural network structure with the classic notion of expected value of perfect information. Our preliminary model learns to select the right question from a set of candidate questions. We propose two future directions for automatically generating clarification questions.

One main avenue for improvement of this work is in evaluation: given that this task is so difficult for humans, but also given that there is no single right question to ask, how can we better measure performance at this task? This is exactly the same question faced in dialog and generation (Paek, 2001; Lowe et al., 2015; Liu et al., 2016; Kannan and Vinyals, 2017). Finally, asking question is a natural component of dialog, and building a collaborative dialog system that can naturally converse with a user is a broad long term goal.

References

Yoav Artzi and Luke Zettlemoyer. 2011. Bootstrapping semantic parsers from conversations. In *Empirical Methods in Natural Language Processing*. pages 421–432.

Mordecai Avriel and AC Williams. 1970. The value of information and stochastic programming. *Operations Research* 18(5):947–954.

Jonathan Ginzburg. 2012. *The interactive stance*. Oxford University Press.

Michael Heilman. 2011. *Automatic factual question generation from text*. Ph.D. thesis, Carnegie Mellon University.

Sepp Hochreiter and Jürgen Schmidhuber. 1997. Long short-term memory. *Neural computation* pages 1735–1780.

Anjuli Kannan and Oriol Vinyals. 2017. Adversarial evaluation of dialogue models. *arXiv preprint arXiv:1701.08198* .

Igor Labutov, Sumit Basu, and Lucy Vanderwende. 2015. Deep questions without deep understanding. In *Association for Computational Linguistics*. pages 889–898.

Chia-Wei Liu, Ryan Lowe, Iulian V Serban, Michael Noseworthy, Laurent Charlin, and Joelle Pineau. 2016. How not to evaluate your dialogue system: An empirical study of unsupervised evaluation metrics for dialogue response generation. In *Empirical Methods in Natural Language Processing*. pages 2122–2132.

Ming Liu, Rafael A Calvo, and Vasile Rus. 2010. Automatic question generation for literature review writing support. In *International Conference on Intelligent Tutoring Systems*. Springer, pages 45–54.

Ryan Lowe, Nissan Pow, Iulian V Serban, and Joelle Pineau. 2015. The ubuntu dialogue corpus: A large dataset for research in unstructured multi-turn dialogue systems. In *Special Interest Group on Discourse and Dialogue*.

Nasrin Mostafazadeh, Ishan Misra, Jacob Devlin, Margaret Mitchell, Xiaodong He, and Lucy Vanderwende. 2016. Generating natural questions about an image. In *Association for Computational Linguistics*. pages 1802–1813.

Tim Paek. 2001. Empirical methods for evaluating dialog systems. In *Proceedings of the workshop on Evaluation for Language and Dialogue Systems-Volume 9*. Association for Computational Linguistics, page 2.

Jeffrey Pennington, Richard Socher, and Christopher D Manning. 2014. Glove: Global vectors for word representation. In *Empirical Methods on Natural Language Processing*.

Matthew Richard John Purver. 2004. *The theory and use of clarification requests in dialogue*. Ph.D. thesis, Citeseer.

Vasile Rus, Paul Piwek, Svetlana Stoyanchev, Brendan Wyse, Mihai Lintean, and Cristian Moldovan. 2011. Question generation shared task and evaluation challenge: Status report. In *Proceedings of the 13th European Workshop on Natural Language Generation*. Association for Computational Linguistics, pages 318–320.

Iulian V Serban, Alessandro Sordoni, Yoshua Bengio, Aaron Courville, and Joelle Pineau. 2016. Building end-to-end dialogue systems using generative hierarchical neural network models. In *Thirtieth AAAI Conference on Artificial Intelligence*.

Ilya Sutskever, Oriol Vinyals, and Quoc V Le. 2014. Sequence to sequence learning with neural networks. In *Advances in neural information processing systems*. pages 3104–3112.

Lucy Vanderwende. 2008. The importance of being important: Question generation. In *Proceedings of the 1st Workshop on the Question Generation Shared Task Evaluation Challenge, Arlington, VA*.

Jun Yin, Xin Jiang, Zhengdong Lu, Lifeng Shang, Hang Li, and Xiaoming Li. 2016. Neural generative question answering. *International Joint Conference on Artificial Intelligence* .

Building a Non-Trivial Paraphrase Corpus
using Multiple Machine Translation Systems

Yui Suzuki   **Tomoyuki Kajiwara**   **Mamoru Komachi**

Graduate School of System Design, Tokyo Metropolitan University, Tokyo, Japan

{suzuki-yui, kajiwara-tomoyuki}@ed.tmu.ac.jp, komachi@tmu.ac.jp

Abstract

We propose a novel sentential paraphrase acquisition method. To build a well-balanced corpus for Paraphrase Identification, we especially focus on acquiring both non-trivial positive and negative instances. We use multiple machine translation systems to generate positive candidates and a monolingual corpus to extract negative candidates. To collect non-trivial instances, the candidates are uniformly sampled by word overlap rate. Finally, annotators judge whether the candidates are either positive or negative. Using this method, we built and released the first evaluation corpus for Japanese paraphrase identification, which comprises 655 sentence pairs.

1 Introduction

When two sentences share the same meaning but are written using different expressions, they are deemed to be a sentential paraphrase pair. Paraphrase Identification (PI) is a task that recognizes whether a pair of sentences is a paraphrase. PI is useful in many applications such as information retrieval (Wang et al., 2013) or question answering (Fader et al., 2013).

Despite this usefulness, there are only a few corpora that can be used to develop and evaluate PI systems. Moreover, such corpora are unavailable in many languages other than English. This is because manual paraphrase generation tends to cost a lot. Furthermore, unlike a bilingual parallel corpus for machine translation, a monolingual parallel corpus for PI cannot be spontaneously built.

Even though some paraphrase corpora are available, there are some limitations on them. For example, the Microsoft Research Paraphrase Corpus

Figure 1: Overview of candidate pair generation.

(MSRP) (Dolan and Brockett, 2005) is a standardized corpus in English for the PI task. However, as Rus et al. (2014) pointed out, MSRP collects candidate pairs using short edit distance, but this approach is limited to collecting positive instances with a low word overlap rate (WOR) (*non-trivial positive instances*, hereafter)[1]. In contrast, the Twitter Paraphrase Corpus (TPC) (Xu et al., 2014) comprises short noisy user-generated texts; hence, it is difficult to acquire negative instances with a high WOR (*non-trivial negative instances*, hereafter)[2].

To develop a more robust PI model, it is important to collect both *"non-trivial"* positive and negative instances for the evaluation corpus. To create a useful evaluation corpus, we propose a novel paraphrase acquisition method that has two viewpoints of balancing the corpus: positive/negative and trivial/non-trivial. To balance between positive and negative, our method has a machine translation part collecting mainly positive instances and a random extraction part collecting negative instances. In the machine translation part, we generate candidate sentence pairs using multiple machine translation systems. In the random extraction part, we extract candidate sentence pairs from a monolingual corpus. To collect both trivial and non-trivial instances, we sample candidate pairs

---

[1]*Non-trivial positive instances* are difficult to identify as semantically equivalent.

[2]*Non-trivial negative instances* are difficult to identify as semantically inequivalent.

Proceedings of the 55th Annual Meeting of the Association for Computational Linguistics- Student Research Workshop, pages 36–42

Vancouver, Canada, July 30 - August 4, 2017. ©2017 Association for Computational Linguistics

https://doi.org/10.18653/v1/P17-3007

using WOR. Finally, annotators judge whether the candidate pairs are paraphrases.

In this paper, we focus on the Japanese PI task and build a monolingual parallel corpus for its evaluation as there is no Japanese sentential paraphrase corpus available. As Figure 1 shows, we use phrase-based machine translation (PBMT) and neural machine translation (NMT) to generate two different Japanese sentences from one English sentence. We expect the two systems provide widely different translations with regard to surface form such as lexical variation and word order difference because they are known to have different characteristics (Bentivogli et al., 2016); for instance, PBMT produces more literal translations, whereas NMT produces more fluent translations.

We believe that when the translation succeeds, the two Japanese sentences have the same meaning but different expressions, which is a positive instance. On the other hand, translated candidates can be negative instances when they include fluent mistranslations. This occurs since adequacy is not checked during an annotation phase. Thus, we can also acquire some negative instances in this manner.

To actively acquire negative instances, we use Wikipedia to randomly extract sentences. In general, it is rare for sentences to become paraphrase when sentence pairs are collected randomly, so it is effective to acquire negative instances in this regard.

Our contributions are summarized as follows:

- Generated paraphrases using multiple machine translation systems for the first time

- Adjusted for a balance from two viewpoints: positive/negative and trivial/non-trivial

- Released[3] the first evaluation corpus for the Japanese PI task

2 Related Work

Paraphrase acquisition has been actively studied. For instance, paraphrases have been acquired from monolingual comparable corpora such as news articles regarding the same event (Shinyama et al., 2002) and multiple definitions of the same concept (Hashimoto et al., 2011). Although these methods effectively acquire paraphrases, there are not many domains that have comparable corpora. In contrast, our method can generate paraphrase

candidates from any sentences, and this allows us to choose any domain required by an application.

Methods using a bilingual parallel corpus are similar to our method. In fact, our method is an extension of previous studies that acquire paraphrases using manual translations of the same documents (Barzilay and McKeown, 2001; Pang et al., 2003). However, it is expensive to manually translate sentences to create large numbers of translation pairs. Thus, we propose a method that inexpensively generates translations using machine translation and Quality Estimation.

Ganitkevitch et al. (2013) and Pavlick et al. (2015) also use a bilingual parallel corpora to build a paraphrase database using bilingual pivoting (Bannard and Callison-Burch, 2005). Their methods differ from ours in that they aim to acquire phrase level paraphrase rules and carry out word alignment instead of machine translation.

There are also many studies on building a large scale corpora utilizing crowdsourcing in related tasks such as Recognizing Textual Entailment (RTE) (Marelli et al., 2014; Bowman et al., 2015) and Lexical Simplification (De Belder and Moens, 2012; Xu et al., 2016). Moreover, there are studies collecting paraphrases from captions to videos (Chen and Dolan, 2011) and images (Chen et al., 2015). One advantage of leveraging crowdsourcing is that annotation is done inexpensively, but it requires careful task design to gather valid data from non-expert annotators. In our study, we collect sentential paraphrase pairs, but we presume that it is difficult for non-expert annotators to provide well-balanced sentential paraphrase pairs, unlike lexical simplification, which only replaces content words. For this reason, annotators classify paraphrase candidate pairs in our study similar to the method used in the TPC and previous studies on RTE.

As for Japanese, there exists a paraphrase database (Mizukami et al., 2014) and an evaluation dataset that includes some paraphrases for lexical simplification (Kajiwara and Yamamoto, 2015; Kodaira et al., 2016). They provide either lexical or phrase-level paraphrases, but we focus on collecting sentence-level paraphrases for PI evaluation. There is also an evaluation dataset for RTE (Watanabe et al., 2013) containing 70 sentential paraphrase pairs; however, as there is a limitation in terms of size, we aim to build a larger corpus.

---

[3]https://github.com/tmu-nlp/paraphrase-corpus

Jaccard	# Sentence	Average Sentence Length			# Sample	# Positive	# Negative	# Unnatural	# Other
		source	PBMT	NMT					
$[0.0, 0.1)$	228	19.42	20.65	19.75	200	2	1 (0)	80	117
$[0.1, 0.2)$	2,117	21.56	24.81	22.01	200	11	14 (0)	147	28
$[0.2, 0.3)$	14,080	21.56	26.50	23.37	200	20	9 (0)	162	9
$[0.3, 0.4)$	51,316	23.48	29.69	26.29	200	24	15 (0)	161	0
$[0.4, 0.5)$	100,674	24.40	31.35	28.08	200	27	16 (0)	151	6
$[0.5, 0.6)$	134,101	23.16	29.90	27.26	200	34	16 (0)	142	8
$[0.6, 0.7)$	100,745	21.04	27.32	25.30	200	38	13 (0)	129	20
$[0.7, 0.8)$	55,610	18.83	24.57	23.04	200	53	12 (40)	131	4
$[0.8, 0.9)$	26,884	16.23	21.31	20.24	200	81	3 (80)	94	22
$[0.9, 1.0)$	8,071	13.79	18.40	17.55	200	73	3 (70)	56	68
$[1.0, 1.0]$	6,174	10.10	13.07	12.96	0	0	0 (0)	0	0
Total	500,000	19.42	24.32	22.35	2,000	363	102 (190)	1,253	282

Table 1: Statistics on our corpus. The number inside ( ) of Negative column is the number of instances extracted from Wikipedia and the other is that of machine-translated instances.

3 Candidate Generation

3.1 Paraphrase Generation using Multiple Machine Translation Systems

We use different types of machine translation systems (PBMT and NMT) to translate source sentences extracted from a monolingual corpus into a target language. This means that each source sentence has two versions in the target language, and we use the sentences as a pair.

To avoid collecting ungrammatical sentences as much as possible, we use Quality Estimation and eliminate inappropriate sentences for paraphrase candidate pairs. At WMT2016 (Bojar et al., 2016) in the Shared Task on Quality Estimation, the winning system YSDA (Kozlova et al., 2016) shows that it is effective for Quality Estimation to employ language model probabilities of source and target sentences, and BLEU scores between the source sentence and back-translation. Therefore, we calculate the language model probabilities of source sentences and translate them in the order of their probabilities. To further obtain better translations, we select sentence pairs in the descending order of machine translation output quality, which is defined as follows:

$$QE_i = \text{SBLEU}(e_i, \text{BT}_{\text{PBMT}}(e_i)) \times \text{SBLEU}(e_i, \text{BT}_{\text{NMT}}(e_i)) \tag{1}$$

Here, e_i denotes the i-th source sentence, BT_{PBMT} denotes the back-translation using PBMT, BT_{NMT} denotes the back-translation using NMT, and SBLEU denotes the sentence-level BLEU score (Nakov et al., 2012). When this score is high, it indicates that the difference in sentence meaning before and after translation is small for each machine translation system.

3.2 Non-Paraphrase Extraction from a Monolingual Corpus

This extraction part of our method is for acquiring non-trivial negative instances. Although the machine translation part of our method is expected to collect non-trivial negative instances too, there will be a certain gap between positive and negative instances. To fill the gap, we randomly collect sentence pairs from a monolingual corpus written in the target language.

To check whether the negative instances acquired by machine translation and those extracted directly from a monolingual corpus are discernible, we asked three people to annotate randomly extracted 100 instances whether a pair is machine-translated or not. The average F-score on the annotation was 0.34. This means the negative instances are not distinguishable, so this does not affect the balance of the corpus.

3.3 Balanced Sampling using Word Overlap Rate

To collect both trivial and non-trivial instances, we carefully sample candidate pairs. We classify the pairs into eleven ranges depending on the WOR and sample pairs uniformly for each range, except for the exact match pairs. The WOR is calculated as follows:

$$\text{Jaccard}(\text{T}_{\text{PBMT}}(e_i), \text{T}_{\text{NMT}}(e_i))$$
$$= \frac{\left| \text{T}_{\text{PBMT}}(e_i) \cap \text{T}_{\text{NMT}}(e_i) \right|}{\left| \text{T}_{\text{PBMT}}(e_i) \cup \text{T}_{\text{NMT}}(e_i) \right|} \tag{2}$$

Label	Example		
Positive	Input:	*My father was a very strong man.*	
	PBMT:	私の父は非常に強い男でした。	*My father was a very strong man.*
	NMT:	父はとても強い男だった。	*My father was a very strong man.*
Negative	Input:	*It is available as a generic medication.*	
	PBMT:	これは、一般的な薬として利用可能です。	*It is available as a generic medicine.*
	NMT:	ジェネリック医薬品として入手できます。	*It is available as a generic medication.*
Unnatural	Input:	*I want to wake up in the morning*	
	PBMT:	私は午前中に目を覚ますしたいです*	*I wake up want to in the morning**
	NMT:	私は朝起きたい	*I want to wake up in the morning*
Other	Input:	*Academy of Country Music Awards :*	
	PBMT:	アカデミーオブカントリーミュージックアワード：	*Academy of Country Music Awards :*
	NMT:	アカデミー・オブ・カントリー・ミュージック賞：	*Academy of Country Music Awards :*

Table 2: Annotation labels and examples.

Here, T_{PBMT} and T_{NMT} denote the sentence in the target language translated by PBMT and NMT respectively.

4 Corpus Creation

4.1 Acquiring Candidate Pairs in Japanese

We built the first evaluation corpus for Japanese PI using our method. We used Google Translate PBMT[4] and NMT[5] (Wu et al., 2016) to translate English sentences extracted from English Wikipedia [6] into Japanese sentences[7]. We calculated the language model probabilities using KenLM (Heafield, 2011), and built a 5-gram language model from the English Gigaword Fifth Edition (LDC2011T07). Then we translated the top 500,000 sentences and sampled 200 pairs in the descending order of machine translation output quality for each range, except for the exact match pairs (Table 1).

4.2 Annotation

We used four types of labels; *Positive*, *Negative*, *Unnatural*, and *Other* (Table 2). When both sentences of a candidate pair were fluent and semantically equivalent, we labeled it as *Positive*. In contrast, when the sentences were fluent but semantically inequivalent, the pair was labeled as *Negative*. *Positive* and *Negative* pairs were included in our corpus. The label *Unnatural* was assigned to pairs when at least one of the sentences was ungrammatical or not fluent. In addition, the label

Other was assigned to sentences and phrases that comprise named entities or that have minor differences such as the presence of punctuation, even though they are paraphrases. *Unnatural* or *Other* pairs were discarded from our corpus.

One of the authors annotated 2,000 machine-translated pairs, then another author annotated the pairs labeled either *Positive* or *Negative* by the first annotator. The inter-annotator agreement (Cohen's Kappa) was κ=0.60. Taking into consideration the fact that PI deals with a deep understanding of sentences and that there are some ambiguous instances without context (e.g., *good child* and *good kid*), the score is considered to be sufficiently high. There were 89 disagreements, and the final label was decided by discussion. As a result, we acquired 363 positive and 102 negative machine-translated pairs.

Although the machine translation part of our method successfully collected non-trivial positive instances, it acquired only a few non-trivial negative instances as we expected. To fill the gap between positive and negative in higher WOR, we randomly collected sentence pairs from Japanese Wikipedia[8] and added 190 non-trivial negative instances. At the end of both parts of our method, we acquired 655 sentence pairs in total, comprising 363 positive and 292 negative instances.

Figures 2 and 3 indicate the distribution of the instances in each corpus. Compared to MSRP and TPC, our corpus covers all ranges of WOR both for positive and negative instances.

---

[4]GOOGLETRANSLATE function on Google Sheets.

[5]https://translate.google.co.jp/

[6]https://dumps.wikimedia.org/enwiki/20160501/

[7]We trained Moses and translated the sentences from Wikipedia; however, it did not work well. This is the reason why we chose Google machine translation systems, which work sufficiently well on Wikipedia.

[8]https://dumps.wikimedia.org/jawiki/20161001/

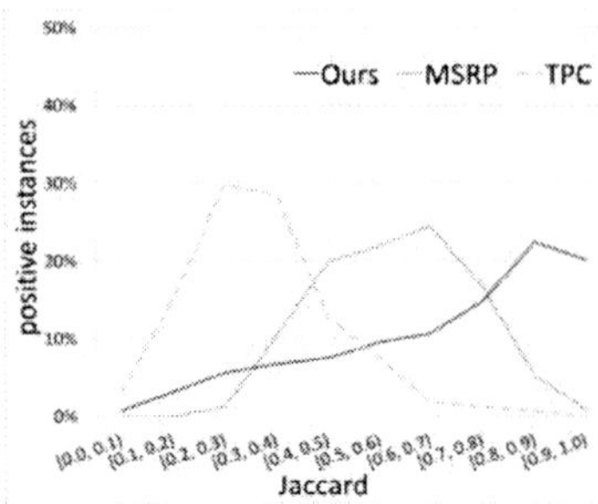

Figure 2: Distributions of positive sentence pairs in each WOR.

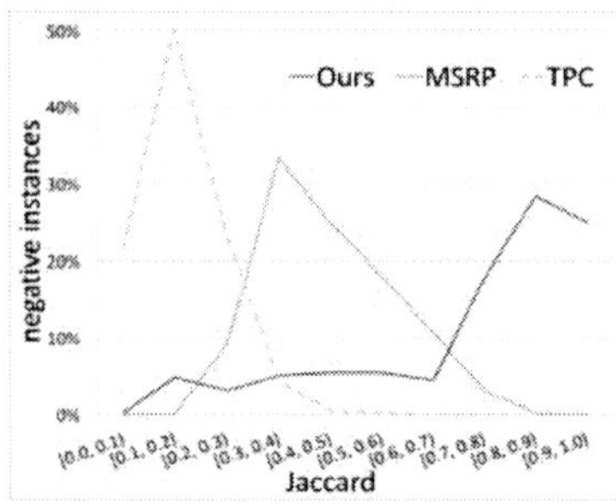

Figure 3: Distributions of negative sentence pairs in each WOR.

Category	%
Content word replacement	63.1
Phrasal/Sentential replacement	25.0
Function word replacement	23.2
Function word insertion/deletion	14.3
Content word insertion/deletion	9.5
Word order	6.5
Lexical entailment	4.2

Table 3: The result of corpus analysis.

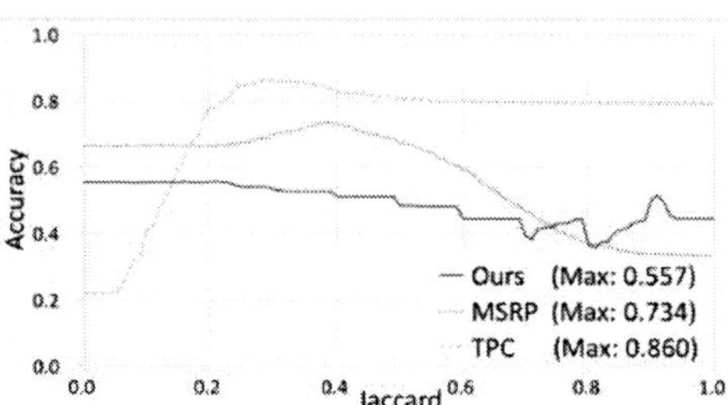

Figure 4: Accuracy of PI using WOR.

5 Discussion

5.1 Corpus Analysis

Table 3 shows the result of corpus analysis on machine-translated instances. We randomly sampled ten pairs from each range of WOR for both positive and negative pairs, i.e., 168 pairs in total, and investigated what type of pairs are included.

We found that most of the data comprises content word replacement (63.1%). Further investigation of this category shows that 30.2% are related to a change in the origin of words and transliterations. In Example # 1 in Table 4, PBMT outputs a transliteration of a *member*, and NMT outputs a Japanese translation. Next, the second most common type of pair is phrasal/sentential replacement (25.0%). When a pair has a bigger chunk of sentence or the sentence as a whole is replaced, it is assigned to this category. This implies that our method, which focuses on sampling by WOR, works to collect non-trivial instances like Examples # 2 and # 3. On the contrary, Example # 4 is an example of instances where machine translations demonstrate each characteristic like that mentioned in Section 1 (PBMT is more literal and

NMT is more fluent), so negative instances are produced as we expected. The outputs are semantically close, but the surface is very different. In this example, the PBMT output entails the NMT output.

5.2 Paraphrase Identification

We conducted a simple PI experiment — an unsupervised binary classification. Here, we classified each sentence pair as either paraphrase or non-paraphrase using WOR thresholds and evaluated its accuracy. Figure 4 shows the results from each corpus. Achieving around accuracy of 80% does not mean that the corpus is well built in any language. In that respect, this result proves that our corpus includes more instances that are difficult to be solved with only superficial clues, which helps develop a more robust PI model.

6 Conclusion

We proposed a paraphrase acquisition method to create a well-balanced corpus for PI. Our method generates positive instances using machine translations, extracts negative instances from a monolingual corpus, and uses WOR to collect both triv-

#	Type of Replacement	Jaccard	Label	Trivial/Non-Trivial	Example	
1	Lexical	0.60	P	Trivial	Input:	*He was a **member** of the Republican Party.*
					PBMT:	彼は共和党のメンバーでした。
					NMT:	彼は共和党の一員だった。
2	Lexical	0.90	N	Non-Trivial	Input:	*There is also a strong Roman Catholic **presence**.*
					PBMT:	強力なローマカトリックの存在感もあります。
					NMT:	強力なローマカトリックの存在もあります。
3	Phrasal	0.07	P	Non-Trivial	Input:	*It is **rarely** used.*
					PBMT:	めったに使われることはありません。
					NMT:	まれに使用されます。
4	Phrasal	0.15	N	Trivial	Input:	*Why do **you work so hard**?*
					PBMT:	なぜあなたは一生懸命働くのですか？
					NMT:	どうしてそんなに頑張ってるの？

Table 4: Examples from our corpus. Bold words/phrases were replaced.

ial and non-trivial instances. With this method, we built the first evaluation corpus for Japanese PI. According to our PI experiment, our method made the corpus difficult to be solved.

Our method can be used in other languages, as long as machine translation systems and monolingual corpora exist. In addition, more candidates could be added by including additional machine translation systems. A future study will be undertaken to explore these possibilities.

Acknowledgments

We thank Naoaki Okazaki, Yusuke Miyao, and anonymous reviewers for their constructive feedback. The first author was partially supported by Grant-in-Aid for the Japan Society for Promotion of Science Research Fellows.

References

Colin Bannard and Chris Callison-Burch. 2005. Paraphrasing with Bilingual Parallel Corpora. In *Proceedings of the 43rd Annual Meeting of the Association for Computational Linguistics*. pages 597–604.

Regina Barzilay and Kathleen R. McKeown. 2001. Extracting Paraphrases from a Parallel Corpus. In *Proceedings of 39th Annual Meeting of the Association for Computational Linguistics*. pages 50–57.

Luisa Bentivogli, Arianna Bisazza, Mauro Cettolo, and Marcello Federico. 2016. Neural versus Phrase-Based Machine Translation Quality: a Case Study. In *Proceedings of the 2016 Conference on Empirical Methods in Natural Language Processing*. pages 257–267.

Ondřej Bojar, Rajen Chatterjee, Christian Federmann, Yvette Graham, Barry Haddow, Matthias Huck, Antonio Jimeno Yepes, Philipp Koehn, Varvara Logacheva, Christof Monz, Matteo Negri, Aurelie Neveol, Mariana Neves, Martin Popel, Matt Post, Raphael Rubino, Carolina Scarton, Lucia Specia, Marco Turchi, Karin Verspoor, and Marcos Zampieri. 2016. Findings of the 2016 Conference on Machine Translation. In *Proceedings of the First Conference on Machine Translation*. pages 131–198.

Samuel R. Bowman, Gabor Angeli, Christopher Potts, and Christopher D. Manning. 2015. A large annotated corpus for learning natural language inference. In *Proceedings of the 2015 Conference on Empirical Methods in Natural Language Processing*. pages 632–642.

David Chen and William Dolan. 2011. Collecting Highly Parallel Data for Paraphrase Evaluation. In *Proceedings of the 49th Annual Meeting of the Association for Computational Linguistics: Human Language Technologies*. pages 190–200.

Jianfu Chen, Polina Kuznetsova, David Warren, and Yejin Choi. 2015. Déjà Image-Captions: A Corpus of Expressive Descriptions in Repetition. In *Proceedings of the 2015 Conference of the North American Chapter of the Association for Computational Linguistics: Human Language Technologies*. pages 504–514.

Jan De Belder and Marie-Francine Moens. 2012. A Dataset for the Evaluation of Lexical Simplification. In *Proceedings of the 13th International Conference on Computational Linguistics and Intelligent Text Processing*. pages 426–437.

William B. Dolan and Chris Brockett. 2005. Automatically Constructing a Corpus of Sentential Paraphrases. In *Proceedings of the Third International Workshop on Paraphrasing*. pages 9–16.

Anthony Fader, Luke Zettlemoyer, and Oren Etzioni. 2013. Paraphrase-Driven Learning for Open Question Answering. In *Proceedings of the 51st Annual Meeting of the Association for Computational Linguistics*. pages 1608–1618.

Juri Ganitkevitch, Benjamin Van Durme, and Chris Callison-Burch. 2013. PPDB: The Paraphrase Database. In *Proceedings of the 2013 Conference of* the North American Chapter of the Association for Computational Linguistics: Human Language Technologies*. pages 758–764.

Chikara Hashimoto, Kentaro Torisawa, Stijn De Saeger, Jun'ichi Kazama, and Sadao Kurohashi. 2011. Extracting Paraphrases from Definition Sentences on the Web. In *Proceedings of the 49th Annual Meeting of the Association for Computational Linguistics: Human Language Technologies*. pages 1087–1097.

Kenneth Heafield. 2011. KenLM: Faster and Smaller Language Model Queries. In *Proceedings of the Sixth Workshop on Statistical Machine Translation*. pages 187–197.

Tomoyuki Kajiwara and Kazuhide Yamamoto. 2015. Evaluation Dataset and System for Japanese Lexical Simplification. In *Proceedings of the ACL-IJCNLP 2015 Student Research Workshop*. pages 35–40.

Tomonori Kodaira, Tomoyuki Kajiwara, and Mamoru Komachi. 2016. Controlled and Balanced Dataset for Japanese Lexical Simplification. In *Proceedings of the ACL 2016 Student Research Workshop*. pages 1–7.

Anna Kozlova, Mariya Shmatova, and Anton Frolov. 2016. YSDA Participation in the WMT'16 Quality Estimation Shared Task. In *Proceedings of the First Conference on Machine Translation*. pages 793–799.

Marco Marelli, Stefano Menini, Marco Baroni, Luisa Bentivogli, Raffaella bernardi, and Roberto Zamparelli. 2014. A SICK cure for the evaluation of compositional distributional semantic models. In *Proceedings of the Ninth International Conference on Language Resources and Evaluation*. pages 216–223.

Masahiro Mizukami, Graham Neubig, Sakriani Sakti, Tomoki Toda, and Satoshi Nakamura. 2014. Building a free, general-domain paraphrase database for Japanese. In *Proceedings of the 17th Oriental Chapter of the International Committee for the Co-ordination and Standardization of Speech Databases and Assessment Techniques (COCOSDA 2014)*. pages 1–4.

Preslav Nakov, Francisco Guzman, and Stephan Vogel. 2012. Optimizing for Sentence-Level BLEU+1 Yields Short Translations. In *Proceedings of COLING 2012, the 24th International Conference on Computational Linguistics: Technical Papers*. pages 1979–1994.

Bo Pang, Kevin Knight, and Daniel Marcu. 2003. Syntax-based Alignment of Multiple Translations: Extracting Paraphrases and Generating New Sentences. In *Proceedings of the 2003 Human Language Technology Conference of the North American Chapter of the Association for Computational Linguistics*. pages 102–109.

Ellie Pavlick, Pushpendre Rastogi, Juri Ganitkevitch, Benjamin Van Durme, and Chris Callison-Burch. 2015. PPDB 2.0: Better paraphrase ranking, fine-grained entailment relations, word embeddings, and style classification. In *Proceedings of the 53rd Annual Meeting of the Association for Computational Linguistics and the 7th International Joint Conference on Natural Language Processing*. pages 425–430.

Vasile Rus, Rajendra Banjade, and Mihai Lintean. 2014. On Paraphrase Identification Corpora. In *Proceedings of the Ninth International Conference on Language Resources and Evaluation*. pages 2422–2429.

Yusuke Shinyama, Satoshi Sekine, and Kiyoshi Sudo. 2002. Automatic Paraphrase Acquisition from News Articles. In *Proceedings of the 2002 Human Language Technologiy Conference*. pages 1–6.

Chenguang Wang, Nan Duan, Ming Zhou, and Ming Zhang. 2013. Paraphrasing Adaptation for Web Search Ranking. In *Proceedings of the 51st Annual Meeting of the Association for Computational Linguistics*. pages 41–46.

Yotaro Watanabe, Yusuke Miyao, Junta Mizuno, Tomohide Shibata, Hiroshi Kanayama, Cheng-Wei Lee, Chuan-Jie Lin, Shuming Shi, Teruko Mitamura, Noriko Kando, Hideki Shima, and Kohichi Takeda. 2013. Overview of the Recognizing Inference in Text (RITE-2) at NTCIR-10. In *Proceedings of the 10th NTCIR Conference*. pages 385–404.

Yonghui Wu, Mike Schuster, Zhifeng Chen, Quoc V. Le, Mohammad Norouzi, Wolfgang Macherey, Maxim Krikun, Yuan Cao, Qin Gao, Klaus Macherey, Jeff Klingner, Apurva Shah, Melvin Johnson, Xiaobing Liu, ukasz Kaiser, Stephan Gouws, Yoshikiyo Kato, Taku Kudo, Hideto Kazawa, Keith Stevens, George Kurian, Nishant Patil, Wei Wang, Cliff Young, Jason Smith, Jason Riesa, Alex Rudnick, Oriol Vinyals, Greg Corrado, Macduff Hughes, and Jeffrey Dean. 2016. Google's Neural Machine Translation System: Bridging the Gap between Human and Machine Translation. In *arXiv preprint arXiv:1609.08144*. pages 1–23.

Wei Xu, Courtney Napoles, Ellie Pavlick, Quanze Chen, and Chris Callison-Burch. 2016. Optimizing Statistical Machine Translation for Text Simplification. *Transactions of the Association for Computational Linguistics* 4:401–415.

Wei Xu, Alan Ritter, Chris Callison-Burch, William B. Dolan, and Yangfeng Ji. 2014. Extracting Lexically Divergent Paraphrases from Twitter. *Transactions of the Association for Computational Linguistics* 2(1):435–448.

Segmentation guided attention networks for Visual Question Answering

Vasu Sharma
Indian Institute of Technology, Kanpur
sharma.vasu55@gmail.com

Labhesh Patel
Abzooba Inc.
labhesh@gmail.com

Ankita Bishnu
Indian Institute of Technology, Kanpur
ankitab.iitk@gmail.com

Abstract

In this paper we propose to solve the problem of Visual Question Answering by using a novel segmentation guided attention based network which we call **SegAttend-Net**. We use image segmentation maps, generated by a Fully Convolutional Deep Neural Network to refine our attention maps and use these refined attention maps to make the model focus on the relevant parts of the image to answer a question. The refined attention maps are used by the LSTM network to learn to produce the answer. We presently train our model on the visual7W dataset and do a category wise evaluation of the 7 question categories. We achieve state of the art results on this dataset and beat the previous benchmark on this dataset by a 1.5% margin improving the question answering accuracy from 54.1% to 55.6% and demonstrate improvements in each of the question categories. We also visualize our generated attention maps and note their improvement over the attention maps generated by the previous best approach.

1 Introduction

Visual Question Answering (VQA) is a recent problem in the intersection of the fields of Computer Vision and Natural Language Processing, where a system is required to answer arbitrary questions about the images, which may require reasoning about the relationships of objects with each other and the overall scene.

There are many potential applications for VQA. The most immediate is as an aid to blind and visually impaired individuals, enabling them to get information about images both on the web and in the real world.

The task of Image Question answering has received a lot of traction from the research community of late (Ren et al. (2015), Gao et al. (2015), Antol et al. (2015a), Malinowski et al. (2015)) due to the inherent challenging nature of the problem which involves combining question understanding in context of the image, scene understanding and common sense reasoning to be able to answer the question effectively. The problem is much more complicated than the purely text based Question answering problem which has been extensively studied in the past (Berant and Liang (2014), Kumar et al. (2015), Bordes et al. (2014), Weston et al. (2014)) and needs the model to be able to combine information from multiple sources and reason about them together.

Most recent approaches are based on Neural Networks, where a Convolutional Neural is first used to extract out image features and then these image features are used along with some RNN model to understand the question and generate an answer. However the problem with such approaches is that they do not know where to look. Recent approaches solve this problem by calculating an attention over the image by using the question embeddings to try and guide the model where to look, however such attention maps are still not very precise and not grounded at the image level. Moreover, there is no way to explicitly train these attention maps and the hope is that the model will implicitly learn them during training. In this paper we propose an approach which tries to guide these attention maps to learn to focus on the right regions in this image by giving them pixel level grounded annotations in the form of segmentation maps which we generate using a Fully Convolutional Deep Neural Network.

Proceedings of the 55th Annual Meeting of the Association for Computational Linguistics- Student Research Workshop, pages 43–48
Vancouver, Canada, July 30 - August 4, 2017. ©2017 Association for Computational Linguistics
https://doi.org/10.18653/v1/P17-3008

The rest of the paper is organized as follows. The existing literature on this problem is presented in Section 2 followed by a description of the datasets we used in Section 3. Section 4 introduces our approach and gives a detailed explanation of how we generate the segment maps and use them to guide our model to learn better attention maps which are subsequently used to perform the task of visual question answering. Finally we present the results in Section 5 and outline the papers conclusions and directions for future research in Section 6.

2 Literature Review

VQA is a fairly recent problem and was proposed by Antol et al. (2015b). Despite being a recent problem, several researchers from across the world have attempted to solve it. However, the performance still remains a long way off from the human performance which means there is still scope for improvement.

One of the early neural network based model for this problem proposed by Malinowski et al. (2015) combines a CNN and a LSTM into an end-to-end architecture that predict answers conditioning on a question and an image. In this model at each time step the LSTM is fed with a vector which is an one hot vector encoding of word in the question and the CNN encoding of the whole image. In Ren et al. (2015), a similar kind of approach was employed, with the main differnce that CNN features was fed to LSTM only once for each question; either before the question or after the last word of the question. This model achieved better accuracy than Malinowski et al. (2015).

In Agrawal et al. (2015) the best model model uses a two layer LSTM to encode the questions and the last hidden layer of VGGNet Simonyan and Zisserman (2014) to encode the images. Both the question and image features are then transformed to a common space and fused by a hadamard product and passed through a fully connected layer followed by a softmax layer to obtain a score over 1000 most frequent answers. The model proposed in Gao et al. (2015) had four components: Two separate LSTM modules for question representation and context of answer generated so far with a shared word embedding layer, a CNN to extract the image representation and a fusing component to fuse the information from other three components and generate the answer. All of these models look at the CNN feature of the whole image whereas to answer the real word questions concentrating to parts of the image is more useful in most of the cases. Many of the proposed VQA systems afterwards have incorporated spatial attention to CNN features, instead of using global features from the entire image. Both Shih et al. (2016); Ilievski et al. (2016) used Edge Boxes Zitnick and Dollr (2014) to generate Bounding Box proposals in the image. In Shih et al. (2016) a CNN was used for local features extraction of the images from each of these boxes. The input to their model was consisting of these CNN features, question features and one of the multiple choice answer. Weighted average score for each of the proposed region's features was used to calculate the score for an answer. In Ilievski et al. (2016) the authors use region proposals for the objects present in the question. At training time the objects labels and bounding boxes are taken from the annotation of COCO dataset and at test time bounding box proposals are classified using ResnetHe et al. (2015). Word2vecMikolov et al. (2013) is used to get a similarity between bounding box labels and objects present in question. Any bounding box with a similarity score greater than 0.5 is successively fed to an LSTM and at last time step the global CNN features for the image is also fed to the LSTM. A separate LSTM was used to represent the question. The output of these two LSTMs are then fed to a fully connected layer to predict the question. In Zhu et al. (2015) the model actually learns which region of the image to attend rather than feeding the model any specific region of the image. Here the LSTM is fed with the CNN feature of the whole image and the question word by word. Based on the image features and hidden state, the model actually learns which part of the image it should look at and generates an attention vector. This attention vector is operated on the CNN feature of the whole image resulting in some focused parts of the image. The model computes the log-likelihood of an answer by a dot product between CNN features of the image and the last LSTM hidden state.

We build on this model by proposing how to generate better attention maps and use them to improve the performance on the VQA task.

Several newer approaches also propose novel methods of computing these attention maps. Notable among these are Z. Yang and Smola. (2015) and J. Lu and Parikh (2016). The former among these uses the question's semantic representation to search for the regions in an image that are related to the answer and used a multilayer approach to attend important parts of the image. In each layer of the attention it actually refines where to look at in the image.

3 Dataset

We did our experimentation on the Visual7W Dataset which was introduced by Zhu et al. (2015). Visual7W is named after the seven categories of questions it contains: What, Where, How, When, Who, Why, and Which. The dataset also provides object level groundings in the form of bounding boxes for the objects occuring in the question. The Visual7W dataset is collected on 47,300 COCO images. In total, it has 327,939 QA pairs, together with 1,311,756 human-generated multiple-choices and 561,459 object groundings from 36,579 categories. In addition, it also provides complete grounding annotations that link the object mentioned in the QA sentences to their bounding boxes in the images and therefore introduce a new QA type with image regions as the visually grounded answers.

We use this dataset for our task as we wanted to study how having pixel level groundings in form of segmentation maps affect each particular question type among how, when, where, why etc. We expect the improvement to be substantial for questions like 'how many' and 'where' which intuitively should benefit most from such pixel level groundings. This study allows us to validate this. We can also compare how these segmentation maps correspond with the provided object level groundings. Hence this dataset is our dataset of choice for this study.

4 Approach

We now present the approach we used to solve the problem of Visual Question Answering. A complete diagrammatic representation of our **SegAttendNet** model is presented in Figure 2. Each component of this model is explained in the subsequent subsections.

4.1 Generating segmentation masks for the image using the question

We first use the question to determine the objects whose segmentation maps we need to extract. This is done by using a POS tagging of the question to determine the nouns occurring in the question. After pre-processing these nouns, we match them to the 60 object categories from the Pascal context dataset Mottaghi et al. (2014) to know which of these objects might occur in the image. We then generate the segmentation maps from the question using the following steps:

- The Image is then fed to a Fully Convolutional Neural Network (FCN) Long et al. (2015), trained on the Pascal Context dataset to perform semantic segmentation on it based on the 60 classes of PASCAL Context dataset

- The FCN-16 feature map is generated using the architecture described in Figure 1. The lower resolution segment map (16X lower spatial resolution than the original image) is obtained from the fuse pooled layer, which combines both local features from lower layers and global features from higher layers to generate a segmentation map. We take a softmax over the 60 channels (corresponding to the 60 object categories) to obtain a probability map over the various classes.

- Now we extract the channels from this segmentation map which correspond to the nouns occurring in the question. We sum the segmentation map probabilities for these channels to obtain a single channel combined segmentation map. The intuition behind summing these channels is that, a particular pixel location in the image can have any of the objects occurring in the question with a probability which is the sum of the probability of each individual object occurring at that location.

- This map is further used in the attention network to refine the attention maps as described in the next subsection.

4.2 Using segmentation maps to guide the attention network for VQA

Once we have generated the segment maps and combined them into a single map based on the objects occurring in the question, we use this map to

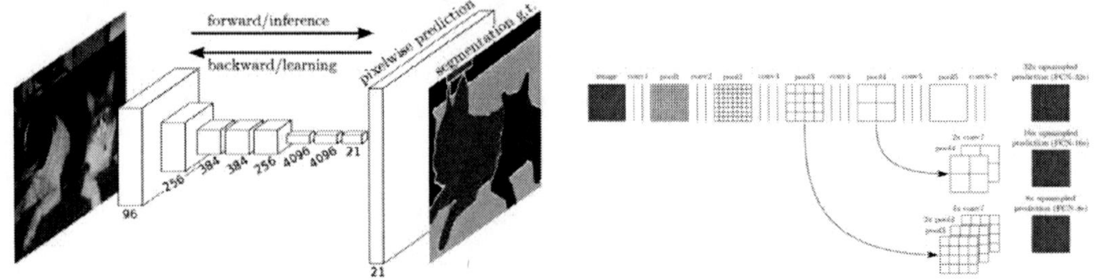

Figure 1: Fully Convolutional Neural Networks for Semantic segmentation

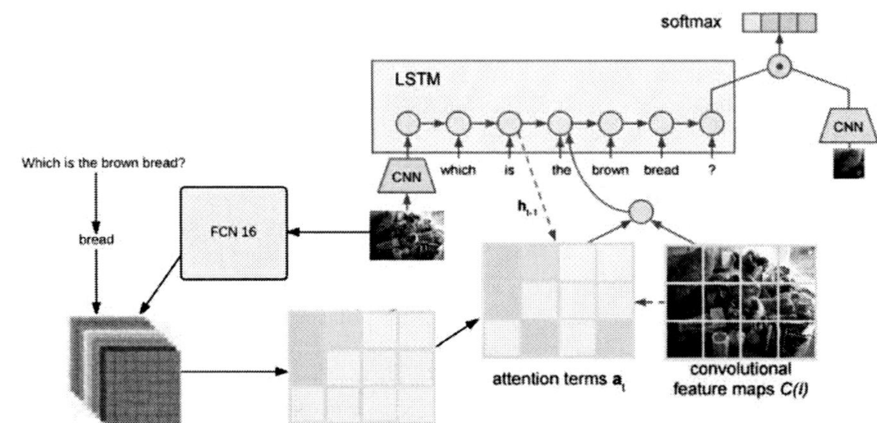

Figure 2: Our SegAttendNet for Visual Question Answering

Model	What	Where	When	Who	Why	How	Overall
Human(Question only)	0.356	0.322	0.393	0.342	0.439	0.337	0.353
Human(Question + Image)	0.965	0.957	0.944	0.965	0.927	0.942	0.964
Logistic Regression (Ques + Image)	0.429	0.454	0.621	0.501	0.343	0.356	0.359
LSTM (Question + Image)	0.489	0.544	0.713	0.581	0.513	0.503	0.521
Visual7W, LSTM-Attn(Ques+Image)	0.529	0.560	0.743	0.602	0.522	0.466	0.541
SegAttendNet(Ours)(Ques+Image)	**0.539**	**0.581**	**0.754**	**0.611**	**0.542**	**0.494**	**0.556**

Table 1: Comparison of results of our model against some existing approaches on the VQA task

guide our attention model to help it know where to look. We use the following steps to combine our segmentation maps with the attention based VQA network:

- The image is first passed through a VGG 16 network Simonyan and Zisserman (2014) in a feed forward manner and the fc7 features are extracted from the VGG network giving us a 4096 dimensional vector. These image features are fed as input to the LSTM at $t = 0$ and forms an initializing mechanism for the LSTM network.

- The question is passed through an LSTM network word by word, with a one hot word embedding being fed to the network at each time step. We also record the LSTM state at each time step. Lets say the previous such state was $h(t-1)$. The LSTM's ability to remember temporal context allows the network to understand the question with reference to the

46

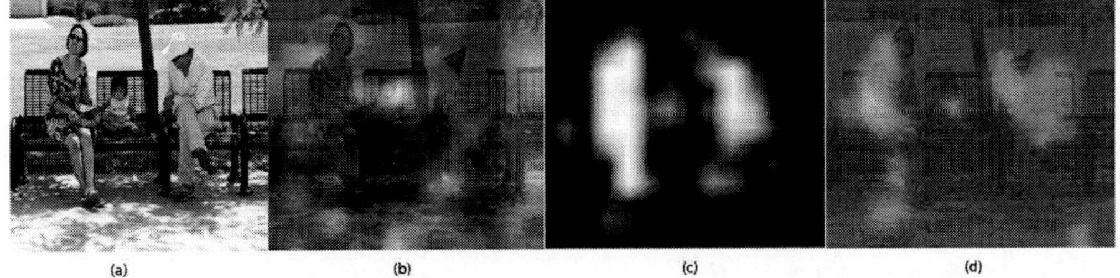

Figure 3: Question: "How many people are in the image?" Answer: "three"
a) Original image b) Attention map generated by previous state of the art approach c) Our low resolution segmentation map guidance d) Attention map generated by our SegAttendnet Model

input image and to subsequently refine it's internal representation at each time step based on the new input it receives.

- The above steps can be represented by the equations:

$$v_0 = W_i[F(I)] + b_i,$$
$$v_i = W_w[OH(t_i)], i = 1, ..., m$$

Here F is the transformation function which uses the VGG's fc7 layer to convert an image into a 4096 dimensional embedding. $OH(.)$ represents he one-hot encoding for the word t_i. The weight matrices W_i and W_w embed the image and word embeddings into d_i and d_w dimensional embedding spaces such that d_i and d_w are both 512. The embedded image vector is used as the initial input to the LSTM network.

- Now lets call our segmentation map obtained from the FCN-16 as $S(I)$. Also let's call the pool5 features extracted from the VGG network as $C(I)$ Now we compute the attention by the following set of equations:

$$e_t = W_a^T \cdot tanh(W_{he}h(t-1) + W_{ce}C(I)$$
$$+ W_{se}S(I)) + b_a$$
$$a_t = softmax(e_t)$$
$$r_t = a^T_t \cdot C(I)$$

Here a_t is the generated attention map which helps the model decide how much attention to pay to various parts of the image by taking a dot product with the convolutional feature map of the image to generate r_t.

- Now this computed attention weighted convolution map is fed back to the LSTM net-

work and the whole process repeats till the whole question is exhausted.

- In the end, the final state of the LSTM network and the pool 5 convolutional features are used to generate the final answer to the question. The end of the question is denoted by the question mark token.

- A decoder LSTM is used for open ended question and a softmax for multiple choice questions. In case of open ended questions, the previous word output is fed back to the LSTM network as input for generating the next answer word.

- A cross entropy loss is used to train the model using Backpropagation using Adam update rule. Hyperparameter tuning is done on the validation set and the results are reported after testing on a held out test set. The train, val and test sets are kept exactly the same as the original Visual7W paper to allow for a fair comparison. We also compare our approach with the human performance on this task.

5 Results

We evaluated our model for the telling questions in the Visual7W dataset using the approach we described in the previous section. The results of the same are presented in Table 1.

We note that our model outperforms the existing best reported result on this dataset by close to 1.5% margin. We also notice that we achieve substantial improvements in all the question categories. A closer observation of Figure 3 also reveals that our intuition that the model will perform substantially better on 'how many' and 'where' kind of questions does seem to be empirically justified as we can see a 3% improvement in the 'how' questions and a 2.1% improvement in the 'where' questions. Visualizing the attention maps also tells us that our attention maps are much more refined than the ones produced by the older approaches.

6 Conclusion and Future Work

In this paper we presented our model SegAttendNet to use segmentation maps to guide our attention model to focus on the right parts of an image to answer a question. We demonstrate that our model outperforms all other approaches on this dataset and attains superior performance in all question categories.

Right now we haven't tried combining our approach with more complicated attention mechanisms like the Stacked Attention Networks and Hierarchical Co-Attention networks. Our approach can easily be extended to the same and can help us achieve even better performances. We also plan to experiment with other much larger datasets which too can let our model train much better.

References

A. Agrawal, S. Antol, J. Lu, M. Mitchell, D. Batra, C. L. Zitnick, and D. Parikh. 2015. Vqa: Visual question answering. *arXiv preprint arXiv:1505.00468* .

S. Antol, A. Agrawal, J. Lu, M. Mitchell, D. Batra, C. L. Zitnick, and D. Parikh. 2015a. Vqa: Visual question answering. *arXiv preprint arXiv:1505.00468* .

Stanislaw Antol, Aishwarya Agrawal, Jiasen Lu, Margaret Mitchell, Dhruv Batra, C. Lawrence Zitnick, and Devi Parikh. 2015b. VQA: Visual Question Answering. In *International Conference on Computer Vision (ICCV)*.

J. Berant and P. Liang. 2014. Semantic parsing via paraphrasing. *In Proceedings of ACL* 2.

A. Bordes, S. Chopra, and J. Weston. 2014. Question answering with subgraph embeddings. *arXiv preprint arXiv:1406.3676* .

H. Gao, J. Mao, J. Zhou, Z. Huang, L. Wang, and W. Xu. 2015. Are you talking to a machine? dataset and methods for multilingual image question answering. *NIPS* .

Kaiming He, Xiangyu Zhang, Shaoqing Ren, and Jian Sun. 2015. Deep residual learning for image recognition. *CoRR* abs/1512.03385. http://arxiv.org/abs/1512.03385.

I. Ilievski, S. Yan, and J. Feng. 2016. A focused dynamic attention model for visual question answering. *arXiv preprint arXiv:1604.01485* .

J. Yang D. Batra J. Lu and D. Parikh. 2016. Hierarchical question-image co-attention for visual question answering. *CoRR.abs/1606.00061* .

A. Kumar, O. Irsoy, J. Su, J. Bradbury, R. English, B. Pierce, P. Ondruska, I. Gulrajani, and R. Socher. 2015. Ask me anything: Dynamic memory networks for natural language processing. *arXiv preprint arXiv:1506.07285* .

Jonathan Long, Evan Shelhamer, and Trevor Darrell. 2015. Fully convolutional networks for semantic segmentation. *CVPR* .

M. Malinowski, M. Rohrbach, and M. Fritz. 2015. Ask your neurons: A neural-based approach to answering questions about images. *arXiv preprint arXiv:1505.01121* .

Tomas Mikolov, Kai Chen, Greg Corrado, and Jeffrey Dean. 2013. Efficient estimation of word representations in vector space. *CoRR* abs/1301.3781. http://arxiv.org/abs/1301.3781.

Roozbeh Mottaghi, Xianjie Chen, Xiaobai Liu, Nam-Gyu Cho, Seong-Whan Lee, Sanja Fidler, Raquel Urtasun, and Alan Yuille. 2014. The role of context for object detection and semantic segmentation in the wild. In *IEEE Conference on Computer Vision and Pattern Recognition (CVPR)*.

M. Ren, R. Kiros, , and R. Zemel. 2015. Exploring models and data for image question answering. *arXiv preprint arXiv:1505.02074* .

K. J. Shih, S. Singh, and D. Hoiem. 2016. Where to look: Focus regions for visual question answering. *CVPR* .

Karen Simonyan and Andrew Zisserman. 2014. Very deep convolutional networks for large-scale image recognition. *CoRR* abs/1409.1556. http://arxiv.org/abs/1409.1556.

J. Weston, S. Chopra, and A. Bordes. 2014. Memory networks. *arXiv preprint arXiv:1410.3916* .

X. He J. Gao L. Deng Z. Yang and A. J. Smola. 2015. Stacked attention networks for image question answering. *CoRR, abs/1511.02274* .

Zhu, O. Groth, M. S. Bernstein, and L. Fei-Fei. 2015. Visual7w: Grounded question answering in images. *CoRR abs/1511.03416* .

C. L. Zitnick and P. Dollr. 2014. Locating object proposals from edges. *ECCV* .

Text-based Speaker Identification on Multiparty Dialogues Using Multi-document Convolutional Neural Networks

Kaixin Ma
Math & Computer Science
Emory University
Atlanta, GA 30322, USA

Catherine Xiao
Math & Computer Science
Emory University
Atlanta, GA 30322, USA

Jinho D. Choi
Math & Computer Science
Emory University
Atlanta, GA 30322, USA

{kaixin.ma, catherine.xiao, jinho.choi}@emory.edu

Abstract

We propose a convolutional neural network model for text-based speaker identification on multiparty dialogues extracted from the TV show, *Friends*. While most previous works on this task rely heavily on acoustic features, our approach attempts to identify speakers in dialogues using their speech patterns as captured by transcriptions to the TV show. It has been shown that different individual speakers exhibit distinct idiolectal styles. Several convolutional neural network models are developed to discriminate between differing speech patterns. Our results confirm the promise of text-based approaches, with the best performing model showing an accuracy improvement of over 6% upon the baseline CNN model.

1 Introduction

Speakers verbalize their thoughts in different ways through dialogues. The differences in their expressions, be they striking or subtle, can serve as clues to the speakers' identities when they are withheld. This paper investigates the possibility of identifying speakers in anonymous multiparty dialogues.

Impressive advancements have been achieved in the field of speech recognition prior to this paper (Sadjadi et al., 2016; Fine et al., 2001; Campbell et al., 2006). Research on dialogue systems has also involved considerable efforts on speaker identification, as it constitutes an important step in building a more natural and human-like system (Raux et al., 2006; Hazen et al., 2003). Research in this area, however, has mostly been focused on acoustic features, which are absent in many situations (e.g., online chats, discussion forums, text messages). In addition, it is commonly acknowledged that natural language texts themselves reflect the personalities of speakers, in addition to their semantic content (Mairesse et al., 2007).

Various experiments have demonstrated significant differences in the linguistic patterns generated by different participants, suggesting the possibility to perform speaker identification with text-based data. An increasing number of large unstructured dialogue datasets are becoming available, although they comprise only the dialogue transcripts without speaker labels (Tiedemann, 2012; Lowe et al., 2015). This paper attempts to identify the six main characters in the dialogues occurring in the first 8 seasons of the TV show, *Friends*. The minor characters in the show are to be identified collectively as *Other*.

For each episode, we first withhold the identity of the speaker to each utterance in its transcript, and have prediction models label the speakers. The accuracy and the F1 score of the labeling against the gold labels are used to measure the model performance. Our best model using multi-document convolutional neural network shows an accuracy of 31.06% and a macro average F1 score of 29.72, exhibiting promising performance on the text-based speaker identification task. We believe that the application of text-based speaker identification is extensive since data collected from online chatting and social media contains no acoustic information. Building accurate speaker identification models will enable the prediction of speaker labels in such datasets.

2 Related Work

Reynolds and Rose (1994) introduced the Gaussian Mixture Models (GMM) for robust text independent speaker identification. Since then, GMM has been applied to a number of datasets and achieved great results (Fine et al., 2001; Campbell et al., 2006). Knyazeva et al. (2015) proposed to perform sequence labeling and structured prediction in TV show speaker identification, and achieved better performance on sequential data. Despite the potential of text-based speaker identification in targeted

Proceedings of the 55th Annual Meeting of the Association for Computational Linguistics- Student Research Workshop, pages 49–55
Vancouver, Canada, July 30 - August 4, 2017. ©2017 Association for Computational Linguistics
https://doi.org/10.18653/v1/P17-3009

Speaker	Utterance
Monica	No . Not after what happened with Steve .
Chandler	What are you talking about ? We love **Schhteve** ! **Schhteve** was **schhexy** !.. Sorry .
Monica	Look , I do n't even know how I feel about him yet . Just give me a chance to figure that out .
Rachel	Well , then can we meet him ?
Monica	Nope . **Schhorry** .

Table 1: An excerpt from the transcripts to the TV show *Friends*.

Internet surveillance, research into this area has been scant. So far, there have been only a handful of attempts at text-based speaker identification. Kundu et al. (2012) proposed to use the K Nearest Neighbor Algorithm, Naive Bayes Classifier and Conditional Random Field to classify speakers in the film dialogues based on discrete stylistic features. Although their classification accuracies increase significantly from the random assignment baseline, there remains significant room for improvement. Serban and Pineau (2015) proposed their text-based speaker identification approach using Logistic Regression and Recurrent Neural Network (RNN) to learn the turn changes in movie dialogues. Their task is fundamentally different from the task of this paper, as their main focus is on the turn changes of dialogues instead of the identities of speakers. To the best of our knowledge, it is the first time the multi-document CNN has been applied to the speaker identification task.

3 Corpus

The Character Mining project provides transcripts to the TV show *Friends*; transcripts to the first 8 seasons of the show are publicly available in JSON format. Moreover, the first 2 seasons are annotated for the character identification task (Chen and Choi, 2016). Each season contains a number of episodes, and each episode is comprised of separate scenes.[1] The scenes in an episode, in turn, are divided at the utterance level. An excerpt from the data is shown in Table 1. In total, this corpus consists of 194 episodes, 2,579 scenes and 49,755 utterances. The utterance distribution by speaker is shown in Figure 1. The percentages for major speakers are fairly consistent. However, the *Other* speaker has a larger percentage in the dataset than any of the major speakers. The frequencies of interactions between pairs of speakers exhibit significant variance. For instance, *Monica* talks with *Chandler*

[1]http://nlp.mathcs.emory.edu/
character-mining

more often than any other speaker, whereas *Phoebe* does not talk with *Rachel* and *Joey* very frequently. It will be of interest to note whether the variance of interaction rates can affect the performance of our identification model.

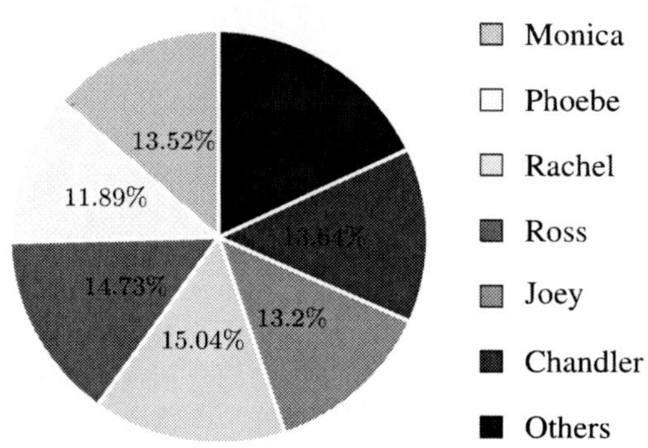

Figure 1: Data distribution

The first dataset is structured such that each utterance is considered as one discrete sample. To test the prediction performance for samples of greater lengths, all utterances of the same speaker in a scene are concatenated together as one single sample in the second dataset. Additional summary of the dataset is presented in Table 2.

4 Approaches

4.1 K Nearest Neighbor

In Kundu et al. (2012), the best result is reported using the K Nearest Neighbor algorithm (KNN), which is selected as the baseline approach for this paper, and implemented according to the original authors' specifications. Each utterance is treated as one sample, and 8 discrete stylistic features defined in the original feature template are extracted from each sample. Cosine similarity is used to locate the 15 nearest neighbors to each utterance. Majority voting of the neighbors, weighted by cosine similarity, is used to make predictions.

4.2 Recurrent Neural Network

A recurrent neural network (RNN) model is also considered in the course of the experiments, where each utterance in the transcripts is handled separately. The RNN model treats the speaker identification task as a variant of sequence classification. For each instance, the concatenation of word embedding vectors is fed into the model, with a dense layer and softmax activation to model the probability for each speaker. The model is unable to demonstrate significantly above random accuracy on labeling, achieving a maximal accuracy of 16.05% after training. We conclude that a simple RNN model is unable to perform speaker identification based on textual data. Variations on the hyperparameters, including the dimension of the RNN, the dimension of word embeddings, and dropout rate, produced no appreciable improvements.

4.3 Convolutional Neural Network

Widely utilized for computer vision, Convolutional Neural Network (CNN) models have recently been applied to natural language processing and showed great results for many tasks (Yih et al., 2014; Kim, 2014; Shen et al., 2014). Speaker identification can be conceptualized as a variant of document classification. Therefore, we elected to use the traditional CNN for our task. The model is a minor modification to the proposal of Kim (2014), which consists of a 1-dimensional convolution layer with different filter sizes, a global max pooling layer, and a fully connected layer. Each utterance is treated as one sample and classified independently.

One of the challenges is the large number of misspellings and colloquialisms in the dataset as a result of the mistakes in the human transcription process and the nature of human dialogues. It is unlikely for these forms to appear in pre-trained word embeddings. The bold instances in Table 1 provide a glimpse into these challenges. It should also be noted that these irregularities oftentimes only deviate slightly from the standard spellings. A character-aware word embedding model is expected to produce similar vectors for the irregular forms and the standard spellings. Most of the colloquialisms appear frequently in the dataset, and the challenge they pose can be resolved by a pre-trained character-aware word embedding model, such as `fastText` (Bojanowski et al., 2016). The word embeddings used in this paper are trained on a dataset consisting of the *New York Times* corpus,

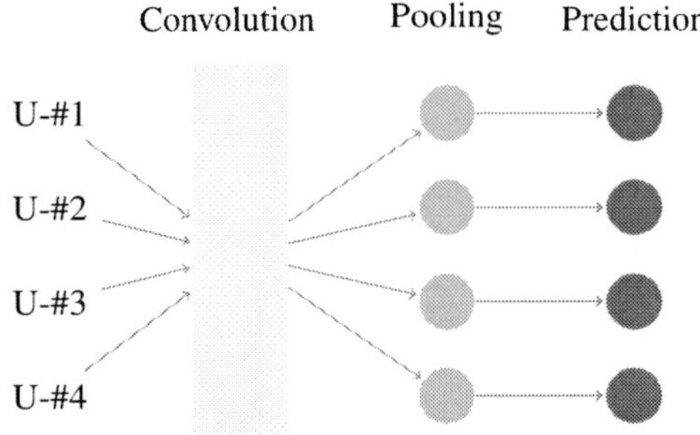

Figure 2: The baseline CNN model.

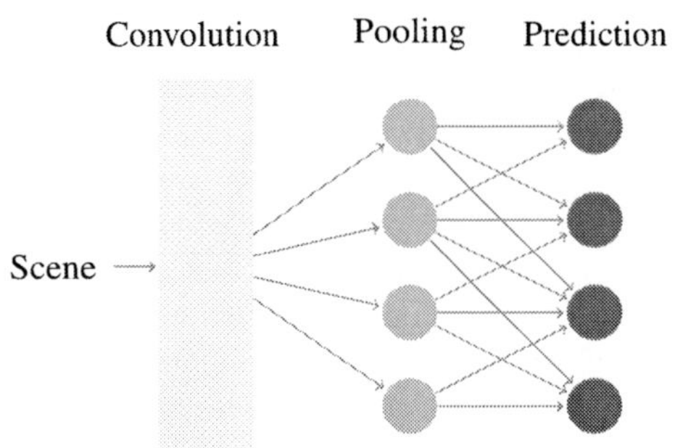

Figure 3: The multi-document CNN model.

the Wikipedia text dump, the Amazon Book Reviews,[2] and the transcripts from several TV shows.

4.4 CNN with Surrounding Utterance

Unlike other types of short documents such as movie reviews, where each sample is independent from the others, dialogues within a typical TV show are highly structured (Knyazeva et al., 2015). Every utterance is highly related to its prior and subsequent utterances, and it is important to take sequential information into account in predicting the speakers. However, contextual information is completely ignored by the basic CNN model. Each batch of input to the model consists of discrete utterances from different episodes and seasons, as shown in Figure 2.

To remedy the loss of contextual information, the CNN model is modified in a manner similar to the one proposed by Lee and Dernoncourt (2016). After the global max pooling layer, each utterance vector is concatenated with both the previous two utterances and the subsequent utterance in the same scene. Then, the vector is fed into the fully con-

---

[2] `snap.stanford.edu/data/web-Amazon.html`

51

Dataset	M	P	R_1	R_2	J	C	O	Total
Training	5,017	4,349	5,308	5,527	4,738	5,268	7,006	37,213
Development	898	799	1,092	821	930	846	931	6,317
Evaluation	810	769	1,082	983	909	673	999	6,225
Training	919	840	934	931	943	994	1,199	6,760
Development	151	148	151	131	148	139	159	1,027
Evaluation	116	116	137	132	129	119	156	905

Table 2: Dataset distribution by speakers. **M**: Monica, **P**: Phoebe, R_1: Rachel, R_2: Ross, **J**: Joey, **C**: Chandler, **O**: Other. Non-main speakers (all the others), are collectively grouped as the *Other* speaker.

nected layer. In this model, some information on the original dialogue sequence is preserved. Each scene is padded to the maximal sequence length, and fed into the model as one batch for both training and decoding. Figure 3 illustrates the structure of the model. Although topics within the scene are closely related, any single utterance is usually only relevant to its surrounding utterances. Based on this observation, including additional utterances in the prediction process can result in noisy input to the prediction model.

In a typical TV show, only a subset of characters are present in any particular scene. To further boost our model's ability to distinguish between speakers, the model optionally considers the set of speakers appearing in the scene. At the decoding stage, the Softmax probabilities for speakers absent from the scene are set to 0. The model benefits from the restrictions on its prediction search space. Such restrictions are applicable in the domain of targeted surveillance, where a vast number of speakers can be precluded from consideration during the identification process. For instance, speaker identification on a surveilled dialogue inside a criminal syndicate need only consider the members of the organization. In the majority of cases, however, the set of possible speakers may be difficult to ascertain. Therefore, we exclude this information in the determination of the best performing model.

4.5 CNN with Utterance Concatenation

Many individual utterances appearing in the dataset are fairly laconic and generic, as exemplified by the last utterance shown in Table 1, rendering them challenging to classify even with the help of contextual information. The proposed solution is to group multiple utterances together as one sample. Specifically, all of the utterances for each speaker in one scene are concatenated in the original dia-

logue order. We assign consistent unknown labels to all speakers in this dataset so that all the utterances in a single scene maintain their trackable provenances from the same speakers. The concatenated individual utterances can be fairly reasonable and consistent speech. As documents increase in length, it becomes easier for the CNN model to capture the speech pattern of each speaker. Once again, this model also optionally restricts its prediction search space to the set of speakers appearing in the scene for each batch of input.

5 Experiments

In the KNN experiment, the transcript to season 8 of *Friends* is used as evaluation data, and the first 7 seasons as training data. In the rest of the experiments, season 8 is used as evaluation data, and season 7 is used as the development set. The first 6 seasons are used as the training dataset. In each experiment, the F1 scores for the speakers, the average F1 score for major speakers, the average F1 score for all speakers, and the accuracy are reported in Tables 3 and 4.

In Kundu et al. (2012), the highest accuracy achieved by the KNN approach on the paper's film dialogue dataset was 30.39% , which is comparable to the best result of this paper. In contrast, the KNN approach did not perform well on the *Friends* dataset. Upon further examination of the KNN model's prediction process, we observe that the cosine similarities between any given utterance and its 15 nearest neighbors are consistently above 98%. The speaker labels are not linearly separable due to the low dimensionality of the feature space. The basic CNN model is able to outperform the baseline by almost 9% because the highly differing n-grams frequencies in the dataset enabled the model to distinguish between speakers. It is also worth noting that when the surrounding utterances

| | Individual F1 Score | | | | | | | | | |
Model	M	P	R$_1$	R$_2$	J	C	O	MF1	F1	ACC
KNN	13.30	12.13	17.34	19.23	14.68	14.61	19.23	15.22	15.80	16.18
RNN	17.87	15.22	14.98	17.51	17.42	13.48	12.02	15.39	15.50	16.05
CNN	20.55	17.52	24.20	24.70	28.15	14.05	31.81	21.36	22.86	25.01
Multi-Document-CNN	20.65	25.20	29.67	35.76	37.29	23.93	35.55	28.75	29.72	**31.06**
CNN-Concatenation	29.35	28.49	33.11	30.05	44.18	26.20	39.42	31.90	32.97	34.19

Table 3: Model performance. **MF1**: Average of F1 scores for major speakers, **F1**: Average of F1 scores for all speakers, **ACC**: Accuracy

| | Individual F1 Score | | | | | | | | | |
Model	M	P	R$_1$	R$_2$	J	C	O	MF1	F1	ACC
Multi-Document-CNN-2	28.13	29.59	41.49	48.15	45.72	36.06	46.98	38.19	39.45	41.36
CNN-Concatenation-2	36.43	33.16	50.09	45.03	53.67	39.90	51.02	43.05	44.19	46.48

Table 4: Model performance where the prediction labels are restricted to speakers present in each scene.

are taken into account, identification accuracy increases significantly from that achieved by the simple CNN. With more contextual information, the model is able to identify speakers with higher accuracy, as individual speakers react differently in comparable situations.

The experiment on the utterance concatenation dataset yields a relatively high identification accuracy, corroborating our theory that the prediction model can better capture different speech patterns on longer documents. When prediction labels are restricted to the speakers present in a scene, accuracy boosts of 10% and 12% are achieved on the two datasets, respectively.

Table 5 shows the confusion matrix produced by the multi-document CNN, i.e., the best performing model. The speakers for whom the model produces higher accuracies (*Ross* and *Other*) are also confused by the model more often than other speakers. The cause can be accounted for by the model's overzealousness in assigning these two labels to utterances due to their relatively large percentages in the training data. In addition, *Monica* and *Chandler* are often confused with each other. Due to their romantic relationship, it is possible that there is a convergence between their idiolectal styles. On the other hand, the confusion rates between *Phoebe* and *Rachel*, and between *Phoebe* and *Joey* are both fairly low. Such results confirm the observation that the frequency of interactions between speaker pairs correlates with the rate of confusion.

6 Conclusion

This paper presents a neural network-based approach to speaker identification in multiparty dialogues relying only on textual transcription data. The promising experimental results confirm the value of textual features in speaker identification on multiparty dialogues. The improvements produced by the consideration of neighboring utterances in the CNN's prediction process indicate that contextual information is essential to the performance of text-based speaker identification. Prior to this paper, Serban and Pineau (2015) used scripted dialogues to identify turn-taking and differences in speakers, where the actual identities of the speakers are irrelevant. However, this paper enables an identification where the names of the speakers are associated with their own utterances, a novel attempt in text-based speaker identification. Because of the ability of the model to uncover speaker identities in the absence of audio data, applications and interests in the intelligence and surveillance community are expected.

Although speaker verification based on acoustic signals is a helpful tool, it can conceivably be defeated by voice modulating algorithms. Whereas text-based speaker identification can discern the involuntary and unconscious cues of speakers. It is of interest to incorporate text-based features in a larger system of speaker identification to enhance its security. Several dialogue emotion recognition systems have incorporated both acoustic and

P S	M	P	R₁	R₂	J	C	O
M	**22.10**	8.40	6.17	17.90	8.27	20.37	16.79
P	12.09	**20.16**	6.63	18.21	4.81	17.95	20.16
R_1	13.22	6.38	**18.39**	19.50	4.25	15.90	22.37
R_2	8.75	4.17	4.68	**45.17**	5.70	14.95	16.58
J	9.13	4.51	6.38	19.03	**29.59**	16.61	14.74
C	18.28	6.39	3.42	10.85	6.84	**34.92**	19.32
O	13.21	3.80	5.01	12.71	4.80	15.02	**45.45**

Table 5: Confusion Matrix between speakers. **S**: true speaker, **P**: predicted speaker.

textual features, and resultant performances show improvements upon previous systems which rely only on one kind of features(Chuang* and Wu, 2004; Polzehl et al., 2009). Similarly, integration of acoustic and textual information in the speaker identification task can result in improved performance in future works.

References

Piotr Bojanowski, Edouard Grave, Armand Joulin, and Tomas Mikolov. 2016. Enriching word vectors with subword information. *arXiv preprint arXiv:1607.04606* .

W. M. Campbell, J. P. Campbell, D. A. Reynolds, E. Singer, and P. A. Torres-Carrasquilloe. 2006. Support vector machines for speaker and language recognition. *Odyssey 2004: The speaker and Language Recognition Workshop* page 210–229.

Henry Yu-Hsin Chen and Jinho D. Choi. 2016. Character Identification on Multiparty Conversation: Identifying Mentions of Characters in TV Shows. In *Proceedings of the 17th Annual Meeting of the Special Interest Group on Discourse and Dialogue.* Los Angeles, CA, SIGDIAL'16, pages 90–100. http://www.sigdial.org/workshops/conference17/.

Ze-Jing Chuang* and Chung-Hsien Wu. 2004. Multi-Modal Emotion Recognition from Speech and Text . *The Association for Computational Linguistics and Chinese Language Processing* .

Shai Fine, Jirí Navrátil, and Ramesh A. Gopinath. 2001. A hybrid gmm/svm approach to speaker identification. In *ICASSP.*

Timothy J. Hazen, Douglas A. Jones, Alex Park, Linda C. Kukolich, and Douglas A. Reynolds. 2003. Integration of speaker recognition into conversational spoken dialogue systems]. *EUROSPEECH* .

Yoon Kim. 2014. Convolutional Neural Networks for Sentence Classification. *In Proceedings of EMNLP* .

Elena Knyazeva, Guillaume Wisniewski, Herve Bredin, and Francois Yvon. 2015. Structured Prediction for Speaker Identification in TV Series. *LIMSI − CNRS − Rue John Von Neumann, Orsay, France. Université Paris Sud* .

Amitava Kundu, Dipankar Das, and Sivaji Bandyopadhyay. 2012. Speaker identification from film dialogues. *IEEE Proceedings of 4th International Conference on Intelligent Human Computer Interaction* .

Ji Young Lee and Franck Dernoncourt. 2016. Sequential Short-Text Classification with Recurrent and Convolutional Neural Networks. *In Proceedings of the NAACL Conference* .

Ryan Lowe, Nissan Pow, Iulian Serban, and Joelle Pineau. 2015. The Ubuntu Dialogue Corpus: A Large Dataset for Research in Unstructured Multi-Turn Dialogue Systems. *In Proceedings of the SIGDIAL Conference* .

Francois Mairesse, Marilyn A. Walker, Matthias R. Mehl, and Roger K. Moore. 2007. Using linguistic cues for the automatic recognition of personality in conversation and text. *Journal of Artificial Intelligence Research* pages 475–500.

Tim Polzehl, Shiva Sundaram, Hamed Ketabdar, Michael Wagner, and Florian Metze. 2009. Emotion classification in children's speech using fusion of acoustic and linguistic features. In *in Proc. Inter-Speech.*

Antoine Raux, Dan Bohus, Brian Langner, Alan W Black, and Maxine Eskenazi. 2006. Doing research on a deployed spoken dialogue system: one year of let's go! experience. *In INTERSPEECH* .

D.A. Reynolds and R.C. Rose. 1994. Robust text-independent speaker identification using Gaussian mixture speaker models. *IEEE transactions on speech and audio processing* pages 73–82.

Seyed Omid Sadjadi, Jason W. Pelecanos, and Sriram Ganapathy. 2016. The ibm speaker recognition system: Recent advances and error analysis. *arXiv preprint arXiv:1605.01635* .

Iulian V. Serban and Joelle Pineau. 2015. Text-Based Speaker Identification For Multi-Participant Open-Domain Dialogue System. *Department of Computer Science and Operations Research, Université de Montréal* .

Y. Shen, X. He, L. Deng J. Gao, and G. Mesnil. 2014. Learning Semantic Representations Using Convolutional Neural Networks for Web Search. *In Proceedings of WWW* .

Jorg Tiedemann. 2012. Parallel data, tools and interfaces in opus. *In Proceedings of LREC* pages 2214–2218.

W. Yih, X. He, and C. Meek. 2014. Semantic Parsing for Single-Relation Question Answering. *In Proceedings of ACL 2014.* .

Variation Autoencoder Based Network Representation Learning for Classification

Hang Li [#1], **Haozheng Wang** [#2], **Zhenglu Yang** [#3] **Masato Odagaki** [†4]

[#]College of Computer and Control Engineering, Nankai University, Tianjin, China

[†] Maebashi Institute of Technology, Japan

[1][2]{hangl,hzwang}@mail.nankai.edu.cn [3]yangzl@nankai.edu.cn [4]odagaki@maebashiit.ac.jp

Abstract

Network representation is the basis of many applications and of extensive interest in various fields, such as information retrieval, social network analysis, and recommendation systems. Most previous methods for network representation only consider the incomplete aspects of a problem, including link structure, node information, and partial integration. The present study introduces a deep network representation model that seamlessly integrates the text information and structure of a network. The model captures highly non-linear relationships between nodes and complex features of a network by exploiting the variational autoencoder (VAE), which is a deep unsupervised generation algorithm. The representation learned with a paragraph vector model is merged with that learned with the VAE to obtain the network representation, which preserves both structure and text information. Comprehensive experiments is conducted on benchmark datasets and find that the introduced model performs better than state-of-the-art techniques.

1 Introduction

Information network representation is an important research issue because it is the basis of many applications, such as document classification in citation networks, functional label prediction in protein-protein interaction networks, and potential friend recommendations in social networks. Although there are not a few recent work proposed to study the issue (Belkin and Niyogi, 2003; Tenenbaum et al., 2001; Cao et al., 2015; Tian et al., 2014; Cao, 2016), it is still far from satisfactory because of the intrinsic difficulty. In essence, the rich and complex information (i.e., link structure and node contents) embedded in information networks poses a significant challenge in the effective representation of networks.

Network-distributed representation learning can be viewed as a problem using low-dimensional vectors to represent nodes in a network. Most network representation methods are based on a network structure. The traditional representation is based on matrix decomposition and uses eigenvectors as representation (Belkin and Niyogi, 2003; Roweis and Saul, 2000; Tenenbaum et al., 2001). Furthermore, they extend to high-order information (Cao et al., 2015). However, these methods are not applicable to large-scale networks, and although many approximate approaches have been developed to solve this problem, they are not effective enough. Some methods are based on optimization objective functions (Tang et al., 2015; Pan et al., 2016; Yang et al., 2015). Although they are suitable for large-scale network data, they adopt shallow models that are limited in terms of performance and are difficult to use to obtain highly non-linear relationships that are vital to the preservation of network structure. Inspired by deep learning techniques in natural language processing, (Perozzi et al., 2014; Grover and Leskovec, 2016) adopted several stunted random walks in networks to generate node sequences serving as sentence corpus and then applied the skip-gram model to these sequences to learn node representation. However, they cannot easily handle additional information during random walks in a network.

To capture highly non-linear structures for large-scale networks, (Tian et al., 2014; Cao, 2016) introduced an autoencoder to model training instead of using a sampling based method to generate linear sequences. Motivated by this

Proceedings of the 55th Annual Meeting of the Association for Computational Linguistics- Student Research Workshop, pages 56–61
Vancouver, Canada, July 30 - August 4, 2017. ©2017 Association for Computational Linguistics
https://doi.org/10.18653/v1/P17-3010

model, we develop the variational autoencoder (VAE) (Kingma and Welling, 2014), which is a deep generation model, instead of a basic autoencoder. Most previous studies utilized only one type of information in networks. The work in (Le and Mikolov, 2014) focused on node content, and others (Grover and Leskovec, 2016; Perozzi et al., 2014) explored link structure. Although a few previous models (Pan et al., 2016; Yang et al., 2015) combined both text information and network structure, they did not preserve the complete network structure and only partially utilized node content. A straightforward method is to learn representations from text features and network structure independently, and then concatenate the two separate representations.

To address the above issues, we introduce a deep generative model to learn network representation by modeling both node content information and network structure comprehensively. First, the representation based on node content through the paragraph vector model is obtained. Then, we feed the network adjacency matrix and representation obtained into a deep generative model, the building block of which is the VAE. After stacking several layers of the VAE, the result of the first layer is chosen before decoding as the final representation. Intuitively, we can obtain the representation containing both content information and structure in a d-dimensional feature space. The experimental evaluation demonstrates the superior performance of the model on the benchmark datasets.

2 Preliminary

Notation: Let $G = (V, E, C)$ denote a given network, where $V = \{v_i\}_{i=1...N}$ is the node set and $E = \{e_{ij}\}$ is the edge set that indicates the relation of nodes. If a direct link exists between v_i and v_j then $e_{ij} = 1$; otherwise, $e_{ij} = 0$ when network is unweighted. $C = \{c_i\}$ is the set of content information. let A denote the adjacency matrix for a network, and let $x = \{e_{i,k}, ..., e_{n,k}\}$ be an adjacency vector. Our goal is to seek a low-dimensional vector $\vec{y}_j$ for each node v_i of a given network.

Autoencoder: We first provide a brief description of a basic autoencoder and the VAE. The basic autoencoder first compresses the input into a small form and then transforms it back into an approximation of the input. The encoding part aims to find the compression representation z of a given

data x, and the decoding part is a reflection of the encoder used to reconstruct the original input x. The VAE (Kingma and Welling, 2014) imposes a prior distribution on the hidden layer vector of the autoencoder and re-parameterizes the network according to the parameters of the prior distribution. Through the parameterization process, the means and variance values of the input data can be learned. We extended VAE to generate two means and variances of input data, which can be considered correspond to the content and structure respectively.

3 Model Description

The architecture of the proposed model is shown in Fig. 1. The whole architecture consists of two main modules, namely, the content2vec module and the union training module. For an information network, such as a paper citation network, we can obtain the node link and content information (e.g., paper abstract). We learn an effective feature representation vector that preserves both structure information and node content information and can thus be applied to many tasks (e.g., paper classification).

3.1 Content2vec Module

We employ the state-of-the-art approach called doc2vec (Le and Mikolov, 2014), which utilizes text to learn vector representations of documents, as our content2vec module. Specifically, if one node contains other information (e.g., author name), we treat it as a word and merge it into the comprehensive text information (e.g., the abstract of the paper in the citation network) as the content of the node. A representation u_i that includes the node content information is obtained from this module.

3.2 Union-training Module

The union training module is the core part of our model, in which content information and structure information are integrated. The details are shown in Fig 1. The VAE is adopted as the main block. Given a network, the adjacency matrix A can be obtained. A can describe the relationship among the nodes and reflect the overall structure of the network. We extract each adjacency vector a_i and concatenate it with the corresponding u_i as the input x_i of our model. Therefore, the content and

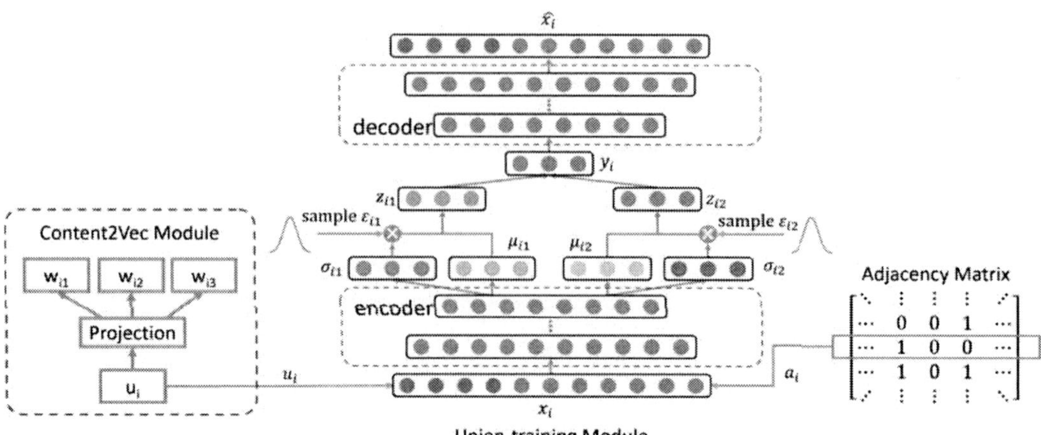

Figure 1: Architecture of our model. w_i can be seen as a word of the content information, u_i is a node in the network, $\boldsymbol{u}_i$ is a representation vector learned by the Content2Vec Module, $\boldsymbol{x}_i$ is a vector of the adjacency matrix. The input of the union-training module is combination of $\boldsymbol{x}_i$ and $\boldsymbol{u}_i$, the encoder and decoder are stack full-connected layer, $\sigma_{i1}, \sigma_{i2}, \mu_{i1}, \mu_{i2}$ can be seen the mean and variance of the distribution of the content and structure data, respectively. ε_{i1} and ε_{i2} are the sample data from two Gaussian distributions.

structure information is able to be learned simultaneously.

During the encoding phase, we adapt several fully connected layers composed of multiple nonlinear mapping functions to map the input data to a highly nonlinear latent space. Therefore, given the input $\boldsymbol{x}_i$, the output h^k for the kth layer is shown as follow:

$$h^1 = \pi(\boldsymbol{W}^1 \boldsymbol{x}_i + \boldsymbol{b}^1)$$
$$h^k = \pi(\boldsymbol{W}^k h^{k-1} + \boldsymbol{b}^k), k = 1, 2...K \tag{1}$$

where π is the nonlinear activation function of each layer. The value of K varies with the data.

In the last layer of encoder, we obtain four output: μ_{i1}, σ_{i1} μ_{i2} and σ_{i2}. They can be treated as the means and variances of the distribution of content information and structure information respectively. Furthermore, we sample two values ε_{i1} and ε_{i2} from two previous distributions (e.g., Gaussian distribution). Then we can obtain the reparameterized $z_i 1$ and $z_2 1$. Through concatenate $z_i 1$ and $z_2 1$, content and structure information can be integrated together, $\boldsymbol{y}_i$ is the representation of the network. Nonlinear operations are not performed in this phase. Thus, the gradient descent method can be safely applied in optimization. The operations can be expressed as follows:

$$z_{ik} = f(\boldsymbol{\mu}_{ik}, \boldsymbol{\sigma}_{ik}, \boldsymbol{\varepsilon}_i), k = 1, 2$$
$$\boldsymbol{y}_i = Merge[\boldsymbol{z}_{i1}, \boldsymbol{z}_{i2}] \tag{2}$$

where f is a linear function that can reparameterize $\boldsymbol{y}_i$, $Merge$ concatenate the two vectors together directly.

The decoding phase is a reflection of the encoder; its output $\hat{\boldsymbol{x}}_i$ should be close to the input $\boldsymbol{x}_i$. The loss function of this module that should be minimized is as follows:

$$\mathcal{L}(\boldsymbol{x}_i) = -\sum_{k=1}^{2} \mathcal{KL}(q(\boldsymbol{z}_{ik}|\boldsymbol{x}_i)||p(\boldsymbol{z}_{ik})) + \mathcal{H}(\boldsymbol{x}_i, \hat{\boldsymbol{x}}_i) \tag{3}$$

where KL is the KL divergence which is always used as a measure of the difference between two distributions, $\mathcal{H}$ is a cross-entropy function that is used to measure the difference between $\boldsymbol{x}_i$ and $\hat{\boldsymbol{x}}_i$.

Finally, We choose the output of the layer $\boldsymbol{y}_i$ as the final representation of each node.

4 Experiments

4.1 Experimental setup

Paper citation networks is a classical social information network. To evaluate the quality of the proposed model, we conduct three important tasks on two benchmark citation network datasets: (1)

Table 1: Macro-F1 score on Citeseer-M10 Network

%p	One-Hot	Deepwalk	Node2vec	Doc2vec	DW+D2V	TADW	TriDNR	Ours
10%	0.254	0.297	0.314	0.503	0.526	0.475	0.683	**0.889**
30%	0.321	0.334	0.331	0.536	0.615	0.488	0.744	**0.913**
50%	0.352	0.346	0.346	0.547	0.633	0.495	0.760	**0.924**
70%	0.363	0.344	0.339	0.534	0.630	0.495	0.773	**0.940**

Table 2: Macro-F1 score on DBLP Network

%p	One-Hot	Deepwalk	Node2vec	Doc2vec	DW+D2V	TADW	TriDNR	Ours
10%	0.328	0.379	0.448	0.574	0.495	0.660	0.724	**0.751**
30%	0.362	0.454	0.473	0.598	0.586	0.687	0.742	**0.753**
50%	0.371	0.459	0.475	0.604	0.614	0.697	0.747	**0.762**
70%	0.372	0.461	0.476	0.605	0.628	0.699	0.748	**0.763**

CiteSeerM10[1]. It contains 10 distinct categories with 10,310 papers and 77,218 citations. Titles are treated as the text information because no more text information is available; and (2) DBLP dataset[2]. We treat abstracts as text information and choose 4 research areas with the same setting as that of (Pan et al., 2016), which are database (SIGMOD, ICDE, VLDB, EDBT, PODS, ICDT, DASFAA, SSDBM, CIKM), data mining (KDD, ICDM, SDM, PKDD, PAKDD), artificial intelligent (IJCAI, AAAI, NIPS, ICML, ECML, ACML, IJCNN, UAI, ECAI, COLT, ACL, KR), computer vision (CVPR, ICCV, ECCV, ACCV, MM, ICPR, ICIP, ICME). Therefore we get a network contains 30,422 nodes and 41,206 edges.

We compare our approach with the following methods:

- **One-Hot** uses adjacency matrix, which carries the structure information as the high-dimension representation, and directly feed into the classifier.

- **DeepWalk** (Perozzi et al., 2014) is exploited by statistical models, which employs truncated random walks to learns nodes embedding by treating walk as the equivalent of sentences.

- **Node2vec** (Grover and Leskovec, 2016) learns the network representation by designing a biased random walk procedure which efficiently explores diverse neighborhoods.

- **Doc2vec** (Le and Mikolov, 2014) is the Paragraph Vector model that learns document representation by predicting the words appeared.

- **DW+D2V** is simply to concatenate the representation result learned by DeepWalk and Doc2vec.

- **TADW** (Yang et al., 2015) is text-based DeepWalk, which incorporates text information into network structure by matrix factorization.

- **TriDNR** (Pan et al., 2016) uses node text, label, and structure to jointly learn node representation.

4.2 Performance on Node Classification

We conduct the paper classification task on two benchmark citation networks to evaluate the performance of our method. To reduce the impact of sophisticated classifiers on the performance, we employ a linear SVM, which is a common technique used by the exiting work (Pan et al., 2016). The results are shown in Table 1 and Table 2, respectively. The reported parameters for our model are set: dimension d=100 on CiteseerM10 and d=300 on DBLP. The dimension for other algorithms is the same as ours, and the other parameters are set as their papers report, i.e., window size b=10 in DeepWalk and Node2vec, in-out parameter q=2 in Node2vec, text weight ∂=0.8 in TADW and TriDNR. We use Macro-F1 which is the same as that adopted by other algorithms to measure the classification performance. The experiments are independently conducted 10 times for each setting, and the average values are reported. The proportion of training data with labels is range from 10% to 70%.

[1]http://citeseerx.ist.psu.edu/
[2]http://arnetminer.org/citation (V4 version is used)

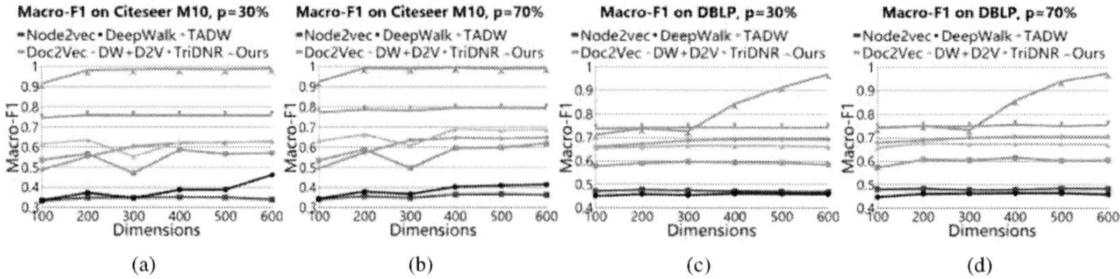

Figure 2: Performance of each strategy on different training proportion p

Our model is evaluated by comparing it with seven approaches. One-Hot uses the original structure data, and its performance is poor because it is discrete and the context relation of nodes can not be captured. DeepWalk and Node2vec are structure-based methods that exhibit inferior performance mainly because they only use the shallow structure information and the network is rather sparse, while the information of the complex non-linear structure cannot be employed. The performance of Doc2vec is not as good as ours which demonstrates the effectiveness of our proposed model. TADW and TriDNR are inferior to our approach, although these two methods also consider the text and structure. Nevertheless, they cannot capture the complex non-linear structure. The reason for the superior of our method is that our model can effectively capture the inter-relationship between node content and link structure, and the intro-relationship among nodes and links, which are essential to learn the representation of networks. Furthermore, our model can capture the information of highly non-linear structure instead of the shallow structure (e.g., Deep-Walk) by exploiting VAE. Moreover, our approach does not require heavy text information which is utilized by the other state-of-the-art strategies (e.g.,TriDNR). Our model exhibits consistent superior performance, and is up to 16% better than the state-of-the-art methods (i.e., the Macro-F1 score of our model is 94% when the proportion of training data with labels is 70% conducted on the Citeseer-M10 Network dataset).

4.3 Parameter Setting

A significant hyperparameter in our model is the dimension d. The performance of different methods with varying dimensions has been evaluated. The result is illustrated in Fig. 2. We obtain very good performance on the CiteSeer-M10 dataset, i.e., the Macro-F1 score is 94% and the performance tends to be stable as b becomes larger. It validates the effectiveness of our algorithm and the reason is due to the ability of our model that can capture the complex network structure and the text information. From Fig. 2, we can see that the performance gets better when d increases from 100 to 600. We think the main reason is because more information can be preserved in higher dimensional space of the datasets.

5 Conclusions

In this paper, we have introduced an effective network representation model, which comprehensively integrates the text information and the network structure. We introduced Paragraph Model as a preliminary module. And we have exploited Variational Autoencoder as the main block of our model, that could capture highly non-linear structure of the network. The comprehensive experimental evaluation on two benchmark datasets has demonstrated the effectiveness of the model.

Acknowledgement

This research is supported by the National Natural Science Foundation of China: U1636116, 11431006, Research Fund for International Young Scientists: 61650110510, Ministry of Education of Humanities and Social Science: 16YJC790123.

References

Mikhail Belkin and Partha Niyogi. 2003. Laplacian eigenmaps for dimensionality reduction and data representation. *Neural Computation* 15(6):1373–1396.

Shaosheng Cao. 2016. deep neural network for learning graph representations. In *AAAI*.

Shaosheng Cao, Wei Lu, and Qiongkai Xu. 2015. Grarep:learning graph representations with global structural information. pages 891–900.

A Grover and J Leskovec. 2016. node2vec: Scalable feature learning for networks. In *SIGKDD*.

Diederik P Kingma and Max Welling. 2014. Auto-encoding variational bayes .

Quoc V Le and Tomas Mikolov. 2014. Distributed representations of sentences and documents. In *ICML*.

Shirui Pan, Jia Wu, Xingquan Zhu, Chengqi Zhang, and Yang Wang. 2016. Tri-party deep network representation. In *IJCAI*.

Bryan Perozzi, Rami Al-Rfou, and Steven Skiena. 2014. Deepwalk: Online learning of social representations. In *SIGKDD*.

Sam T. Roweis and Lawrence K. Saul. 2000. Nonlinear dimensionality reduction by locally linear embedding. *Science* 290(5500):2323–2326.

Jian Tang, Meng Qu, Mingzhe Wang, Ming Zhang, Jun Yan, and Qiaozhu Mei. 2015. Line: Large-scale information network embedding. In *WWW*.

Joshua B. Tenenbaum, Vin De Silva, and John C. Langford. 2001. A global geometric framework for nonlinear dimensionality reduction. *Science* 290(5500):2319–2323.

F. Tian, B. Gao, Q. Cui, E. Chen, and T. Y. Liu. 2014. Learning deep representations for graph clustering. *Inproceedings* .

Cheng Yang, Zhiyuan Liu, Deli Zhao, Maosong Sun, and Edward Y Chang. 2015. Network representation learning with rich text information. In *IJCAI*.

Blind phoneme segmentation with temporal prediction errors

Paul Michel[1]*   **Okko Rasanen**[2]   **Roland Thiollière**[3]   **Emmanuel Dupoux**[3]

[1]Carnegie Mellon University, [2]Aalto University, [3]LSCP / ENS / EHESS / CNRS

`pmichel1@cs.cmu.edu`, `okko.rasanen@aalto.fi`,
`rolthiolliere@gmail.com`, `emmanuel.dupoux@gmail.com`

Abstract

Phonemic segmentation of speech is a critical step of speech recognition systems. We propose a novel unsupervised algorithm based on sequence prediction models such as Markov chains and recurrent neural networks. Our approach consists in analyzing the error profile of a model trained to predict speech features frame-by-frame. Specifically, we try to learn the dynamics of speech in the MFCC space and hypothesize boundaries from local maxima in the prediction error. We evaluate our system on the TIMIT dataset, with improvements over similar methods.

1 Introduction

One of the main difficulty of speech processing as opposed to text processing is the continuous, time-dependent nature of the signal. As a consequence, pre-segmentation of the speech signal into words or sub-words units such as phonemes, syllables or words is an essential first step of a variety of speech recognition tasks.

Segmentation in phonemes is useful for a number of applications (annotation of speech for the purpose of phonetic analysis, computation of speech rate, keyword spotting, etc), and can be done in two ways. Supervised methods are based on an existing phoneme or word recognition system, which is used to decode the incoming speech into phonemes. Phonemes boundaries can then be extracted as a by-product of the alignment of the phoneme models with the speech. Unsupervised methods (also called blind segmentation) consist in finding phonemes boundaries using the acoustic signals only. Supervised methods depend

---

This work was done when the author was an intern at LSCP / ENS / EHESS / CNRS

on the training of acoustic and language models, which requires access to large amounts of linguistic resources (annotated speech, phonetic dictionary, text). Unsupervised methods do not require these resources and are therefore appropriate for so-called under-resourced languages, such as endangered languages, or languages without consistent orthographies.

We propose a blind phoneme segmentation method based on short term statistical properties of the speech signal. We designate peaks in the error curve of a model trained to predict speech frame by frame as potential boundaries. Three different models are tested. The first is an approximated Markov model of the transition probabilities between categorical speech features. We then replace it by a recurrent neural network operating on the same categorical features. Finally, a recurrent neural network is directly trained to predict the raw speech features. This last model is especially interesting in that it couples our statistical approach with more common spectral transition based methods (Dusan and Rabiner (2006) for instance).

We first describe the various models used and the pre- and post-processing procedures, before presenting and discussing our results in the light of previous work.

2 Related work

Most previous work on blind phoneme segmentation (Esposito and Aversano, 2005; Estevan et al., 2007; Almpanidis and Kotropoulos, 2008; Rasanen et al., 2011; Khanagha et al., 2014; Hoang and Wang, 2015) has focused on the analysis of the rate of change in the spectral domain. The idea is to design robust acoustic features that are supposed to remain stable within a phoneme, and change when transitioning from one phoneme to

Proceedings of the 55th Annual Meeting of the Association for Computational Linguistics- Student Research Workshop, pages 62–68
Vancouver, Canada, July 30 - August 4, 2017. ©2017 Association for Computational Linguistics
https://doi.org/10.18653/v1/P17-3011

the next. The algorithm then define a measure of change, which is then used to detect phoneme boundaries.

Apart from this line of research, three main approaches have been explored. The first idea is to use short term statistical dependencies. In Räsänen (2014), the idea was to first discretize the signal using a clustering algorithm and then compute discrete sequence statistics, over which a threshold can be defined. This is the idea that we follow in the current paper. The second approach is to use dynamic programming methods inspired by text segmentation (Wilber, 1988), in order to derive optimal segmentation (Qiao et al., 2008). In this line of research, however, the number of segments is assumed to be known in advance, so this cannot count as blind segmentation. The third approach consists in jointly segmenting and learning the acoustic models for phonemes (Kamper et al., 2015; Glass, 2003; Siu et al., 2013). These models are much more computationally involved than the other methods. Interestingly they all use a simpler, blind segmentation as an initialization phase. Therefore, improving on pure blind segmentation could be useful for joint models as well.

The principal source of inspiration for our work comes from previous work by Elman (1990) and Christiansen et al. (1998) published in the 90s. In the former, the author uses recurrent neural networks to train character-based language models on text and notices that "The error provides a good clue as to what the recurring sequences in the input are, and these correlate highly with words." (Elman, 1990). More precisely, the error tends to be higher at the beginning of new words than in the middle. In the latter, the author uses Elman recurrent neural networks to predict boundaries between words given the character sequence and phonological cues.

Our work uses the same idea, using prediction error as a cue for segmentation, but with two important changes: we apply it to speech instead of text, and we use it to segment in terms of phoneme units instead of word units.

3 System

3.1 Pre-processing

We used two kinds of speech features : 13 dimensional MFCCs (Davis and Mermelstein, 1980) (with 12 mel-cepstrum coefficients and 1 energy coefficient) and categorical one-hot vectors de-

rived from MFCCs inspired by Räsänen (2014).

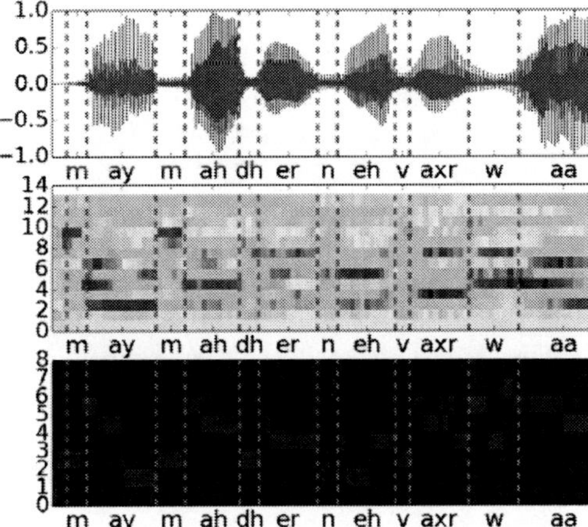

Figure 1: Visual representation of the various features on 100 frames from the TIMIT corpus. From top to bottom are the waveform, the 13-dimensional MFCCs and the 8-dimensional one hot encoded categorical features.

The latter are computed according to Räsänen (2014) : K-means clustering[1] is performed on a random subset of the MFCCs (10,000 frames were selected at random), with a target number of clusters of 8, then each MFCC is identified to the closest centroid. Each frame is then represented by a cluster number $c \in \{1, \ldots, 8\}$, or alternatively by the corresponding one-hot vector of dimension 8. These hyper-parameters were chosen according to Räsänen (2014).

Figure 1 allows for a visual comparison of the three signals (waveform, MFCC, categorical).

The entire dataset is split between a training and a testing subset. A randomly selected subset of the training part is used as validation data to prevent overfitting.

3.2 Training phase

A frame-by-frame prediction model is then learned on the training set. The three different models used are described below :

Pseudo-markov model When trying to predict the frame x_t given the previous frames $x_0^{t-1} := x_{t-1}, \ldots, x_0$, a simplifying assumption is to model the transition probabilities with a Markov

---

[1] In particular, we use the K-means++ (Arthur and Vassilvitskii, 2007) algorithm, and pick the best outcome of 10 random initializations

chain of higher order K, i.e. $p(x_t|x_0^{t-1}) = p(x_t | x_{t-K}^{t-1})$. Provided each frame is part of a finite alphabet, a finite (albeit exponential in K) number of transition probabilities must be learned.

However, as the order rises, the ratio between the size of the data and the number of transition probability being learned makes the exact calculation more difficult and less relevant.

In order to circumvent this issue, we approximate the K-order Markov chain with the mean of 1-order markov chain of the lag-transition probabilities $p(x_t|x_{t-i})$ for $1 \leqslant i \leqslant K$, so that

$$p(x_t|x_0^{t-1}) = \frac{1}{K} \sum_{i=1}^{K} p(x_t|x_{t-i}) \qquad (1)$$

with $p(x_t|x_{t-i}) = \frac{f(x_t, x_{t-i})}{f(x_{t-i})}$.

In practice, we chose $K = 6$, thus ensuring that the markov model's attention is of the same order of magnitude than the length of a phoneme.

Compared to Räsänen (2014), this model only uses information from previous frames and as such is completely online.

Recurrent neural network on categorical features Alternatively to Markov chains, the transition probability $p(x_t|x_0^{t-1})$ can be modeled by a recurrent neural network (RNN). RNN can theoretically model indefinite order temporal dependencies, hence their advantage over Markov chains for long sequence modeling.

Given a set of examples $\{(x_t, (x_0^{t-1})) \mid t \in \{0, \ldots, t_{max}\}\}$, the networks parameters are learned so that the error $E(x_t, \text{RNN}(x_0^{t-1}))$ is minimized using back propagation through time (Werbos, 1990) and stochastic gradient descent or a variant thereof (we have found RMSProp (Tieleman and Hinton, 2012) to give the best results).

In our case, the network itself consists of two LSTM layers (Hochreiter and Schmidhuber, 1997) stacked on one another followed by a linear layer and a softmax. The input and output units have both dimension 8, whereas all other layers have the same hidden dimension 40. Dropout (Srivastava et al., 2014) with probability 0.2 was used after each LSTM layer to prevent overfitting.

A pitfall of this method is the tendency of the network to predict the last frame it is fed. This is due to the fact that the sequences of categorical features extracted from speech contain a lot of constant sub-sequences length $\geqslant 2$.

As a consequence, around 80% of the data fed to the network consists of sub-sequences where $x_t = x_{t-1}$. Despite the fact that phone boundaries are somewhat correlated with changes of categories (around 65% of the time), this leads the network to a local minimum where it only tries to predict the same characters.

To mitigate this effect, examples where $x_t = x_{t-1}$ were removed with probability 0.8, so that the number of transitions was slightly skewed towards category transitions. The model still passed over all frames during training but the error was back-propagated for only 46% of them. This change lead to substantial improvement.

Recurrent neural network on raw MFCCs The recurrent neural network model can be adapted to raw speech features simply by changing the loss function from categorical cross-entropy to mean squared error, which is the direct translation from a categorical distribution to a Gaussian density ($2\|\mathbf{x} - \mathbf{y}\|_2^2 + d$ is the Kullback-Leibler divergence of two d-dimensional normal distributions centered in $\mathbf{x}$ and $\mathbf{y}$ with the same scalar covariance matrix).

We used the same architecture than in the categorical case, simply removing the softmax layer and decreasing the hidden dimension size to 20. In this case, no selection of the samples is needed since the sequences vary continuously.

3.3 Test phase

Each model is run on the test set and the prediction error is calculated at each time step according to the formula :

$$E_{\text{markov}}(t) = -\log\left(\sum_{i=1}^{K} p(x_t|x_{t-i})\right)$$

$$E_{\text{RNN-cat}}(t) = -\sum_{i=1}^{d} \mathbb{1}_{x_t=i} \log(\text{RNN}(x_0^{t-1})) \qquad (2)$$

$$E_{\text{RNN-MFCC}}(t) = \frac{1}{d} \left\|\mathbf{x}_t - \text{RNN}(\mathbf{x}_0^{t-1})\right\|_2^2$$

In each case this corresponds, up to a scaling factor constant across the dataset, to the Kullback-Leibler divergence between the predicted and actual probability distribution for x_t in the feature space.

Since all three systems predict probabilities conditioned by the preceding frames, they cannot be expected to give meaningful results for the first

Algorithm	P	R	F	R-val
Periodic	57.5	91.0	70.5	46.9
Rasanen (2014)	68.4	70.6	69.5	73.7
Markov	70.7	77.3	73.9	76.4
RNN (Cat.)	68.7	77.1	72.7	74.6
RNN (Cont.)	70.3	72.4	71.3	75.3

Table 1: Final results (in%) evaluated with cropped tolerance windows

Algorithm	P	R	F	R-val
Periodic	62.2	98.3	76.2	49.8
Rasanen (2014)	74.0	70.0	73.0	76.0
Markov	74.8	81.9	78.2	80.1
RNN (Cat.)	72.5	81.4	76.7	78.0
RNN (Cont.)	77.6	72.7	75.0	78.6

Table 2: Final results (in%) evaluated with overlapping tolerance windows. The scores reported for *Rasanen (2014)* are the paper results.

frames of each utterance. To be consistent, the first 7 frames (70 ms) of the error signal for each utterance were set to 0.

A peak detection procedure is then applied to the resulting error. As we are looking for sudden bursts in the prediction error, a local maximum is labeled as a potential boundary if and only if the difference between its value and the one of the previous minimum is superior to a certain threshold δ.

4 Experiments

4.1 Dataset

We evaluated our methods on the TIMIT dataset Fischer et al. (1986). The TIMIT dataset consists of 6300 utterances ($\sim$ 5.4 hours) from 630 speakers spanning 8 dialects of the English language. The corpus was divided into a training and test set according to the standard split. The training set contains 4620 utterances (172,460 boundaries) and the test set 1680 (65,825 boundaries).

4.2 Evaluation

The performance evaluation of our system is based on precision (P), recall (R) and F-score, defined as the harmonic mean of precision and recall. A drawback of this metric is that high recall, low precision results, such as the ones produces by hypothesizing a boundary every 5 ms ($P : 58\%$, $R : 91\%$) yield high F-score (70%).

Other metrics have been designed to tackle this issue. One such example is the R-value (Räsänen et al., 2009) :

$$\text{R-val} = 1 - \frac{\sqrt{(1-R)^2 + OS^2} + |\frac{R+1-OS}{\sqrt{2}}|}{2} \quad (3)$$

Where $OS = \frac{R}{P} - 1$ is the over-segmentation measure. The R value represents how close the segmentation is from the ideal 0 OS, 1 R point and the P=1 line in the R, OS space. Further details can be found in Räsänen et al. (2009).

Determining whether gold boundary is detected or not is a crucial part of the evaluation procedure. On our test set for instance, which contains 65,825 gold boundaries partitioned into 1,680 files, adding or removing one correctly detected boundary per utterance leads to a change of $\pm$ 2.5% in precision. This means that minor changes in the evaluation process (such as removing the trailing silence parts of each file, removing the opening and closing boundary) yield non-trivial variations in the end result.

A common condition for a gold boundary to be considered as 'correctly detected' is to have a proposed boundary within a 20 ms distance on either side. Without any other specification, this means that a proposed boundary may be matched to several gold boundaries, provided these are within 40 ms from each other, leading to an increase of up to 4% F-score in some of our results (74%—78%). Unfortunately this point is seldom detailed in the literature.

We decided to use the procedure described in Räsänen et al. (2009) to match gold boundaries and hypothesized boundaries : overlapping tolerance windows are cropped in the middle of the two boundaries.

4.3 Results

The current state of the art in blind phoneme segmentation on the TIMIT corpus is provided by Hoang and Wang (2015). It evaluates to 78.16% F-score and 81.11 R-value on the training part of the dataset, using an evaluation method similar to our own.

In Tables 1 and 2 we compare our best results to the previous statistical approach evoked in Räsänen (2014) and the naive periodic boundaries segmentation (one boundary each 5 ms). Since Räsänen (2014) used an evaluation method allowing for tolerance windows to overlap, we provide our results with both evaluation methods (full windows and cropped windows) for the sake of consistency.

Another main difference with Räsänen (2014) is that its results are given on the core test set of TIMIT, whereas our results are given on the full test set.

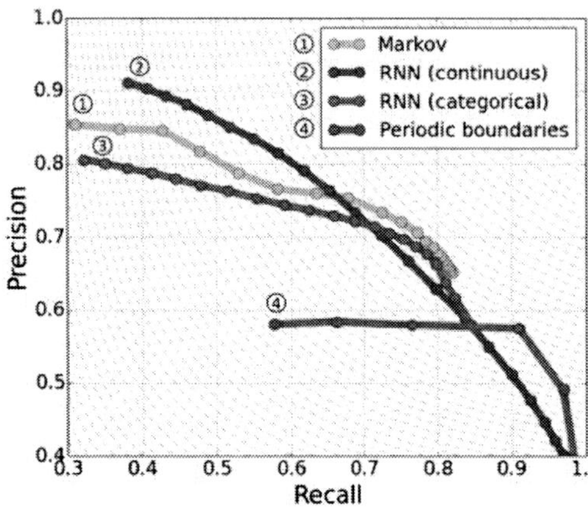

Figure 2: Precision/recall curves for our various models when varying the peak detection threshold δ

Figure 2 provides an overview of the precision/recall scores when varying the peak detection threshold (and, in case of periodic boundaries, the period). This gives some insight about the actual behavior of the various algorithms, especially in the high precision, low recall region where the RNN on actual MFCCs seems to outperform the methods based on discrete features.

We provide Figure 3 as a qualitative assessment of the error profiles of all three algorithms on one specific utterance. Notably, the error profile of the markov model contains distinct isolated peaks of similar height. As expected, the error curve is much more noisy in the case of the RNN on MFCCs, due to the greater variability in the feature space.

5   Discussion

In terms of optimal F-score and R values, the simple Markov model outperformed the previously published paper using short term sequential statistics (Räsänen, 2014), as well as the recurrent neural networks. However, these optimal values may mask the differential behavior of these algorithms in different sections of the precision/recall curve.

In particular, it is interesting to notice that the neural network based model trained on the raw MFCCs gave very good results in the low recall, high precision domain. Indeed, the precision can reach 90% with a recall of 40%. Such a regime could be useful, for instance, if blind phoneme segmentation is used to help with word segmentation.

The reason of the higher precision of neural networks may be that it combines the sensitivity of this model to sequential statistical regularities of the signal, but also to the spectral variations, i.e. the error is also correlated to the spectral changes, meaning that some peaks are associated with a high error because the euclidean distance $\|x_{t+1} - x_t\|_2$ itself is big. This is why the height difference is much more significant in this case.

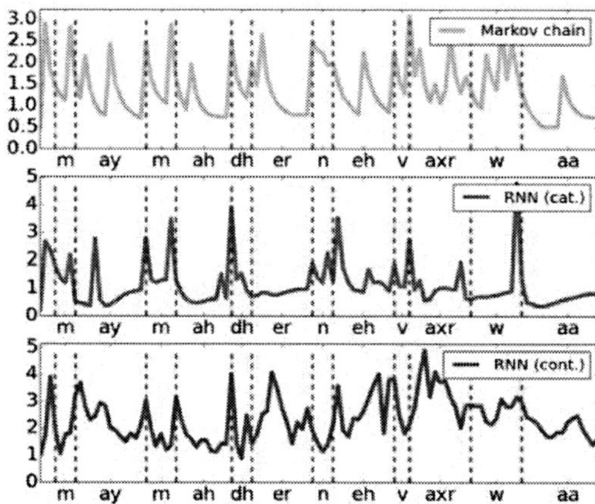

Figure 3: Comparison of error signals (gold boundaries are indicated in red)

Although we only reported the best results, we also tested our model on two other neural network architectures : a single vanilla RNN and a single LSTM cell. Both architecture did not yield significantly different results ($\sim$ 1—2% F-score, mainly dropping precision). Similarly, different hidden dimension were tested. In the extreme cases (very low - 8 - or high - 128 - dimension), the output signal proved too noisy to be of any significance, yielding results comparable to naive periodic segmentation.

It is worth mentioning that our approach doesn't make any language specific assumption, and as such similar results are to be expected on other languages. We leave the confirmation of this assumption to future work.

6   Conclusions

We have presented a lightweight blind phoneme segmentation method predicting boundaries at peaks of the prediction loss of transition probabilities models. The different models we tested produced satisfying results while remaining computationally tractable, requiring only one pass over the data at test time.

Our recurrent neural network trained on speech features in particular hints at a way of combining both the statistical and spectral information into a single model.

On a machine learning point of view, we highlighted the use that can be made of side channel information (in this case the test error) in order to extract structure from raw data in an unsupervised setting.

Future work may involve exploring different RNN models, assessing the stability of these methods on simpler features such as raw spectrograms or waveforms, or exploring the representation of each frame in the hidden layers of the networks.

7   Acknowledgements

The authors would like to thank the anonymous reviewers for their insightful and constructive comments which helped shape the final version of this paper.

This project is supported by the European Research Council (ERC-2011-AdG-295810 BOOTPHON), the Agénce Nationale pour la Recherche (ANR-10-LABX-0087 IEC, ANR-10-IDEX-0001-02 PSL*), the Fondation de France, the Ecole de Neurosciences de Paris, the Region Ile de France (DIM cerveau et pensée), and an AWS in Education Research Grant award.

References

George Almpanidis and Constantine Kotropoulos. 2008. Phonemic segmentation using the generalised gamma distribution and small sample bayesian information criterion. *Speech Communication* 50(1):38–55.

David Arthur and Sergei Vassilvitskii. 2007. k-means++: The advantages of careful seeding. In *Proceedings of the eighteenth annual ACM-SIAM symposium on Discrete algorithms*. Society for Industrial and Applied Mathematics, pages 1027–1035.

Morten H Christiansen, Joseph Allen, and Mark S Seidenberg. 1998. Learning to segment speech using multiple cues: A connectionist model. *Language and cognitive processes* 13(2-3):221–268.

Steven Davis and Paul Mermelstein. 1980. Comparison of parametric representations for monosyllabic word recognition in continuously spoken sentences. *IEEE transactions on acoustics, speech, and signal processing* 28(4):357–366.

Sorin Dusan and Lawrence R Rabiner. 2006. On the relation between maximum spectral transition positions and phone boundaries. In *Proceedings of Interspeech*. Citeseer.

Jeffrey L Elman. 1990. Finding structure in time. *Cognitive Science* 14(2):179–211.

Anna Esposito and Guido Aversano. 2005. Text independent methods for speech segmentation. In *Nonlinear Speech Modeling and Applications*, Springer, pages 261–290.

Yago Pereiro Estevan, Vincent Wan, and Odette Scharenborg. 2007. Finding maximum margin segments in speech. In *2007 IEEE International Conference on Acoustics, Speech and Signal Processing-ICASSP'07*. IEEE, volume 4, pages IV–937.

William M. Fischer, George R. Doddington, and Kathleen M Goudie-Marshall. 1986. The darpa speech recognition research database: Specifications and status. In *Proceedings of DARPA Workshop on Speech Recognition*. pages 93–99.

James R Glass. 2003. A probabilistic framework for segment-based speech recognition. *Computer Speech & Language* 17(2):137–152.

Dac-Thang Hoang and Hsiao-Chuan Wang. 2015. Blind phone segmentation based on spectral change detection using legendre polynomial approximation. *The Journal of the Acoustical Society of America* 137(2):797–805.

Sepp Hochreiter and Jürgen Schmidhuber. 1997. Long short-term memory. *Neural computation* 9(8):1735–1780.

Herman Kamper, Aren Jansen, and Sharon Goldwater. 2015. Fully unsupervised small-vocabulary speech recognition using a segmental bayesian model. In *Proceedings of Interspeech*.

Vahid Khanagha, Khalid Daoudi, Oriol Pont, and Hussein Yahia. 2014. Phonetic segmentation of speech signal using local singularity analysis. *Digital Signal Processing* 35:86–94.

Yu Qiao, Naoya Shimomura, and Nobuaki Minematsu. 2008. Unsupervised optimal phoneme segmentation: Objectives, algorithm and comparisons. In *2008 IEEE International Conference on Acoustics, Speech and Signal Processing*. IEEE, pages 3989–3992.

Okko Räsänen. 2014. Basic cuts revisited: Temporal segmentation of speech into phone-like units with statistical learning at a pre-linguistic level. In *Proceedings of the 36th Annual Conference of the Cognitive Science Society. Quebec, Canada.*

Okko Rasanen, Toomas Altosaar, and Unto Laine. 2011. *Blind segmentation of speech using nonlinear filtering methods.* INTECH Open Access Publisher.

Okko Räsänen, Unto Kalervo Laine, and Toomas Altosaar. 2009. An improved speech segmentation quality measure: the r-value. In *Proceedings of Interspeech.*

Man-hung Siu, Herbert Gish, Arthur Chan, William Belfield, and Steve Lowe. 2013. Unsupervized training of an HMM-based self-organizing recognizer with applications to topic classification and keyword discovery. *Computer Speech & Language* preprint.

Nitish Srivastava, Geoffrey E Hinton, Alex Krizhevsky, Ilya Sutskever, and Ruslan Salakhutdinov. 2014. Dropout: a simple way to prevent neural networks from overfitting. *Journal of Machine Learning Research* 15(1):1929–1958.

Tijmen Tieleman and Geoffrey Hinton. 2012. Lecture 6.5-rmsprop: Divide the gradient by a running average of its recent magnitude. *COURSERA: Neural Networks for Machine Learning* 4(2).

Paul J Werbos. 1990. Backpropagation through time: what it does and how to do it. *Proceedings of the IEEE* 78(10):1550–1560.

Robert Wilber. 1988. The concave least-weight subsequence problem revisited. *Journal of Algorithms* 9(3):418–425.

Automatic Generation of Jokes in Hindi

Srishti Aggarwal
LTRC, KCIS
IIIT Hyderabad
srishti.aggarwal@research.iiit.in

Radhika Mamidi
LTRC, KCIS
IIIT Hyderabad
radhika.mamidi@iiit.ac.in

Abstract

When it comes to computational language generation systems, humour is a relatively unexplored domain, especially more so for Hindi (or rather, for most languages other than English). Most researchers agree that a joke consists of two main parts - the setup and the punchline, with humour being encoded in the incongruity between the two. In this paper, we look at *Dur se Dekha* jokes, a restricted domain of humorous three liner poetry in Hindi. We analyze their structure to understand how humour is encoded in them and formalize it. We then develop a system which is successfully able to generate a basic form of these jokes.

1 Introduction

The Oxford dictionary has defined humour as the quality of being amusing or comic, especially as expressed in literature or speech. It is an essential element of human interactions. The understanding and sense of humour varies widely across time, space and people. The same properties which make it interesting and compelling also make its structure rich and complex, making it an interesting topic of study.

Verbal humour is the most commonly used form of humour in the everyday use of natural language. Joke, a sub-class of verbal humour, is commonly considered the prototypical form of verbal humour, produced orally in conversations or published in collections (Dynel, 2009). Most researchers (Sherzer (1985), Attardo and Chabanne (1992), Attardo (1994, 2001), Suls (1972)) agree with Raskin (1985) that jokes comprise a setup and a punchline. The setup builds a narrative and induces some form of expectation, while the punch-

line is the final portion of the text, which violates that expectation, thereby generating humour due to the production of incongruity and its consequent resolution.

As intelligent systems advance further and find their way into increasingly more domains the need to process human natural languages increases; a challenging part of this is processing humour. Hence, in this paper, we attempt to build a system, which generates humorous texts in a restricted domain of *Dur se Dekha* type jokes, a form of humorous three liner poetry[1] in Hindi. This kind of poetry was popular in the Indian culture at one point but is almost lost now, with only a few repeated examples available online.

2 Related Work

Till date, there has been limited contribution towards construction of computational humour generation systems. One of the first attempts in generating humour was the program JAPE (Binsted and Ritchie (1997), Ritchie (2003)). JAPE used an algorithm to generate funny punning riddles, or more specifically phonologically ambiguous riddles, having noun phrase punchlines.

HAHAcronym generator (Stock and Strapparava, 2003) was another attempt at computational humour generation, whose goal was to automatically generate new versions of existing acronyms, which were ensured to be humorous using incongruity theories.

Aside from this, Taylor and Mazlack (2004), worked on humour comprehension on a restricted domain of "knock-knock" jokes. Although the heuristic based approach was able to effectively identify the word-play instances which was the first task, it faced difficulty in the knock-knock joke identification part, again stressing the chal-

---

[1]A three line poem is called a tercet.

Proceedings of the 55th Annual Meeting of the Association for Computational Linguistics- Student Research Workshop, pages 69–74
Vancouver, Canada, July 30 - August 4, 2017. ©2017 Association for Computational Linguistics
https://doi.org/10.18653/v1/P17-3012

lenge in humour analysis.

More Recently, Valitutti et al. (2016), attempts to generate humorous texts by substitution of a single word in a short text, within some constraints. The results showed that taboo words made a text recognizable as humorous.

Petrović and Matthews (2013) attempted to build a fully unsupervised humour generation system which generates a specific form of jokes using big data. This is a first attempt at unsupervised joke generation which gave promising results.

While there have been some attempts to formalize humour in English and a handful of other languages, to the best of our knowledge, no such prior research work has been attempted in Hindi.

3 *Dur se Dekha*

Dur se Dekha is a focused form of poetic three liner jokes in the Hindi language. These jokes have a typical structure, with the humour lying in the incongruity of the punchline against the expectation of the listener. A typical *Dur se Dekha* joke consists of three parts. The structure of a typical *Dur se Dekha* joke can be surmised as follows:

Part$_1$: *Dur se dekha to* $\underline{NP_1/VP_1}$ *tha,*
Part$_2$: *Dur se dekha to* $\underline{NP_1/VP_1}$ *tha,*
Part$_3$: *Paas jaakar dekha to* $\underline{NP_2/VP_2}$ *tha.*

Translation:

Part$_1$: From afar I saw $\underline{NP_1/VP_1}$,
Part$_2$: From afar I saw $\underline{NP_1/VP_1}$,
Part$_3$: On going closer it turned out to be $\underline{NP_2/VP_2}$

A *Dur se Dekha* joke employs stylistic features like alliteration, repetition and rhyme, which have previously been associated with humour appreciation (Bucaria, 2004; Mihalcea and Strapparava, 2006).

The first part is the setup of the joke, the second is a repetition of the first. This repetition puts emphasis on the first. The beginning of the third part raises the listeners expectation, and it is what comes at the end that creates humour in this joke. That is the element of surprise, the punch line.

Alliteration exists in the first and the third word of the template. Also, the setup and the punchline normally rhyme and contradict in meaning and sentiment, which are two more indicators of humour present in these jokes. This is also precisely why these jokes lose their humour when translated into another language.

On further analysis, we classified these jokes into two main types, which are explained below with examples.

Type 1.a:

Part$_1$: *Dur se dekha to* $\underline{NP_1}$ *tha,*
Part$_2$: *Dur se dekha to* $\underline{NP_1}$ *tha,*
Part$_3$: *Paas jaakar dekha to* $\underline{NP_2}$ *tha.*

An example of the basic form of this type would be:

Joke$_1$: *Dur se dekha to Dharmendra tha, dur se dekha to Dharmendra tha, paas jaakar dekha to bandar tha.*[2]

Joke$_1$(translated): From afar I saw Dharmendra, from afar I saw Dharmendra, on going closer it turned out to be a monkey.

A more complex example of the same type is:

Joke$_2$: *Dur se dekha to Gabbar Singh ka adda tha, dur se dekha to Gabbar Singh ka adda tha, paas jaakar dekha to aapka chadda tha.*[3]

Joke$_2$(translated): From afar I saw Gabbar Singh's haunt, from afar I saw Gabbar Singh's haunt, on going closer it turned out to be your underpants.

Type 1.b:

Part$_1$: *Dur se dekha to* $\underline{VP_1}$ *tha,*
Part$_2$: *Dur se dekha to* $\underline{VP_1}$ *tha,*
Part$_3$: *Paas jaakar dekha to* $\underline{VP_2}$ *tha.*

Examples of jokes belonging to this category are:

Joke$_3$: *Dur se dekha to ande ubal rahe the, dur se dekha to ande ubal rahe the, paas jaakar dekha to ganje uchal rahe the.*[4]

Joke$_3$(translated): From afar I saw eggs boiling, from afar I saw eggs boiling, on going closer it turned out to be bald men jumping.

---

[2] http://www.jokofy.com/2595/door-se-dekha-to-funny-shayari/
[3] http://www.shayri.com/forums/showthread.php?t=27592
[4] http://www.shayri.com/forums/showthread.php?t=27592

Joke[4]: *Dur se dekha to hasina baal bana rahi thi, dur se dekha to hasina baal bana rahi thi, paas jaakar dekha to gaay puch hila rahi thi.*[5]

Joke[4](translated): From afar I saw a beautiful girl grooming her hair, from afar I saw a beautiful girl grooming her hair, on going closer it turned out to be cow swinging its tail.

Type 2: The structure being the same as Type 1, but differing in the how humour is encoded in the joke.

Part[1]: *Dur se dekkha to NP/VP[1] tha,*
Part[2]: *Dur se dekha to NP/VP[1] tha,*
Part[3]: *Paas jaakar dekha to NP/VP[2] tha.*

For example:

Joke[5]: *Dur se dekha to kuch nahi dikha, dur se dekha to kuch nahi dikha, paas jaakar dekha to kuch tha hi nahi.*[6]

Joke[5](translated): From afar I could see nothing, from afar I could see nothing, on going closer it actually turned out to be nothing.

Joke[6](translated): Dur se dekha to baarish ho rahi thi, dur se dekha to baarish ho rahi thi, paas gaya to bheeg gaya.[7]

Joke[6]: *From afar I saw that it was raining, from afar I saw that it was raining, on going closer I got drenched.*

The difference between Type[1] and Type[2] jokes lies in the way humour is encoded in them. Type[1] jokes are humorous because of how the punch line contrasts with the subject of the setup in terms of the sentiment. The incongruity between the subject (what something seems to be from far away) versus the punchline (what it actually turns out to be), induces surprise and amusement in the listener. The use of celebrity names further makes a joke funnier. On the other hand, for Type[2] jokes, humour lies in the unconventionality of the punchline. The listener expects a conventional punchline, something conflicting the subject, what

he gets instead is an affirmation of the subject (Joke[5]), or maybe a consequence of the subject in the real world (Joke[6]). This is not unlike the way humour is encoded in some shaggy dog jokes, "a nonsensical joke that employs in the punchline a psychological non sequitur ... to trick the listener who expects conventional wit or humour" (Brunvand, 1963).

For the purposes of this study, we will be looking at only Type[1] jokes.

4 Experimental Design

We are attempting to build a system that would generate the Type[1] jokes mentioned in the previous section. As of now this system generates only the most basic form of Type[1a] jokes (such as Joke[1]), but will be expanded upon to cover as many types as possible.

The Joke generation process has four steps:

Step[1]: Template selection
Step[2]: Setup Formation
Step[3]: Punchline Formation
Step[4]: Compilation

These steps are explained in the subsections below.

4.1 Template Selection

We created a collection of three templates for the two types of jokes we are working on (Type[1a] and Type[1b]), along with a few minor variations in terms of auxiliary verbs, postpositions etc. These varied templates were added to naturalize the final jokes, and as a measure against joke fatigue.

4.2 Setup Formation

We manually created a lexicon of words from different semantic categories - human and non human. For humans, we compiled a list of names of popular celebrities, both male and female, from different domains - actors, politicians, players as well as popular fictional characters. For the second category in the lexicon we picked some generic adjectives, and words (mostly nouns) from the Hindi language that would have a negative sentiment when associated with a human, for example, names of animals, or vegetables.

For the form of Type[1a] jokes we have been working on, one word is picked randomly from this lexicon. This is the setup, the subject for our joke.

---

[5]http://desipoetry.com/door-se-dekha-series/
[6]http://desipoetry.com/door-se-dekha-series/
[7]http://www.shayri.com/forums/showthread.php?t=27592

4.3 Punchline Formation

We select a single word from the lexicon as our punchline. This selection is done following three constraints explained below:

1. Category constraint: The semantic category of the punchline should be of a different category than the subject.

2. Gender Constraint: As all non-human things are assigned a gender out of male/female, the gender of the punchline has to be the same as the gender of the subject. This is important in Hindi as it plays an important part in subject-verb agreement.

3. Form constraint: A typical characteristic of this type of jokes is that the subject of the setup and the punchline are lexically similar, giving a poetic effect to the joke. So, we first look for a rhyming word for the punchline. If a rhyming word isn't found, we use Levenshtein distance to find a phonetically similar word which is then used as the punchline.

4.4 Compilation

The template, the setup and the punchline is taken and put together to generate the resultant joke.

Given below are a couple of examples of the jokes generated by our system using the above mentioned algorithm:

Joke$_7$: *Dur se dekha to mowgli tha, dur se dekha to mowgli that, paas jaakr dekha to chimpanzi tha.*

Joke$_7$(translated): From afar I saw mowgli, from afar I saw mowgli, on going near I saw it was a chimpanzi.

Joke$_8$: *Dur se dekha to mussadi tha, dur se dekha to mussadi that, paas jaakr dekha to fissadi nikla.*

Joke$_8$(translated): From afar I saw Mr. Mussadi, from afar I saw Mr.Musadi, on going near he turned out to be a loser.

5 Evaluation and Results

We evaluated our system in 2 parts. We first drew a comparison between human created jokes available and the ones generated by our system. Second, we varied our constraints to see how that lead

Experimental Conditions	Funniness (mean $\pm$ std.dev.)
Form + Gender + Category	2.40 ± 0.53
Gender + Category	2.11 ± 0.54
Form + Gender	1.97 ± 0.49
Form + Category	1.68 ± 0.24

Table 1: Mean Funniness values, and standard deviations of computer generated jokes as different constraints are applied.

to changes in humour perception of the resultant jokes.

Since, in our sample set, we had only 5 instances of the subtype of *Dur se Dekha* jokes that we are working on, we took all of those 5 and an equivalent number of jokes generated by our system and put them in a survey in a random order. We then asked 15 participants to rate how natural each joke felt to them on a scale of 1 to 5 (with 5 being completely natural and 1 being completely unnatural).

The analyses of the responses showed us that the average score of the jokes generated by our system was comparable to the average of our exemplar human made jokes. With jokes from our system having an average score of 3.16/5, our system only marginally underperforms the human jokes with an average score of 3.33/5. Another interesting observation is that of all the jokes present in the survey, the one with the highest score was one of the computer generated jokes.

In the second part of the evaluation, we want to look at how the three proposed constraints affect the resultant text. For this, we created a set of 80 jokes - 20 from the system with all three constraints, and 20 each obtained removing one variation at a time. We then conducted a survey this entire set. Each person who then took the survey got a different randomly generated subset of jokes to rate, with each joke being evaluated by 5 people. In this survey, the evaluators were asked to judge how funny they found each joke to be on a scale of 1 to 5 (with 1 being not funny at all, to 5 being hilarious). The results of this evaluation have been summarized in Table 1.

From Table 1, we see that people found our jokes only mildly funny. We believe that the simplicity, the lack of a deeper semantic meaning is the reason for this. Varying the constraints, we see that the jokes work best when they adhere to all three constraints. We infer from the table that Gender constraint contributes the most to humor in our jokes, while Form constraint contributes the least.

We were unable to perform an inter-rater agreement analysis because each joke was rated by a different set of people. Instead, we chose to include the standard deviations for each set in our analysis.

6 Future Extensions

Our joke generator is giving encouraging results for the basic form of the jokes but it still has a long way to go to improve domain coverage, and only then will it be possible to evaluate how well the system works.

The lexicon needs to be expanded to add adjectives, adverbs and verbs so that noun phrases and verb phrases can be formed and used as the subject and the punchline. We also plan on adding associated features of nouns, in terms of their physical representation in the world, which would help add semantic significance to the results. This will require much more sophisticated algorithms. This task is especially challenging due to a lack of availability of language resources and tools for Hindi. We will need to develop phrase generators for Hindi for the task. Also, as the punchline should have the sentiment opposite to the subject line, more thought needs to put into what that means for complete phrases.

The lexicon can be updated regularly. In fact, we can make our system such that it automatically picks up trending celebrity names, adjectives and verbs from social media websites and use them as subjects for the joke. This will be instrumental in avoiding joke fatigue and would help our system keep up with the fast changing culture these days.

Also, a much more extensive evaluation should be done for the system when it is capable of generating more complex jokes. Naturalness of the jokes, as well as their funniness needs to be evaluated on a larger scale. Using crowdsourcing for such an evaluation would be a good choice to learn more about the bigger picture.

7 Summary and Conclusion

Computational linguistics is a widely explored field these days, with translation, summarization and comprehension being a few of the many areas of interest. Because of its complexity, and huge amount of variations, verbal humour has been explored only mildly in computational language processing, with only a few attempts at generating humour. This job is also made difficult due to the lack of any robust theoretical foundations to base a system on. Further, there has essentially been no work of significance in the domain for Hindi.

Our *Dur se Dekha* joke generator is a first step towards the exploration of humour in Hindi language generation. In this paper, we took a focused form of humorous tercets in Hindi - *Dur se Dekha*, and performed an analysis of its structure and humour encoding. We then created a lexicon, and came up with an algorithm to form the various elements of the joke following specific constraints. We saw that the jokes generated by our system gave decent results in terms of naturalness and humour to serve as a baseline for future work.

Finally, we discussed possible extensions for our system to make it more complete and comprehensive.

Acknowledgments

The authors would like to thank all the evaluators for their time and help in rating the jokes. We would also like to thank Kaveri Anuranjana for all the time she spent helping us put this work on paper.

References

Salvatore Attardo. 1994. *Linguistic theories of humor*, volume 1. Walter de Gruyter.

Salvatore Attardo. 2001. *Humorous texts: A semantic and pragmatic analysis*, volume 6. Walter de Gruyter.

Salvatore Attardo and Jean-Charles Chabanne. 1992. Jokes as a text type.

Kim Binsted and Graeme Ritchie. 1997. Computational rules for generating punning riddles. *HUMOR-International Journal of Humor Research* 10(1):25–76.

Jan Harold Brunvand. 1963. A classification for shaggy dog stories. *The Journal of American Folklore* 76(299):42–68.

Chiara Bucaria. 2004. Lexical and syntactic ambiguity as a source of humor: The case of newspaper headlines. *Humor* 17(3):279–310.

Marta Dynel. 2009. Beyond a joke: Types of conversational humour. *Language and Linguistics Compass* 3(5):1284–1299. https://doi.org/10.1111/j.1749-818X.2009.00152.x.

Rada Mihalcea and Carlo Strapparava. 2006. Learning to laugh (automatically): Computational models for humor recognition. *Computational Intelligence* 22(2):126–142.

Saša Petrović and David Matthews. 2013. Unsupervised joke generation from big data. In *Proceedings of the 51st Annual Meeting of the Association for Computational Linguistics (Volume 2: Short Papers)*. Association for Computational Linguistics, Sofia, Bulgaria, pages 228–232. http://www.aclweb.org/anthology/P13-2041.

Victor Raskin. 1985. Semantic mechanisms of humor. *Reidel, Dordrecht* .

Graeme Ritchie. 2003. The jape riddle generator: technical specification. *Institute for Communicating and Collaborative Systems* .

Joel Sherzer. 1985. Puns and jokes. *Handbook of discourse analysis* 3:213–221.

Oliviero Stock and Carlo Strapparava. 2003. Hahacronym: Humorous agents for humorous acronyms. *Humor* 16(3):297–314.

Jerry M Suls. 1972. A two-stage model for the appreciation of jokes and cartoons: An information-processing analysis. *The psychology of humor: Theoretical perspectives and empirical issues* 1:81–100.

Julia M Taylor and Lawrence J Mazlack. 2004. Computationally recognizing wordplay in jokes. In *Proceedings of the Cognitive Science Society*. volume 26.

Alessandro Valitutti, Antoine Doucet, Jukka M Toivanen, and Hannu Toivonen. 2016. Computational generation and dissection of lexical replacement humor. *Natural Language Engineering* 22(5):727–749.

Word Embedding for Response-To-Text Assessment of Evidence

Haoran Zhang
Department of Computer Science
University of Pittsburgh
Pittsburgh, PA 15260
colinzhang@cs.pitt.edu

Diane Litman
Department of Computer Science & LRDC
University of Pittsburgh
Pittsburgh, PA 15260
litman@cs.pitt.edu

Abstract

Manually grading the Response to Text Assessment (RTA) is labor intensive. Therefore, an automatic method is being developed for scoring analytical writing when the RTA is administered in large numbers of classrooms. Our long-term goal is to also use this scoring method to provide formative feedback to students and teachers about students' writing quality. As a first step towards this goal, interpretable features for automatically scoring the evidence rubric of the RTA have been developed. In this paper, we present a simple but promising method for improving evidence scoring by employing the word embedding model. We evaluate our method on corpora of responses written by upper elementary students.

1 Introduction

In Correnti et al. (2013), it was noted that the 2010 Common Core State Standards emphasize the ability of young students from grades 4-8 to interpret and evaluate texts, construct logical arguments based on substantive claims, and marshal relevant evidence in support of these claims. Correnti et al. (2013) relatedly developed the Response to Text Assessment (RTA) for assessing students' analytic response-to-text writing skills. The RTA was designed to evaluate writing skills in Analysis, Evidence, Organization, Style, and MUGS (Mechanics, Usage, Grammar, and Spelling) dimensions. To both score the RTA and provide formative feedback to students and teachers at scale, an automated RTA scoring tool is now being developed (Rahimi et al., 2017).

This paper focuses on the Evidence dimension of the RTA, which evaluates students' ability to find and use evidence from an article to support their position. Rahimi et al. (2014) previously developed a set of interpretable features for scoring the Evidence rubric of RTA. Although these features significantly improve over competitive baselines, the feature extraction approach is largely based on lexical matching and can be enhanced.

The contributions of this paper are as follows. First, we employ a new way of using the word embedding model to enhance the system of Rahimi et al. (2014). Second, we use word embeddings to deal with noisy data given the disparate writing skills of students at the upper elementary level.

In the following sections, we first present research on related topics, describe our corpora, and review the interpretable features developed by Rahimi et al. (2014). Next, we explain how we use the word embedding model for feature extraction to improve performance by addressing the limitations of prior work. Finally, we discuss the results of our experiments and present future plans.

2 Related Work

Most research studies in automated essay scoring have focused on holistic rubrics (Shermis and Burstein, 2003; Attali and Burstein, 2006). In contrast, our work focuses on evaluating a single dimension to obtain a rubric score for students' use of evidence from a source text to support their stated position. To evaluate the content of students' essays, Louis and Higgins (2010) presented a method to detect if an essay is off-topic. Xie et al. (2012) presented a method to evaluate content features by measuring the similarity between essays. Burstein et al. (2001) and Ong et al. (2014) both presented methods to use argumentation mining techniques to evaluate the students' use of evidence to support claims in persuasive essays. However, those studies are different from

Proceedings of the 55th Annual Meeting of the Association for Computational Linguistics- Student Research Workshop, pages 75–81
Vancouver, Canada, July 30 - August 4, 2017. ©2017 Association for Computational Linguistics
https://doi.org/10.18653/v1/P17-3013

this work in that they did not measure how the essay uses material from the source article. Furthermore, young students find it difficult to use sophisticated argumentation structure in their essays.

Rahimi et al. (2014) presented a set of interpretable rubric features that measure the relatedness between students' essays and a source article by extracting evidence from the students' essays. However, evidence from students' essays could not always be extracted by their word matching method. There are some potential solutions using the word embedding model. Rei and Cummins (2016) presented a method to evaluate topical relevance by estimating sentence similarity using weighted-embedding. Kenter and de Rijke (2015) evaluated short text similarity with word embedding. Kiela et al. (2015) developed specialized word embedding by employing external resources. However, none of these methods address highly noisy essays written by young students.

3 Data

Our response-to-text essay corpora were all collected from classrooms using the following procedure. The teacher first read aloud a text while students followed along with their copy. After the teacher explained some predefined vocabulary and discussed standardized questions at designated points, there is a prompt at the end of the text which asks students to write an essay in response to the prompt. Figure 1 shows the prompt of RTA_{MVP}

Two forms of the RTA have been developed, based on different articles that students read before writing essays in response to a prompt. The first form is RTA_{MVP} and is based on an article from *Time for Kids* about the Millennium Villages Project, an effort by the United Nations to end poverty in a rural village in Sauri, Kenya. The other form is RTA_{Space}, based on a developed article about the importance of space exploration. Below is a small excerpt from the RTA_{MVP} article. Evidence from the text that expert human graders want to see in students' essays are in bold.

"Today, Yala Sub-District **Hospital has medicine, free of charge, for all of the most common diseases. Water is connected to the hospital**, which also has a **generator for electricity. Bed nets are used** in every sleeping site in Sauri."

	$Space$	MVP_L	MVP_H
Score 1	538	535	317
	(26%)	(30%)	(27%)
Score 2	789	709	488
	(38%)	(39%)	(42%)
Score 3	512	374	242
	(25%)	(21%)	(21%)
Score 4	237	186	119
	(11%)	(10%)	(10%)
Total	2076	1804	1166
Double-Rated	2076	847	1156
Kappa	0.338	0.490	0.479
QWKappa	0.651	0.775	0.734

Table 1: The distribution of Evidence scores, and grading agreement of two raters.

Two corpora of RTA_{MVP} from lower and higher age groups were introduced in Correnti et al. (2013). One group included grades 4-6 (denoted by MVP_L), and the other group included grades 6-8 (denoted by MVP_H). The students in each age group represent different levels of writing proficiency. We also combined these two corpora to form a larger corpus, denoted by MVP_{ALL}. The corpus of the RTA_{Space} is collected only from students of grades 6-8 (denoted by $Space$).

Based on the rubric criterion shown in Table 2, the essays in each corpus were annotated by two raters on a scale of 1 to 4, from low to high. Raters are experts and trained undergraduates. Table 1 shows the distribution of Evidence scores from the first rater and the agreement (Kappa, and Quadratic Weighted Kappa) between two raters of the double-rated portion. All experiment performances will be measured by Quadratic Weighted Kappa between the score from prediction and the first rater. The reason to only use the score of the first rater is that the first rater graded more essays. Figure 1 shows an essay with a score of 3.

4 Rubric Features

Based on the rubric criterion for the evidence dimension, Rahimi et al. (2014) developed a set of interpretable features. By using this set of features, a predicting model can be trained for automated essay scoring in the evidence dimension.

Number of Pieces of Evidence (NPE): A good essay should mention evidence from the article as much as possible. To extract the NPE feature, they manually craft a topic word list based on the arti-

	1	2	3	4
Number of Pieces of evidence	Features one or no pieces of evidence (NPE)	Features at least 2 pieces of evidence (NPE)	Features at least 3 pieces of evidence (NPE)	Features at least 3 pieces of evidence (NPE)
Relevance of evidence	Selects inappropriate or irrelevant details from the text to support key idea (SPC); references to text feature serious factual errors or omissions	Selects some appropriate and relevant evidence to support key idea, or evidence is provided for some ideas, but not actually the key idea (SPC); evidence may contain a factual error or omission	Selects pieces of evidence from the text that are appropriate and relevant to key idea (SPC)	Selects evidence from the text that clearly and effectively supports key idea
Specificity of evidence	Provides general or cursory evidence from the text (SPC)	Provides general or cursory evidence from the text (SPC)	Provides specific evidence from the text (SPC)	Provides pieces of evidence that are detailed and specific (SPC)
Elaboration of Evidence	Evidence may be listed in a sentence (CON)	Evidence provided may be listed in a sentence, not expanded upon (CON)	Attempts to elaborate upon evidence (CON)	Evidence must be used to support key idea / inference(s)
Plagiarism	Summarize entire text or copies heavily from text (in these cases, the response automatically receives a 1)			

Table 2: Rubric for the Evidence dimension of RTA. The abbreviations in the parentheses identify the corresponding feature group discussed in the Rubric Features section of this paper that is aligned with that specific criteria (Rahimi et al., 2017).

cle. Then, they use a simple window-based algorithm with a fixed size window to extract this feature. If a window contains at least two words from the topic list, they consider this window to contain evidence related to a topic. To avoid redundancy, each topic is only counted once. Words from the window and crafted list will only be considered a match if they are exactly the same. This feature is an integer to represent the number of topics that are mentioned by the essay.

Concentration (CON): Rather than list all the topics in the essay, a good essay should explain each topic with details. The same topic word list and simple window-based algorithm are used for extracting the CON feature. An essay is concentrated if the essay has fewer than 3 sentences that mention at least one of the topic words. Therefore, this feature is a binary feature. The value is 1 if the essay is concentrated, otherwise it is 0.

Specificity (SPC): A good essay should use relevant examples as much as possible. For matching SPC feature, experts manually craft an example list based on the article. Each example belongs to one topic, and is an aspect of a specific detail about the topic. For each example, the same window-based algorithm is used for matching. If the window contains at least two words from an example, they consider the window to mention this example. Therefore, the SPC feature is an integer vector. Each value in the vector represents how many examples in this topic were mentioned by the essay. To avoid redundancy, each example is only to be counted at most one time. The length of the vector is the same as the number of categories of examples in the crafted list.

Word Count (WOC): The SPC feature can capture how many evidences were mentioned in the essay, but it cannot represent if these pieces of evidence support key ideas effectively. From previous work, we know longer essays tend to have higher scores. Thus, they use word count as a potentially helpful fallback feature. This feature is an integer.

5 Word Embedding Feature Extraction

Based on the results of Rahimi et al. (2014), the interpretable rubric-based features outperform competitive baselines. However, there are limitations in their feature extraction method. It cannot extract all examples mentioned by the essay due to the use of simple exact matching.

First, students use their own vocabularies other than words in the crafted list. For instance, some students use the word "power" instead of "electricity" from the crafted list.

Second, according to our corpora, students at the upper elementary level make spelling mistakes, and sometimes they make mistakes in the same way. For example, around 1 out of 10 students misspell "poverty" as "proverty" instead. Therefore, evidence with student spelling mistakes cannot be extracted. However, the evidence dimension of RTA does not penalize students for misspelling words. Rahimi et al. (2014) showed that manual spelling corrections indeed improves performance, but not significantly.

Finally, tenses used by students can sometimes be different from that of the article. Although a stemming algorithm can solve this problem, sometimes there are words that slip through the process.

Prompt: The author provided one specific example of how the quality of life can be improved by the Millennium Villages Project in Sauri, Kenya. Based on the article, did the author provide a convincing argument that winning the fight against poverty is achievable in our lifetime? Explain why or why not with 3-4 examples from the text to support your answer.

Essay: In my opinion I think that they will achieve it in lifetime. During the years threw **2004 and 2008 they made progress**. People didnt have the money to buy the stuff in 2004. *The hospital was packed with patients* and they didnt have alot of treatment in 2004. In 2008 it changed the *hospital had medicine, free of charge*, and **for all the common dieases**. *Water was connected to the hospital* and has a *generator for electricity*. **Everybody has net** in their site. *The hunger crisis has been addressed* with **fertilizer and seeds**, as well as the *tools needed to maintain the food. The school has no fees* and *they serve lunch*. To me thats sounds like it is going achieve it in the lifetime.

Figure 1: The prompt of RTA_{MVP} and an example essay with score of 3.

For example, "went" is the past tense of "go", but stemming would miss this conjugation. Therefore, "go" and "went" would not be considered a match.

To address the limitations above, we introduced the Word2vec (the skip-gram (SG) and the continuous bag-of-words (CBOW)) word embedding model presented by Mikolov et al. (2013a) into the feature extraction process. By mapping words from the vocabulary to vectors of real numbers, the similarity between two words can be calculated. Words with high similarity can be considered a match. Because words in the same context tend to have similar meaning, they would therefore have higher similarity.

We use the word embedding model as a supplement to the original feature extraction process, and use the same searching window algorithm presented by Rahimi et al. (2014). If a word in a stu-dent's essay is not exactly the same as the word in the crafted list, the cosine similarity between these two words is calculated by the word embedding model. We consider them matching, if the similarity is higher than a threshold.

In Figure 1, the phrases in italics are examples extracted by the existing feature extraction method. For instance, "water was connected to the hospital" can be found because "water" and "hospital" are exactly the same as words in the crafted list. However, "for all the common dieases" cannot be found due to misspelling of "disease". Additional examples that can be extracted by the word embedding model are in bold.

6 Experimental Setup

We configure experiments to test several hypotheses: H1) the model with the word embedding trained on our own corpus will outperform or at least perform equally well as the baseline (denoted by $Rubric$) presented by Rahimi et al. (2014). H2) the model with the word embedding trained on our corpus will outperform or at least perform equally well as the model with off-the-shelf word embedding models. H3) the model with word embedding trained on our own corpus will generalize better across students of different ages. Note that while all models with word embeddings use the same features as the $Rubric$ baseline, the feature extraction process was changed to allow non-exact matching via the word embeddings.

We stratify each corpus into 3 parts: 40% of the data are used for training the word embedding models; 20% of the data are used to select the best word embedding model and best threshold (this is the development set of our model); and another 40% of data are used for final testing.

For word embedding model training, we also add essays not graded by the first rater ($Space$ has 229, MVP_L has 222, MVP_H has 296, and MVP_{ALL} has 518) to 40% of the data from the corpus in order to enlarge the training corpus to get better word embedding models. We train multiple word embedding models with different parameters, and select the best word embedding model by using the development set.

Two off-the-shelf word embeddings are used for comparison. Mikolov et al. (2013b) presented vectors that have 300 dimensions and were trained on a newspaper corpus of about 100 billion words. The other is presented by Baroni et al. (2014) and includes 400 dimensions, with the context window size of 5, 10 negative samples and subsampling.

We use 10 runs of 10-fold cross validation in the final testing, with Random Forest (max-depth = 5) implemented in Weka (Witten et al., 2016) as the classifier. This is the setting used by Rahimi et al. (2014). Since our corpora are imbalanced with respect to the four evidence scores being predicted (Table 1), we use SMOTE oversampling method (Chawla et al., 2002). This involves creating "synthetic" examples for minority classes. We only oversample the training data. All experiment performances are measured by Quadratic Weighted Kappa (QWKappa).

7   Results and Discussion

We first examine H1. The results shown in Table 3 partially support this hypothesis. The skip-gram embedding yields a higher performance or performs equally well as the rubric baseline on most corpora, except for MVP_H. The skip-gram embedding significantly improves performance for the lower grade corpus. Meanwhile, the skip-gram embedding is always significantly better than the continuous bag-of-words embedding.

Second, we examine H2. Again, the results shown in Table 3 partially support this hypothesis. The skip-gram embedding trained on our corpus outperform Baroni's embedding on $Space$ and MVP_L. While Baroni's embedding is significantly better than the skip-gram embedding on MVP_H and MVP_{ALL}.

Third, we examine H3, by training models from one corpus and testing it on 10 disjointed sets of the other test corpus. We do it 10 times and average the results in order to perform significance testing. The results shown in Table 4 support this hypothesis. The skip-gram word embedding model outperform all other models.

As we can see, the skip-gram embedding outperforms the continuous bag-of-words embedding in all experiments. One possible reason for this is that the skip-gram is better than the continuous bag-of-words for infrequent words (Mikolov et al., 2013b). In the continuous bag-of-words, vectors from the context will be averaged before predicting the current word, while the skip-gram does not. Therefore, it remains a better representation for rare words. Most students tend to use words that appear directly from the article, and only a small portion of students introduce their own vocabularies into their essays. Therefore, the word embedding is good with infrequent words and tends to work well for our purposes.

In examining the performances of the two off-the-shelf word embeddings, Mikolov's embedding cannot help with our task, because it has less preprocessing of its training corpus. Therefore, the embedding is case sensitive and contains symbols and numbers. For example, it matches "2015" with "000". Furthermore, its training corpus comes from newspapers, which may contain more high-level English that students may not use, and professional writing has few to no spelling mistakes. Although Baroni's embedding also has no spelling mistakes, it was trained on a corpus containing more genres of writing and has more preprocessing. Thus, it is a better fit to our work compared to Mikolov's embedding.

In comparing the performance of the skip-gram embedding and Baroni's embedding, there are many differences. First, even though the skip-gram embedding partially solves the tense problem, Baroni's embedding solves it better because it has a larger training corpus. Second, the larger training corpus contains no or significantly fewer spelling mistakes, and therefore it cannot solve the spelling problem at all. On the other hand, the skip-gram embedding solves the spelling problem better, because it was trained on our own corpus. For instance, it can match "proverty" with "poverty", while Baroni's embedding cannot. Third, the skip-gram embedding cannot address a vocabulary problem as well as the Baroni's embedding because of the small training corpus. Baroni's embedding matches "power" with "electricity", while the skip-gram embedding does not. Nevertheless, the skip-gram embedding still partially addresses this problem, for example, it matches "mosquitoes" with "malaria" due to relatedness. Last, Baroni's embedding was trained on a corpus that is thousands of times larger than our corpus. However, it does not address our problems significantly better than the skip-gram embedding due to generalization. In contrast, our task-dependent word embedding is only trained on a small corpus while outperforming or at least performing equally well as Baroni's embedding.

Overall, the skip-gram embedding tends to find examples by implicit relations. For instance, "winning against poverty possible achievable lifetime" is an example from the article and in the meantime

		Off-the-Shelf		On Our Corpus	
Corpus	**Rubric(1)**	**Baroni(2)**	**Mikolov(3)**	**SG(4)**	**CBOW(5)**
Space	0.606(2)	0.594	0.606(2)	**0.611(2,5)**	0.600(2)
MVP_L	0.628	0.666(1,3,5)	0.623	**0.682(1,2,3,5)**	0.641(1,3)
MVP_H	**0.599(3,4,5)**	0.593(3,4,5)	0.582(5)	0.583(5)	0.556
MVP_{ALL}	0.624(5)	**0.645(1,3,4,5)**	0.634(1,5)	0.634(1,5)	0.614

Table 3: The performance (QWKappa) of the off-the-shelf embeddings and embeddings trained on our corpus compared to the rubric baseline on all corpora. The numbers in parenthesis show the model numbers over which the current model performs significantly better. The best results in each row are in bold.

			Off-the-Shelf		On Our Corpus	
Train	**Test**	**Rubric(1)**	**Baroni(2)**	**Mikolov(3)**	**SG(4)**	**CBOW(5)**
MVP_L	MVP_H	0.582(3)	0.609 (1,3,5)	0.555	**0.615(1,2,3,5)**	0.596(1,3)
MVP_H	MVP_L	0.604	0.629(1,3,5)	0.620(1,5)	**0.644(1,2,3,5)**	0.605

Table 4: The performance (QWKappa) of the off-the-shelf embeddings and embeddings trained on our corpus compared to the rubric baseline. The numbers in parenthesis show the model numbers over which the current model performs significantly better. The best results in each row are in bold.

the prompt asks students "Did the author provide a convincing argument that winning the fight against poverty is achievable in our lifetime?". Consequently, students may mention this example by only answering "Yes, the author convinced me.". However, the skip-gram embedding can extract this implicit example.

8   Conclusion and Future Work

We have presented several simple but promising uses of the word embedding method that improve evidence scoring in corpora of responses to texts written by upper elementary students. In our results, a task-dependent word embedding model trained on our small corpus was the most helpful in improving the baseline model. However, the word embedding model still measures additional information that is not necessary in our work. Improving the word embedding model or the feature extraction process is thus our most likely future endeavor.

One potential improvement is re-defining the loss function of the word embedding model, since the word embedding measures not only the similarity between two words, but also the relatedness between them. However, our work is not helped by matching related words too much. For example, we want to match "poverty" with "proverty", while we do not want to match "water" with "electricity", even though students mention them together frequently. Therefore, we could limit this measurement by modifying the loss function of the word embedding. Kiela et al. (2015) presented a specialized word embedding by employing an external thesaurus list. However, it does not fit to our task, because the list contains high-level English words that will not be used by young students.

Another area for future investigation is improving the word embedding models trained on our corpus. Although they improved performance, they were trained on a corpus from one form of the RTA and tested on the same RTA. Thus, another possible improvement is generalizing the model from one RTA to another RTA.

Acknowledgments

We would like to show our appreciation to every member of the RTA group for sharing their pearls of wisdom with us. We are also immensely grateful to Dr. Richard Correnti, Deanna Prine, and Zahra Rahimi for their comments on an earlier version of the paper.

The research reported here was supported, in whole or in part, by the Institute of Education Sciences, U.S. Department of Education, through Grant R305A160245 to the University of Pittsburgh. The opinions expressed are those of the authors and do not represent the views of the Institute or the U.S. Department of Education.

References

Yigal Attali and Jill Burstein. 2006. Automated essay scoring with e-rater® v. 2. *The Journal of Technology, Learning and Assessment* 4(3).

Marco Baroni, Georgiana Dinu, and Germán Kruszewski. 2014. Don't count, predict! a systematic comparison of context-counting vs. context-predicting semantic vectors. In *ACL (1)*. pages 238–247.

Jill Burstein, Karen Kukich, Susanne Wolff, Chi Lu, and Martin Chodorow. 2001. Enriching automated essay scoring using discourse marking. .

Nitesh V Chawla, Kevin W Bowyer, Lawrence O Hall, and W Philip Kegelmeyer. 2002. Smote: synthetic minority over-sampling technique. *Journal of artificial intelligence research* 16:321–357.

Richard Correnti, Lindsay Clare Matsumura, Laura Hamilton, and Elaine Wang. 2013. Assessing students' skills at writing analytically in response to texts. *The Elementary School Journal* 114(2):142–177.

Tom Kenter and Maarten de Rijke. 2015. Short text similarity with word embeddings. In *Proceedings of the 24th ACM International on Conference on Information and Knowledge Management*. ACM, pages 1411–1420.

Douwe Kiela, Felix Hill, and Stephen Clark. 2015. Specializing word embeddings for similarity or relatedness. In *EMNLP*. pages 2044–2048.

Annie Louis and Derrick Higgins. 2010. Off-topic essay detection using short prompt texts. In *Proceedings of the NAACL HLT 2010 Fifth Workshop on Innovative Use of NLP for Building Educational Applications*. Association for Computational Linguistics, pages 92–95.

Tomas Mikolov, Kai Chen, Greg Corrado, and Jeffrey Dean. 2013a. Efficient estimation of word representations in vector space. *arXiv preprint arXiv:1301.3781* .

Tomas Mikolov, Ilya Sutskever, Kai Chen, Greg S Corrado, and Jeff Dean. 2013b. Distributed representations of words and phrases and their compositionality. In *Advances in neural information processing systems*. pages 3111–3119.

Nathan Ong, Diane Litman, and Alexandra Brusilovsky. 2014. Ontology-based argument mining and automatic essay scoring. In *Proceedings of the First Workshop on Argumentation Mining*. pages 24–28.

Zahra Rahimi, Diane Litman, Richard Correnti, Elaine Wang, and Lindsay Clare Matsumura. 2017. Assessing students use of evidence and organization in response-to-text writing: Using natural language processing for rubric-based automated scoring. *International Journal of Artificial Intelligence in Education* pages 1–35.

Zahra Rahimi, Diane J Litman, Richard Correnti, Lindsay Clare Matsumura, Elaine Wang, and Zahid Kisa. 2014. Automatic scoring of an analytical response-to-text assessment. In *International Conference on Intelligent Tutoring Systems*. Springer, pages 601–610.

Marek Rei and Ronan Cummins. 2016. Sentence similarity measures for fine-grained estimation of topical relevance in learner essays. *arXiv preprint arXiv:1606.03144* .

Mark D Shermis and Jill C Burstein. 2003. *Automated essay scoring: A cross-disciplinary perspective*. Routledge.

Ian H Witten, Eibe Frank, Mark A Hall, and Christopher J Pal. 2016. *Data Mining: Practical machine learning tools and techniques*. Morgan Kaufmann.

Shasha Xie, Keelan Evanini, and Klaus Zechner. 2012. Exploring content features for automated speech scoring. In *Proceedings of the 2012 Conference of the North American Chapter of the Association for Computational Linguistics: Human Language Technologies*. Association for Computational Linguistics, pages 103–111.

Domain Specific Automatic Question Generation from Text

Katira Soleymanzadeh
International Computer Institute
Ege University
Izmir, Turkey
`Katirasole@gmail.com`

Abstract

The goal of my doctoral thesis is to automatically generate interrogative sentences from descriptive sentences of Turkish biology text. We employ syntactic and semantic approaches to parse descriptive sentences. Syntactic and semantic approaches utilize syntactic (constituent or dependency) parsing and semantic role labeling systems respectively. After parsing step, question statements whose answers are embedded in the descriptive sentences are going to be formulated by using some predefined rules and templates. Syntactic parsing is done using an open source dependency parser called MaltParser (Nivre et al. 2007). Whereas to accomplish semantic parsing, we will construct a biological proposition bank (BioPropBank) and a corpus annotated with semantic roles. Then we will employ supervised methods to automatic label the semantic roles of a sentence.

1 Introduction

"Cognition is the mental action or process of acquiring knowledge and understanding through thought, experience, and the senses." (Stevenson, 2010) . Thought is triggered by asking questions and attempt to find answer of questions cause knowledge acquisition. Researches indicate that questioning is a powerful teaching technique. Lecturers benefit from questions for students' knowledge evaluation, student's stimulation to thinking on their own and encourage students to self-learning. Also, students can review and memorize information previously learned by questioning themselves.

Generating questions manually need much time and effort for lecturers. Moreover, student face considerable problems exercising and memorizing lessons. To address these challenges, Automatic question generation (AQG) systems can provide sample questions to alleviate lecturer's effort and help students in self-learning.

Our motivation in generating questions automatically is to facilitate lecturer effort and help students to practice on course materials more efficiently. Our goal in my thesis is building a system for question generation from Turkish biological text. We take biology text as input of our system and generate questions which will rank based on questions quality.

AQG is one of the challenging problems in natural language processing especially when semantic analysis is needed to generate comprehensive questions like how and why. To the best of our knowledge, AQG approaches in Turkish have been proposed by Cabuk et al. (2003) and Orhan et al. (2006). Both of these studies just have used syntactic approach without any semantic analysis for generating questions. However, generating questions from biological text, which contain complex process, cannot rely on syntactic approach merely. Relation between entities in a biological process make it difficult to analyze in syntactic level. Understanding these process needs some level of semantic analysis. In my proposal, we plan to generate comprehensive questions like how and why in addition to when, where, who and whom. Therefore, we need syntactic and semantic analysis of descriptive sentences.

Syntactic analysis of a sentence determines the structure of phrases of a text and converts it into a more structured representation, the parse tree. Characterizing "who" did "what" to "whom," "where," "when," "how" and "why" is semantic analysis of a sentence. Semantic role labeling (SRL) is a task of automatically identifying

Proceedings of the 55th Annual Meeting of the Association for Computational Linguistics- Student Research Workshop, pages 82–88
Vancouver, Canada, July 30 - August 4, 2017. ©2017 Association for Computational Linguistics
https://doi.org/10.18653/v1/P17-3014

semantic relations between predicate and its related arguments in the sentence. Assigning pre-defined set of semantic roles such as Agent, Patient and Manner to arguments is defined as predicate-argument structure (PAS) identification problem.

Lexical resources like PropBank (Palmer et al. 2005) and FrameNet (Baker et al. 1998) are needed to label semantic role of arguments. The Turkish lexical semantic resource (TLSR) were built by Isguder Şahin and Adalı (2014). TLSR is in general domain and does not cover biological field. Moreover, size of TLSR is small compared to PropBank in other languages. At present the number of annotated verb frame and sense are 759 and 1262 respectively. Domain sensitivity of SRL systems have been emphasized by many researchers (Albright et al. 2013; Carreras & Màrquez 2005; Johansson & Nugues 2008; Pradhan et al. 2008). Pradham et al. (2008) showed that the performance of SRL systems dropped dramatically by almost 10% when domain of testing data is different from training data. Albraight et al (2013) indicated the accuracy enhancement of SRL systems with the existence of in-domain annotations of data. Therefore, to automatically generating questions from biological text using semantic parsing, we first need to build an SRL system in the biological domain. To this end we will construct a lexical resource for the biology domain along with a corpus annotated with semantic roles in semi-automatic manner. Furthermore, there is not automatic SRL system in Turkish yet. So, we plan to design a supervised SRL system too.

In AQG step, we parse descriptive sentence using syntactic and semantic parser. Automatic SRL system which will construct in the first phase of my thesis, will employ to parse descriptive sentence semantically. Syntactic parsing of descriptive sentence will do by an open source dependency parser called MaltParser (Nivre et al. 2007). Semantic role labels and syntactic tags will use to identify content to generate relevant question (i.e. if semantic role label is "Arg0" then the question type will be "who"). In the question formation step, some predefined rules and template will utilize. The quality of the generated questions will measure based on its syntactic and semantic correctness and its relevancy to the given sentence.

2 Background

In order to generating interrogative sentences from descriptive sentences, syntactic and semantic approaches are taken. Constituency or dependency parser are used to parse a descriptive sentence in syntactic approach. Afterward, with respect to the label of phrase, appropriate type of question is selected. There are several AQG system that have utilized syntactic approach. Mitkov et al. (2006) proposed multiple choice question generation system to assess students' grammar knowledge by utilizing syntactic approach. Heilman and Smith (2009) described a syntactic and rule based approach to automatically generate factual questions to evaluate students' reading comprehension. Liu et al. (2012) developed template based AQG system by using syntactic approach, called G-Asks, to improve students' writing skill. Cabuk et.al. (2003) employed a syntactic parser to get stem, derivational and inflectional affixes of words of sentence. Predefined rules were used to identify phrases of sentence. In the last step questions were generated by transforming rules based on identified phrases of previous step. Orhan et al. (2006) generate template based math questions for students of elementary school.

In order to generate questions using semantic approach, semantic role of arguments is labeled firstly. Then proper question type is selected according to the semantic labels. Mannem et al. (2010) utilized SRL and Named Entity Recognition (NER) system to generate rule based questions. Lindberg et al. (2013) generated template based questions for educational purpose by using a semantic approach. By the use of a semantic approach, Mazidi and Nielsen (2014) generated questions in specific domains such as chemistry, biology and earth science. After analyzing text by the SRL and constituency parsing system, relevant questions are generated based on predefined templates.

Lecturer assess students' reading comprehension by utilizing questions. Generating pedagogical questions are time consuming and a lot of lecturer effort is needed. The main goal of my thesis is to automatically generate question using both of syntactic and semantic approach to alleviate these efforts. To the best of our knowledge, generating questions by employing semantic approach will do for the first time in Turkish. My thesis is similar to Mazidi and Nielsen's work in terms of utilizing semantic approach but is different in question formation step.

Due to the need for an SRL system in semantic question generation systems, we plan to design a supervised SRL system. Supervised, unsupervised and semi-supervised machine learning methods are applied in building SRL systems. In supervised method, after extracting features from training data, a 1-N (N is number of roles), a classifier (such as support vector machine (SVM), Maximum entropy (MaxEnt) and Naïve Bayes (NB)) is used to label semantic roles. Garg and Henderson (2012) used Bayes method to SRL where dependency parses are used to extract features. Albright et al. (2013) constructed a corpus annotated with semantic roles of clinical narratives that is called MiPAQ. Monachesi et al. (2007) extracted features from dependency parser to use in supervised K-nearest neighbor algorithms to SRL.

In semi-supervised methods, a small amount of data is annotated with their semantic roles that is called seed data. The classifier is trained using the seed data. Unlabeled data is classified using this system and the most confident predictions are added to expand the initial training data. This expansion is carried out iteratively a few times. Semi-supervised self-training and co-training methods were used in many SRL research (Do Thi et al. 2016; Kaljahi & Samad 2010; Lee et al. 2007) recently and they showed their performance in in-domain data. In those study standard supervised algorithms was used as classifier and the features were extracted by constituency parser.

The features extracted from constituency parses defined by Gildea and Jurafsky (2002) are used as basic features in most SRL system. Predicate, phrase type, headword, constituency parse path, phrase position and voice of predicate are some basic features. They mentioned that using syntactic parses is necessary for extracting features.

A role-annotated corpus together with lexical resources in PropBank and FrameNet, are used as training data in many supervised SRL systems in English. Semantic roles of all verbs and their several senses in the Penn Treebank corpus was annotated in the PropBank corpus. Basic roles such as Agent and Patient are listed by Arg0, Arg1, …, Arg5 and adjunct roles like Time and Location are labeled as ArgM (ArgM-TMP, ArgM-LOC, …). Table 1 show the basic and adjunct semantic roles defined in PropBank with their related question type. Since sentences in PropBank is taken from

Wall Street Journal [WSJ], then the performance of supervised classifier outside the domain of the WSJ is decreased. Several methods are utilized to construct a semantically annotated corpus: direct annotation, using parallel corpus and using semi-supervised methods. Bootstrapping approach is applied by Swier and Stevenson (2004) to annotate verbs in general domain. Pado and Lapata (2009) exploited translation of English FrameNet to construct relevant corpus in another language. Monachesi et al. (2007) used semi-supervised method and translation of English PropBank to construct corpus in Dutch. Afterwards annotated sentences was corrected by annotators to use as training corpus in supervised methods.

	Argument	**Question type**
Basic	Arg0	Who?
	Arg1	Whom?
	Arg2	What?
Adjunct	Arg-TMP	When?
	Arg-LOC	Where?
	Arg-MNR	How?
	Arg-PRP/CAU	Why?

Table 1: PropBank's some basic and adjunct semantic roles.

Since accuracy of SRL system drop dramatically in outside the domain of the annotated corpus domain in English, building comprehensive lexical resources in biology domain will improve SRL system in Turkish for biological text. Due to the lots of effort to construct such lexical resource, we will build it in semi-automatic manner by employing self-training semi supervised method where dependency parses will use to extract features. In my proposal, we will use standard supervised method (SVM, MaxEnt and NB) to build SRL system to evaluate their performance in Turkish.

3   Methodology

Before diving in to automatic generating questions in biology domain, we will construct a semantically annotated corpus and SRL system. The following sections will describe our proposed methods in detail to do these issues.

3.1   Corpus Construction

We first consider the annotation of semantic roles in biology domain. To address this issue, first we collect biology texts from different sources like article, textbook and etc. Articles and textbooks will take from "Journal of Biyolojik Çeşitlilik ve Koruma"[1] and "Biyoloji ders kitabı 9, 10, 11, 12"[2], respectively. Afterwards we tag the part of speech (POS) of sentences to identify the predicate and then create lexical recourses with their predicate-argument structure (PAS). Kisla's tool (2009) is employed to POS tagging and morphologic analyzing of sentence. The predicates are selected by their frequency and their importance in domain. English PropBank structure and guidelines are used as reference structure to annotate PAS in Turkish. As a pilot study, we chose 500 sentences from biology high school textbook and tagged their POS. After identifying predicate, we ranked them based on their frequency. Some of selected predicates and their PAS are shown in tables 2 and 3 respectively.

Verb	Frequency
Sentezlemek (Synthesize)	23
İnceltmek (Thinning)	22
Adlandırmak (Naming)	20

Table 2: Some of the selected verbs

Since the annotation process is expensive and time consuming, we address this problem with using self-training method to create corpus in semi-automatic manner. The aim of semi-supervised method is to learn from small amount of annotated data and use large amount of unannotated data to develop the training data. SRL is a done in three steps: predicate identification, argument identification and argument classification. In first step we use POS tagging to identify predicate and its sense will be decided with some filtering rules. In Turkish "-imek, etmek, eylemek, olmak ve kılmak" (to do, make, render, to be) are auxiliaries that give predicate role to some noun words and are called auxiliary verbs. When encountering these verbs, we consider this verb with its preceding word as a predicate. For example, "sentezlenmiş olmak" (is synthesized) is the predicate of "Substrat düzeyinde fosforilasyonla 2 ATP de sentezlenmiş olur.". (2 ATP is synthesized by phosphorylation at the substrate level.)

To accomplish argument identification following rules are applied to select candidate arguments:

- Phrases are considered as argument if there is a dependency relation between them and the predicate.

- Existence of collocation is examined to consider as a candidate argument.

Note that these assumptions will not cover all candidate argument, but will be improved during this thesis.

Roleset id: Sentez.01 , (Synthesize) (kimya)
Element veya başka maddeleri bir arayı getirerek yapay olarak bileşik cisimler oluşturma, bireşim "(create)"
Roles:
   Arg0-PAG: oluşturan (creator)
      Arg1-PRD: oluşan şey (thing created)
      Arg2-VSP: kaynak (source)

Table 3: Annotation of semantic role of predicate "sentez" (Synthesize)

Argument classification is done by self-training. Yarowsky and Florian (2002) utilized self-training for word sense disambiguation problem in 1995. Yarowsky's experimental results showed that the performance of self-training method is almost as high as supervised methods. Our intuition is that by utilizing self-training method, the effort to label semantic roles will reduce substantially. Self-training method is implemented in the following steps. First of all, seed data that is annotated manually by expert is used to train the classifier. After initial training step, all unlabeled data are classified and more appropriate data are selected to add to seed data to improve classifier performance by using more training data. Standard machine learning classifiers, SVM, MaxEnt and NB are used in the self-training method. In our proposal, we do following steps to select more accurate labeled data to expand training data: All unlabeled data are classified using three different classifiers. When two of them are agree about argument label and assigned probability of label is above predetermined threshold value, then this label is considered as true label and added to initial training data. If previous condition is not satisfied, then true label is the one which its assigned probability is maximum among the others and above predefined

---

[1] http://www.biodicon.com/

[2] http://www.eba.gov.tr/

threshold. Semi-automatic labeled data is corrected by annotators afterwards.

Determining effective and convenient features play an essential role in building SRL systems. These features drive from syntactic or semantic parsing systems. In our proposal we will use dependency parser to extract features. In our study we define features shown in Table 4 along with base features defined by Gildea and Jurafsky (2002). The effect of more features such as NE and biology terms will examine to improve performance of SRL system.

3.2 Automatic Question Generation

AQG is performed in three steps: content selection (which part of sentence must be asked), determine question type based on selected content and construct question. In my thesis, first the declarative sentence is labeled by our proposed SRL system. Based on labeled roles, content and question type are selected. In QG step, predetermined templates and rules are applied. We plan to generate templates manually as well as automatically. "Niye <X> <yüklem>?" (why <X> <predicate>?) and "Ne zaman <X> <yüklem>?" (when <X> <predicate>) are examples of templates. If there are no proper template for generating a question, then a rule based method is applied. In rule based method, Turkish question structure is considered to form question. In the first step, the selected content will be removed from the sentence. Then question type is chosen depending on the identified semantic role. For example, "kim" (who) is used if the semantic role label is Arg0. In the third step, selected content is replaced by question word. Finally, the grammar of generated question will be checked. In QG phase, to avoid generating vague question like "canlı dağılımı için ne önemlidir?" (what is important for live distribution?) from sentence "Bu canlı dağılımı için önemlidir." (This is important for live distribution.) some filtering rules will apply. As an example, the sentences which begin with "Bu, Şu, O" (this, that, it) will not considered as descriptive sentence to generate question. Moreover, to add complexity to question we will use paraphrase of phrases.

4 Evaluations

To evaluate the SRL system, precision, recall, F1 and accuracy will be calculated. The following components are evaluated for the quality of the whole system:

- Argument identification performance

- Argument classification performance when arguments are known

- Performance of system when training data is in news domain and test data is in biology domain and vice versa.

- Performance of self-training method in news and biology domain

Rus at al. (2010) evaluated generated questions with the parameters, relevance, question type, syntactic correctness and fluency, ambiguity and variety. All parameters are among 1 and 4 which 1 is the best and 4 is the worst score. In my thesis we will evaluate generated questions by these parameters and the parameters that will define. 'questions importance in education' can be one of these parameters. We will ask three experts to evaluate generated questions manually.

5 Conclusion

Questions are used to assess the level of students' understanding of the given lecture by the lecturer from pedagogical view. Therefore, automatically generating question alleviate lecturer's effort to generate interrogative sentences. Moreover, tutoring system and question answering are some applications which benefit from questions too.

In my thesis, we propose syntactic and sematic approach to generate questions from descriptive sentences. To do this, a three-phase approach will take. Since generating question in semantic approach needs semantic analysis of sentences, we will construct a lexical semantic resource along with a semantically annotated corpus in biology domain, firstly. In the second phase, we built an SRL system to parse a sentence semantically. Finally, syntactically and semantically parsed descriptive sentences will be used to generate interrogative sentences. It is the first time that semantic approach is utilized for AQG in Turkish. Semantically annotated corpus in biology domain can use in several applications such as information extraction, question answering and summarization. Investigating the performance of biology corpus encourage researcher to transfer our proposed methodology to construct such semantic corpus in other domains like chemistry, geography and etc.

Feature	Description
YükKök	Stem of predicate
YükPOS	Predicate's POS tag
Voice	Predicate's voice
YükYapı	Compound, simple, derivative structure of predicate
Konum	Position of head-word
Baş-ad	Argument's head-word
Baş-adPOS	POS tag of argument's head-word
Baş-ad Kök	Stem of argument's head-word
Bağlılık İlişkisi	Dependency relation of argument's head-word
Bağlılık Yolu	Dependency path between arguments and predicate
Bağlılık Yolunun uzunluğu	Length of dependency path between arguments and predicate
SolPOS	POS tag of the argument's leftmost word
SağPOS	POS tag of the argument's rightmost word
Kelimeye eklenen ek	Morphologic analysis of head-word
Pos Yolu	POS tags between arguments and predicate

Table 4: The features will be used in argument classification

References

Albright, Daniel, Arrick Lanfranchi, Anwen Fredriksen, William F Styler, Colin Warner, Jena D Hwang, Jinho D Choi, Dmitriy Dligach, Rodney D Nielsen & James Martin. 2013. Towards comprehensive syntactic and semantic annotations of the clinical narrative. Journal of the American Medical Informatics Association 20.922-30.

Baker, Collin F, Charles J Fillmore & John B Lowe. 1998. The berkeley framenet project. Paper presented to the Proceedings of the 36th Annual Meeting of the Association for Computational Linguistics and 17th International Conference on Computational Linguistics-Volume 1, 1998. http://aclweb.org/anthology/P98-1013.

Çabuk, Hüseyin, Çiğdem Yüksel, Zeki Mocan, Banu Diri & M Fatih Amasyalı. 2003. Metin Analizi Ve Sorgulama (MAvS). Koç Üniversitesi İstanbul 11.

Carreras, Xavier & Lluís Màrquez. 2005. Introduction to the CoNLL-2005 shared task: Semantic role labeling. Paper presented to the Proceedings of the Ninth Conference on Computational Natural Language Learning, 2005. http://aclweb.org/anthology/W05-0620.

Do Thi, Ngoc Quynh, Steven Bethard & Marie-Francine Moens. 2016. Facing the most difficult case of Semantic Role Labeling: A collaboration of word embeddings and co-training. Paper presented to the Proceedings of the 26th International Conference on Computational Linguistics, 2016. http://aclweb.org/anthology/C16-1121.

Garg, Nikhil & James Henderson. 2012. Unsupervised semantic role induction with global role ordering. Paper presented to the Proceedings of the 50th Annual Meeting of the Association for Computational Linguistics: Short Papers-Volume 2, 2012. http://aclweb.org/anthology/P12-2029.

Gildea, Daniel & Daniel Jurafsky. 2002. Automatic labeling of semantic roles. Computational linguistics 28.245-88. http://aclweb.org/anthology/J02-3001.

Heilman, Michael & Noah A Smith. 2009. Question generation via overgenerating transformations and ranking. DTIC Document.

Isguder Sahin, Gozde Gul & Esref Adalı. 2014. Using Morphosemantic Information in Construction of a Pilot Lexical Semantic Resource for Turkish. In Proceedings of the 21st International Conference on Computational Linguistics.929-36. http://aclweb.org/anthology/W14-5807.

Johansson, Richard & Pierre Nugues. 2008. The effect of syntactic representation on semantic role labeling. Paper presented to the Proceedings of the 22nd International Conference on Computational Linguistics-Volume 1, 2008. http://aclweb.org/anthology/C08-1050.

Kaljahi, Zadeh & Rasoul Samad. 2010. Adapting self-training for semantic role labeling. Paper presented to the Proceedings of the ACL 2010 Student Research Workshop, 2010. http://aclweb.org/anthology/P10-3016.

Kisla, T. 2009. An integrated method for morphological analyse and part of speech tagging in Turkish. Doctoral dissertation, Ege University, Izmir, Turkey

Lee, Joo-Young, Young-In Song & Hae-Chang Rim. 2007. Investigation of weakly supervised learning for semantic role labeling. Paper presented to the Advanced Language Processing and Web Information Technology, 2007. ALPIT 2007. Sixth International Conference on, 2007.

Lindberg, David, Fred Popowich, John Nesbit & Phil Winne. 2013. Generating natural language questions to support learning on-line.

Liu, Ming, Rafael A Calvo & Vasile Rus. 2012. G-Asks: An intelligent automatic question generation system for academic writing support. Dialogue & Discourse 3.101-24.

Mannem, Prashanth, Rashmi Prasad & Aravind Joshi. 2010. Question generation from paragraphs at UPenn: QGSTEC system description. Paper presented to the Proceedings of QG2010: The Third Workshop on Question Generation, 2010.

Mazidi, Karen & Rodney D Nielsen. 2014. Linguistic Considerations in Automatic Question Generation. Paper presented to the ACL (2), 2014. http://aclweb.org/anthology/P14-2053.

Mitkov, Ruslan, Li An Ha & Nikiforos Karamanis. 2006. A computer-aided environment for generating multiple-choice test items. Natural Language Engineering 12.177-94.

Monachesi, Paola, Gerwert Stevens & Jantine Trapman. 2007. Adding semantic role annotation to a corpus of written Dutch. Paper presented to the Proceedings of the Linguistic Annotation Workshop, 2007. http://aclweb.org/anthology/W07-1513.

Nivre, Joakim, Johan Hall, Jens Nilsson, Atanas Chanev, Gülsen Eryigit, Sandra Kübler, Svetoslav Marinov & Erwin Marsi. 2007. MaltParser: A language-independent system for data-driven dependency parsing. Natural Language Engineering 13.95-135.

Orhan, Zeynep, Ceydanur Öztürk & Nihal Altuntaş. 2006. SınavYazar: Đlköğretim için Otomatik Sınav ve Çözüm Üretme Aracı SınavYazar: A Tool for Generating Automatic Exams and Solutions for Primary Education.

Padó, Sebastian & Mirella Lapata. 2009. Cross-lingual annotation projection for semantic roles. Journal of Artificial Intelligence Research 36.307-40.

Palmer, Martha, Daniel Gildea & Paul Kingsbury. 2005. The proposition bank: An annotated corpus of semantic roles. Computational linguistics 31.71-106. http://aclweb.org/anthology/J05-1004.

Pradhan, Sameer S, Wayne Ward & James H Martin. 2008. Towards robust semantic role labeling. Computational linguistics 34.289-310. http://aclweb.org/anthology/J08-2006.

Rus, Vasile, Brendan Wyse, Paul Piwek, Mihai Lintean, Svetlana Stoyanchev & Cristian Moldovan. 2010. Overview of the first question generation shared task evaluation challenge. Paper presented to the Proceedings of the Third Workshop on Question Generation, 2010. http://aclweb.org/anthology/W10-4234.

Stevenson, A. (2010). *Oxford dictionary of English*. Oxford University Press, USA.

Swier, Robert S & Suzanne Stevenson. 2004. Unsupervised semantic role labelling. Paper presented to the Proceedings of EMNLP, 2004. http://aclweb.org/anthology/W04-3213.

Yarowsky, David & Radu Florian. 2002. Evaluating sense disambiguation across diverse parameter spaces. Natural Language Engineering 8.293.

SoccEval: An Annotation Schema for Rating Soccer Players

Jose Ramirez   **Matthew Garber**   **Xinhao Wang**

Department of Computer Science

Brandeis University

{jramirez, mgarber, xinhao}@brandeis.edu

Abstract

This paper describes the SoccEval Annotation Project, an annotation schema designed to support machine-learning classification efforts to evaluate the performance
of soccer players based on match reports
taken from online news sources. In addition to factual information about player
attributes and actions, the schema anno-
tates subjective opinions about them. After explaining the annotation schema and
annotation process, we describe a machine
learning experiment. Classifiers trained on
features derived from annotated data performed better than a baseline trained on
unigram features. Initial results suggest
that improvements can be made to the annotation scheme and guidelines as well as
the amount of data annotated. We believe
our schema could be potentially expanded
to extract more information about soccer
players and teams.

1 Introduction

The underlying goal of the SoccEval Annotation
Project was to evaluate the ability and performance of a soccer player from both objective descriptions of their actions as well as subjective descriptions of the players themselves, using soccer
news articles as a source. We used these attributes
to rank players based on their overall quality.

Our annotation scheme was designed to support
both these efforts by creating a corpus annotated
with these descriptions in order to facilitate extraction of relevant features to rate players, as well as
the most relevant attributes of individual players.

A previous soccer-related annotation scheme
exists: the SmartWeb Ontology-based Annotation
System (SOBA) which was designed to extract

information on soccer-related entities, including
players and events associated with them (Buitelaar
et al., 2006).

However, SOBA only includes factual information about events. We created a player-specific annotation scheme that takes into account not only
facts and events about a player, but also subjective evaluations, attaching a polarity value to these
evaluations that can then be used not simply to extract information about a player, but to make judgments on the quality of the players.

2 Annotation Specification

To do the annotation task, our annotators used
MAE (Multi-document Annotation Environment)
(Rim, 2016), an open source, lightweight annotation tool which allows users to define their own
annotation tasks and output annotations in stand-
off XML.

For annotation, MAE allows the creation of
tags which define general categories. Tags then
have attributes which serve as sub-categories from
which a value can be selected. MAE supports the
creation of two types of tags: extent tags and link
tags. Extent tags mark a span of text, while link
tags link two or more extent tags.

All extent tags have Spans and Text attributes.
Spans refers to the range of indexes in the document for the text that an extent tag covers. Text
contains the actual text.

This annotation project focuses on various
descriptions and evaluations of soccer players.
Descriptions from news articles can typically be
divided into two types, facts and opinions[1]. Based

---

[1] This split between Fact and Opinion tags is inspired in
part by the example of the MPQA Corpus (Wilson et al.,
2016), which has separate Objective Speech Event Frames
and Subjective Frames. The MPQA Corpus also inspired the
use of Player IDs, as well as the decision not to impose strict
rules for text span lengths.

Proceedings of the 55th Annual Meeting of the Association for Computational Linguistics- Student Research Workshop, pages 89–94
Vancouver, Canada, July 30 - August 4, 2017. ©2017 Association for Computational Linguistics
https://doi.org/10.18653/v1/P17-3015

on these categories, four extent tags and one link tag were created to capture the performance of a player.

The following 2 sample sentences will be used in explaining the tags in detail:

Sample sentence 1: Ward-Prowse almost levelled with a dangerous free-kick to the far corner that drew a fine save from Mignolet.

Sample sentence 2: Blessed with formidable speed and strength to go with his rare skill, the 25-year-old was always worth watching.

2.1 Player Tag

The Player tag is used to mark all mentions of a player directly by his name.

There are two attributes in the Player tag in addition to the default Spans and Text attributes. PlayerID is an ID that is assigned to each unique player. Name is an optional attribute created solely for the purpose of helping annotators distinguish players by entering any comments or notes they want for this Player tag.

2.2 Coref Tag

The Coref tag is an extent tag that is used to mark all references to a player by something other than his name. The Coref tag contains 3 attributes – Spans, Text and PlayerID. PlayerID is assigned the exact same ID as the player being referred to.

2.3 Fact Tag

The Fact tag is used to mark all text spans that describe events within a match that are connected to a player.

There are three attributes associated with this tag in addition to Spans and Text: Type, Time, and FactID. Type includes goal, assist, pass, shot, movement, positioning, substitute out, substitute in, injury, tackle, save and foul. The Time attribute is for represents the time of the event with relation to the match. Its possible values are: distance past, last season, current season, last match, present or future. FactID is generally unique. However, in certain cases where the same event is mentioned multiple times, the same FactID is assigned.

2.4 Opinion Tag

The Opinion tag is used to mark subjective attitudes toward a player.

There are five attributes associated with this tag besides Spans and Text: Type, Polarity, Time, Hypothetical, and Reported. Type groups different opinions into the following categories: soccer skill, accomplishment, general attribute, impact on team, growth or decline and other opinion. Polarity is the sentiment toward a player in this opinion tag, which can either positive or negative. The Time attribute is the same as that in Fact tag. The Hypothetical attribute is used only when the Opinion is either a prediction or counterfactive. The Reported attribute is a Boolean to distinguish if the Opinion is being reported by someone within the article, such as a secondary source who is not the writer of the article himself.

2.5 TargetLink Tag

TargetLink is a link tag that links a fact or opinion to a player or coreference tag.

2.6 Sample Annotation

Below is a simplified annotated version of the two sample sentences:

Annotated sample sentence 1:
[Ward-Prowse]$_{Player1}$ almost levelled with a dangerous [free-kick]$_{Fact:shot}$ to the far corner that drew a fine [save]$_{Fact:save}$ from [Mignolet]$_{Player2}$.

TargetLink:
T1: [free-kick] − [Ward-Prowse]
T2: [save] − [Mignolet]

Annotated sample sentence 2:
Blessed with
[formidable speed]$_{opinion:particularskill\_positive}$ and
[strength]$_{opinion:generalattribute\_positive}$ to go with
[his]$_{coref1}$
[rare skill]$_{opinion:particularskill\_positive}$,
[the 25-year-old]$_{coref2}$ was always
[worth watching]$_{opinion:otheropinion\_positive}$.

TargetLink:
T1: [formidable speed] − [his]
T2: [strength] − [his]
T3: [rare skill] − [his]
T4: [worth watching] − [the 25-year-old]

3 Corpus Selection and Annotation

Documents were taken from two sources, Goal.com[2] and The Guardian[3]. Initially, a total of 465 documents were collected, 361 of which were taken from The Guardian, while the rest were taken from Goal.com.

The articles focused on three clubs from the English Premier League: Chelsea, Tottenham Hotspur, and Liverpool. The majority of the articles were match reports, though there were also a few end-of-season player and team reviews as well. The final corpus included 34 documents taken from both sources, almost all of which were match reports covering games in which Chelsea had played (there was also one end-of-season player review).

While not part of the corpus per se, player ratings for the corresponding matches were retrieved from Goal.com. Each rating document measured the performance of each player during that match on a scale from 0.0 to 5.0, in increments of 0.5.

All the articles given out were connected to one team, Chelsea. This was done with the intention of making it easier for annotators to keep track of player names.

4 Annotation Guidelines

There are a few aspects of our annotation guidelines which are worth noting.
First, we gave annotators free choice in determining the length of the text span worth annotating. Since descriptions of players, especially subjective ones, come in many forms, we thought it would be best to leave that unspecified. We believed that nonetheless, annotators would generally agree on a rough span of text to be annotated, even if their spans were not exactly the same. We did note in the guidelines that Fact spans were likely to be noun phrases, while Opinion spans would most often either be noun phrases or verb phrases.
We recognized that our team of annotators was generally unfamiliar with soccer, though we assumed a basic knowledge. When dealing with unfamiliar terms, we instructed our annotators to research the unfamiliar terminology using Wikipedia, Google, or other online sources.
In practice, we realized that some of our Opinion attributes were more general than others, and some

of the categories were likely to overlap: for example, an accomplishment could also serve as an example of a player's growth. In these cases, we instructed our annotators to follow a priority system from more specific attributes to more general ones. So in the example here, we would instruct our annotators to prioritize the less vague "accomplishment" attribute instead of the "growth/decline" one.

5 Inter-Annotator Agreement

To evaluate inter-annotator agreement on our annotated corpus, we used Krippendorff's alpha (Krippendorff, 2004)

Tag	IAA score
Player	0.9728
Coref	0.5828
Fact	0.4735
Opinion	0.4041

Table 1: IAA scores for tags (Krippendorff's alpha)

Attribute	IAA score
Player::playerID	0.9197
Fact:: time	0.8971
Opinion::reported	0.7639
Opinion::polarity	0.6747
Fact:: type	0.6366
Opinion::time	0.6031
Fact::FactID	0.4991
Opinion::type	0.4997
Coref::playerID	0.4989
Opinion::hypothetical	0.4122
Player::name	NaN

Table 2: IAA scores for tags and their attributes (Krippendorff's alpha)

Regarding attributes for Fact tags, we had relatively good agreement on Fact type, which was important, as well as strong agreement on time, which was relatively easy for annotators to detect. Agreement in attributes for Opinion tags was lower compared to that in attributes of Fact tags, reflecting the wider degree of subjectivity, but perhaps also the higher degree of ambiguity in our annotation guidelines. However, we did obtain good agreement for polarity values, as well as reported speech attributes. The agreement in polarity

[2]http://www.goal.com/en-us
[3]http://www.theguardian.com/

values was particularly important, since our machine learning experiments made use of polarities in creating features from the opinion tags.

Finally, the score for the Hypothetical attribute is misleading, simply because one of our annotators seems to have marked every Opinion tag with this attribute. Otherwise, we observed during adjudication that annotators were relatively consistent in marking Hypothetical attributes.

6 Adjudication Process

We included Fact tags in our gold standard if at least one annotator tagged it. Occasionally, if a span of text should obviously have been marked as a Fact but had not been tagged by any annotators, we nonetheless tagged it as a Fact in our gold standard. In many cases this involved relatively obvious readings of events such as goals, saves, and other facts which we believe the annotators should easily have caught according to our guidelines. We attempted to do this very sparingly, though. On the other hand, we only included Opinion tags if at least two annotators tagged a span. With regard to attributes, we generally opted for "majority rules". If there was complete disagreement about the attribute, we selected the one that to us seemed most appropriate.

We usually selected the span that the majority of annotators agreed on, which usually was the minimal relevant span.

7 Experiments

An experiment was performed using the previously mentioned player ratings. Players that were explicitly mentioned in a document were classified by the rating obtained from Goal.com.

7.1 Baseline

Three types of baseline models were trained utilizing Scikit-learn (Pedregosa et al., 2011) embedded in NLTK (Bird et al., 2009) wrappers: a support vector machine (SVM) model, a maximum entropy (MaxEnt) model, and a decision tree (DT) model. All baseline models were trained with boolean unigram features, though stopwords were removed before feature extraction. No dimension reduction was performed other than what inherently occurred in each type of model.

For each match report, a sub-document was created for each player mentioned in the match report. Each player's sub-document included every sentence explicitly mentioning that player's name. In a naive model of coreference, sentences containing anaphora were added to the sub-document of the most recently mentioned player. Each sub-document was paired with the rating for that player for that match.

Micro-precision was high for all models, though this was largely due to the fact that they tended to predict a score of 3.0, which was by far the most common player rating. The MaxEnt and Decision Tree models performed roughly equally well, though neither could be considered a successful model.

It is worth noting that no model was able to predict ratings at the high and low extremes due to a sparsity of data for the ratings.

Classifier	Precision	Recall	F1
SVM (Micro)	0.327	0.327	0.327
SVM (Macro)	0.0764	0.169	0.0968
MaxEnt (Micro)	0.297	0.297	0.297
MaxEnt (Macro)	0.121	0.163	0.127
DT (Micro)	0.281	0.281	0.281
DT (Macro)	0.15	0.166	0.148

Table 3: Scores for different baseline classifiers

Rating	Precision	Recall	F1
2.0	0.0294	0.0294	0.0294
2.5	0.121	0.154	0.128
3.0	0.345	0.464	0.375
3.5	0.324	0.327	0.307
4.0	0.159	0.115	0.126

Table 4: Scores for Decision Tree baseline by rating [5]

7.2 Classifiers

Different types of classifiers were applied to the annotated corpus, including maximum entropy (MaxEnt), linear regression (LR), support vector machine (SVM) and random forest (RF). Precision, recall and F1 score were calculated for each classifier, with 17-fold cross-validation, which tested 2 files each time. Since regression predicts a continuous scaling measure instead of a discrete 5 point scale, the prediction of a regression was converted to the nearest rating point. For example,

---

[5] Scores for ratings not shown were all 0.0.

if linear regression output 3.33, it was converted into 3.5.

7.3 Feature Extraction

Multiple attempts were made to achieve a better score. In the initial attempt, the following features were used:

- Normalized percentage of different types of facts in a single article

- Normalized percentage of different types of opinions in a single article

- Total mentions of each player in a single article

The following issues have also been taken into consideration and the model is slighted adjusted accordingly.

Correlation: There were certain degrees of correlation between some features, though due to the limited amount of data these correlations were unstable. However, removing one of two significantly correlated features made no notable improvement in the accuracy of the classifiers.

Dimension reduction: In order to remove redundancies in the features, singular vector decomposition was applied to the feature matrix before doing linear regression. However, linear regression with SVD actually performed slightly worse than linear regression without SVD.

LR, SVM and MaxtEnt performed equally well in terms of their micro-averages, although MaxEnt achieved the best score, 0.367, by a very small margin. While this was only slightly better than baseline, the macro F1-score for the LR model was 0.204, which was a more notable improvement.

Classifier	Precision	Recall	F1
LR (Micro)	0.364	0.364	0.364
LR (Macro)	0.219	0.252	0.204
LR-SVD (Micro)	0.328	0.328	0.328
LR-SVD (Macro)	0.216	0.216	0.187
SVM (Micro)	0.363	0.363	0.363
SVM (Macro)	0.206	0.233	0.194
MaxEnt (Micro)	0.367	0.367	0.367
MaxEnt (Macro)	0.147	0.219	0.160
RF (Micro)	0.283	0.283	0.283
RF (Macro)	0.176	0.188	0.171

Table 5: Scores for different classifiers

8 Challenges

8.1 Challenges in Annotation

One issue with the annotation process was the use of British English and soccer jargon in match reports. Annotators who are not familiar with British English vocabulary and soccer terms reported difficulties in understanding some of the match reports.

Another issue was the ambiguity between certain categories in the annotation scheme. For example, in Fact tags, type "assist" and type "goal" are a subsets of "pass" and "shot" respectively. In Opinion tags, "accomplishment" overlaps "growth/decline", since accomplishments are often indicative of a player's improvement.

The lack of precision in the annotation guidelines regarding the span of the text to be tagged resulted in wide disagreements over spans.

Finally, some of the categories were not often used by the annotators. This mainly resulted from the fact that we initially designed our DTD based on the categories found in match reports and player reviews from the Guardian, which include more opinions and subjective judgments. However, the Goal.com match reports focused more heavily on reporting facts, with few subjective judgments on the part of the writer. However, if we were to expand the corpus to include a more diverse range of sources, we might see cases where Opinion tags would be useful.

8.2 Challenges in Machine Learning

One issue was the limited amount of annotated files. This directly led to unstable results where in some cases, certain features are strongly correlated or the F1 score exceeds 0.6, while in other cases, the features have no correlation at all or the F1 score is lower than the baseline.

The second issue was whether the features being extracted are fundamentally a good predictor for a players rating. Since the rating is based on the actual performance of a player, and the match reports will not cover every detail happened in a match, this incomplete description may or may not be sufficient to predict the rating accurately. In addition, the ratings were collected from one of the sources from which the corpus was built, which may contain its own bias.

Furthermore, as the ratings themselves are determined by sports writers, they are themselves inherently subjective and problematic as a gold standard label, since two different writers might disagree on a rating for a specific player. The Goal.com ratings that we used as a reference label are themselves created by the Goal.com staff and factor in sub-ratings in subjective traits such as 'vision', 'work rate', and 'killer instinct'. Unless we use hard data only as a criterion for determining ratings (ie. counts of specific actions like appearances, goals, saves, etc.), the ratings themselves which we are evaluating will be unreliable as a gold standard label. One possible solution to obtain more agreement on labels might be to restrict the number of labels to two or three instead, instead of going by increments of 0.5. That might help obtain a more reliable gold standard for labels, since there would likely be more agreement on star players vs. terrible players, as opposed to the difference between a 3.0 and a 3.5. We might lose a certain level of granularity, but our labels would likely be more grounded in reality.

Another issue is the methodologies of the classifiers. Discriminant classifiers or decision trees treat ratings as a nominal measure. Therefore, the interval information of ratings will be lost. Although regression keeps such information, it has a stricter requirement for the relationships among features and the target in order to get a better result.

9 Conclusion

This annotation project focuses on a player's performance as described by soccer news articles. By capturing the actions of a particular player as well as subjective evaluations about them, a rating prediction can be made. Models based on the current scheme performed appreciably better than the baseline. However, they still did not perform particularly well, due to the factors mentioned above.

Increasing the corpus size and variety on players performances and ratings are two changes that can be made in the future which would potentially give a more stable result. We might potentially change the rating system to restrict the number of labels, as mentioned above.

We can also improve the current annotation scheme by narrowing the number of fact or opinion types and eliminating redundant attributes. We can select annotators who are knowledgeable enough about soccer to easily understand match reports. Alternatively, in order to lower the cognitive load caused by unfamiliarity with the sport and its jargon, we can create an appendix within the guidelines introducing annotators to the basic rules and vocabulary of soccer.

In terms of further applications, this project can be expanded to include a model for rating teams. If we apply syntactic parsing, we could also extract salient characteristics of players to determine what makes a good player. Finally, in addition to ratings, external statistics of a player, such as transfer value, salary, growth/decline, etc., could also be incorporated into the model to provide a more comprehensive summary of a player.

References

Steven Bird, Ewan Klein, and Edward Loper. 2009. *Natural Language Processing with Python*. O'Reilly Media.

Paul Buitelaar, Thomas Eigner, Greg Gulrajani, Alexander Schutz, Melanie Siegel, Nicolas Weber, Philipp Cimiano, Günther Ladwig, Matthias Mantel, and Honggang Zhu. 2006. Generating and visualizing a soccer knowledge base. In *EACL '06 Proceedings of the Eleventh Conference of the European Chapter of the Association for Computational Linguistics: Posters & Demonstrations*. pages 123–126. http://www.aclweb.org/anthology/E06-2010.

Klaus Krippendorff. 2004. Measuring the reliability of qualitative text analysis data. *Quality & quantity* 38:787–800.

Fabian Pedregosa, Gaël Varoquaux, Alexandre Gramfort, Vincent Michel, Bertrand Thirion, Olivier Grisel, Mathieu Blondel, Peter Prettenhofer, Ron Weiss, Vincent Dubourg, Jake Vanderplas, Alexandre Passos, David Cournapeau, Matthieu Brucher, Matthieu Perrot, and Édouard Duchesnay. 2011. Scikit-learn: Machine learning in python. *Journal of Machine Learning Research* 12:2825–2830.

Kyeongmin Rim. 2016. Mae2: Portable annotation tool for general natural language use. In *Proceedings of 12th Joint ACL-ISO Workshop on Interoperable Semantic Annotation*. pages 75–80.

Theresa Wilson, Janyce Wiebe, and Claire Cardie. 2016. Mpqa opinion corpus. In James Pustejovsky and Nancy Ide, editors, *Handbook of Linguistic Annotation*, Springer, New York.

Accent Adaptation for the Air Traffic Control Domain

Matthew Garber, Meital Singer, Christopher Ward
Brandeis University
Waltham, MA 02453, USA
{mgarber,tsinger,cmward}@brandeis.edu

Abstract

Automated speech recognition (ASR) plays a significant role in training and simulation systems for air traffic controllers. However, because English is the default language used in air traffic control (ATC), ASR systems often encounter difficulty with speakers' non-native accents, for which there is a paucity of data. This paper examines the effects of accent adaptation on the recognition of non-native English speech in the ATC domain. Accent adaptation has been demonstrated to be an effective way to model under-resourced speech, and can be applied to a variety of models. We use Subspace Gaussian Mixture Models (SGMMs) with the Kaldi Speech Recognition Toolkit to adapt acoustic models from American English to German-accented English, and compare it against other adaptation methods. Our results provide additional evidence that SGMMs can be an efficient and effective way to approach this problem, particularly with smaller amounts of accented training data.

1 Introduction

As the field of speech recognition has developed, ASR systems have grown increasingly useful for the ATC domain. The majority of air traffic communication is verbal (Hofbauer et al., 2008), meaning ASR has the potential to be an invaluable tool not just in assisting air traffic controllers in their daily operations, but also for training purposes and workload analysis (Cordero et al., 2012).

Due to a constrained grammar and vocabulary, ATC ASR systems have relatively low word er-ror rates (WER) when compared to other domains, such as broadcast news (Geacăr, 2010). These systems can also be limited at run-time by location (e.g. place names, runway designations), further constraining these parameters and increasing accuracy.

Despite the effectiveness of existing systems, air traffic control has little tolerance for mistakes in day-to-day operations (Hofbauer et al., 2008). Furthermore, these systems generally perform worse in real-world conditions, where they have to contend with confounding factors such as noise and speaker accents (Geacăr, 2010).

In this paper, we attempt to ameliorate the issue of speaker accents by examining the usefulness of accent adaptation in the ATC domain. We compare the relatively new innovation of SGMMs (Povey et al., 2011a) against older adaptation techniques, such as maximum a posteriori (MAP) estimation, as well as pooling, a type of multi-condition training.

We perform experiments using out-of-domain American English data from the HUB4 Broadcast News Corpus (Fiscus et al., 1998), as well as German-accented English data taken from the AT-COSIM corpus (Hofbauer et al., 2008) and provided by UFA, Inc., a company specializing in ATC training and simulation.

The paper is organized as follows: in Section 2, we describe previous accent adaptation techniques as well as the structure of SGMMs and how they can be adapted on new data. In Section 3, we outline our experiments and show how accent adaptation with SGMMs outperforms other methods when using smaller amounts of data. Section 4 concludes the paper and presents paths for future study.

Proceedings of the 55th Annual Meeting of the Association for Computational Linguistics- Student Research Workshop, pages 95–99
Vancouver, Canada, July 30 - August 4, 2017. ©2017 Association for Computational Linguistics
https://doi.org/10.18653/v1/P17-3016

2 Background

2.1 Accent Adaptation

The ideal ASR system for non-native accented speech is one trained on many hours of speech in the target accent. However, for a variety of reasons, there is often a paucity of such data. Several different techniques have been employed to model accented speech in spite of this lack of data.

One method is to manually adjust the pronunciation lexicon to match the accented phone set (Humphries et al., 1996). Unfortunately, this is both time- and labor-intensive as it requires mappings to be generated from one phoneset to another, either probabilistically or using expert knowledge.

Another technique is interpolate models, with one trained on native accented speech and the other trained on non-native accented speech (Witt and Young, 1999). While this has been shown to reduce word error rate (Wang et al., 2003), it does not fully adapt the native model to the new accent.

An effective and versatile method, and the one we implement here, is to directly adapt a native acoustic model on the non-native speech. There exist a few different ways to accomplish this, such as MAP estimation for HMM-GMMs, Maximum Likelihood Linear Regression (MLLR) for Gaussian parameters (Witt and Young, 1999), and re-estimating the state-specific parameters of an SGMM. These techniques have the advantage of requiring little other than a trained native accent model and a non-trivial amount of non-native accented data.

2.2 SGMM Adaptation

Unlike a typical GMM, the parameters of an SGMM are determined by a combination of globally-shared parameters and state-specific parameters. The model can be expressed as follows:

$$p(\mathbf{x}|j) = \Sigma_{m=1}^{M_j} c_{jm} \Sigma_{i=1}^{I} w_{jmi} \mathcal{N}(\mathbf{x}; \boldsymbol{\mu}_{jmi}, \boldsymbol{\Sigma}_i)$$

$$\boldsymbol{\mu}_{jmi} = \mathbf{M}_i \mathbf{v}_{jm}$$

$$w_{jmi} = \frac{\exp \mathbf{w}_i^T \mathbf{v}_{jm}}{\Sigma_{l=1}^{I} \exp \mathbf{w}_l^T \mathbf{v}_{jm}}$$

where $\mathbf{x}$ is the feature vector, j is the speech state, c_{jm} is the state-specific weight, $\mathbf{v}_{jm}$ is the state-specific vector, and $\boldsymbol{\mu}_{jmi}$, $\mathbf{M}_i$, and $\mathbf{w}_i$ are all globally-shared parameters. SGMMs are generally initialized using a Universal Background Model (UBM), which is trained separately from the SGMM.

SGMMs can be further extended beyond the model described above to include speaker-specific vectors and projections. Other speaker adaptation techniques, such as feature-space Maximum Likelihood Linear Regression (fMLLR, also known as CMLLR), can be applied on top of these extensions to further increase the accuracy of the model.

Though it is possible to perform MAP adaptation using SGMMs, their unique structure allows a different and more effective technique to be applied (Povey et al., 2011a). Initially, all of the model's state-specific and globally-shared parameters are trained on out-of-domain data. The state-specific parameter $\mathbf{v}_{jm}$ can then be re-estimated on the non-native speech using maximum likelihood. This adaptation method has been successfully applied to multi-lingual SGMMs (Povey et al., 2011a) as well as different native accents of the same language (Motlicek et al., 2013), and is the technique we use here to adapt the native-accented SGMMs on non-native speech.

Though there exist other ways of adapting SGMMs (Juan et al. (2015) created a multi-accent SGMM by combining UBMs that had been separately trained on the native and non-native data), we do not implement those methods here.

3 Experiments

All experiments were performed using the Kaldi Speech Recognition Toolkit (Povey et al., 2011b).

3.1 Data

Speech Data

For acoustic model training, data was taken from three separate sources:

- Approximately 75 hours of US English audio was taken from the 1997 English Broadcast News Corpus (HUB4), which consists of various radio and television news broadcasts.

- About 20 hours of German-accented data, which is purely in-domain ATC speech, was supplied by UFA.

- An additional 6 hours of German-accented speech was taken from the ATCOSIM corpus, which consists of audio recorded during real-time ATC simulations.

System	Native (Unadapted)		Non-native Only		Pooled (Unadapted)		Native (Adapted)		Pooled (Adapted)	
	WER	SER	WER	SER	WER	SER	WER	SER	WER	SER
HMM-GMM	25.73	74.39	5.74	34.43	6.76	39.24	6.55	37.43	5.38	32.77
+ fMLLR	12.61	58.40	4.64	30.64	5.40	34.53	5.12	33.17	4.51	29.30
SGMM	13.78	58.43	4.15	26.23	4.97	30.99	4.13	26.65	3.71	24.44
+ fMLLR	10.02	51.76	3.46	23.57	4.38	29.15	4.09	27.57	3.25	22.38

Table 1: Error rates of different models trained with 6.5 hours of adaptation data.

System	Native (Unadapted)		Non-native Only		Pooled (Unadapted)		Native (Adapted)		Pooled (Adapted)	
	WER	SER	WER	SER	WER	SER	WER	SER	WER	SER
HMM-GMM	25.73	74.39	3.90	25.16	4.99	31.11	5.95	35.18	4.29	27.54
+ fMLLR	12.61	58.40	3.36	23.00	4.16	27.84	4.79	31.36	3.66	24.91
SGMM	13.78	58.43	3.12	21.34	3.82	25.29	3.71	24.71	3.00	21.10
+ fMLLR	10.02	51.76	2.77	20.03	3.34	23.18	3.64	25.16	2.88	20.45

Table 2: Error rates of different models trained with 26 hours of adaptation data.

Test data consisted of just under 4 hours of German-accented speech provided by UFA. All audio was downsampled to 16 kHz.

Language Model Data

We interpolated a language model trained on the UFA and ATCOSIM utterances with one trained on sentences generated from an ATC grammar supplied by UFA. Both LMs were 5-gram models with Witten-Bell smoothing. The interpolated model was heavily weighted towards the natural utterances (with $\lambda = 0.95$), since the main purpose of the generated utterances was to add coverage for words and n-grams that were not present in the natural data.

Lexicon

The lexicon was largely derived from the CMU Pronouncing Dictionary. Additional pronunciations were supplied by UFA, and several were written by hand.

3.2 Experimental Setup

The baseline acoustic model was a regular HMM-GMM and was trained with the usual 39 MFCC features, including delta and acceleration features. Experiments were conducted both with and without pooling the adaptation data with the US English data, since pooling data prior to adaptation has been shown to give better results for both MAP and SGMM maximum likelihood adaptation (Motlicek et al., 2013), as well as for other adaptation techniques (Witt and Young, 1999).

We conducted two experiments, each with a different amount of adaptation data. The first experiment included only a 6.5-hour subset of the total adaptation data, which was created by randomly selecting speakers from both the ATCOSIM corpus and the UFA data. The second included all 26 hours of adaptation data. HMM-GMM models were adapted using MAP estimation and SGMMs were adapted using the method outlined above.

For each amount of adaptation data, we trained several different models, testing all combinations of the following variables:

- Whether the model was trained solely on the native-accented data, trained solely on the adaptation data, trained on the combined data but not adapted, trained of the native data and then adapted, or trained on the combined data and then adapted.

- Whether an HMM-GMM or SGMM was used (as well as the corresponding adaptation method).

- Whether the model was trained with speaker-dependent fMLLR transforms.

3.3 Experimental Results

With 6.5 hours of German accented data, both the MAP-adapted and SGMM-adapted pooled systems saw modest reductions in word error rate, as can be seen in Table 1. MAP adaptation provided a 6.3% relative improvement over the corresponding accented-only model[1], though WER was reduced by only 2.8% when fMLLR was implemented. Pooled SGMMs were more versatile and amenable to adaptation, with a relative reduction in WER of 10.6%, and a relative improvement of

---

[1]Unless otherwise specified, reduction in error rate is relative to the model with the same parameters (SGMM, fMLLR, etc.) but trained on the non-native accented data only, rather than relative to a single baseline.

6.1% when using fMLLR. Changes in sentence error rate (SER) between models correlated with the changes in WER, reaching a minimum of 22.38% with the adapted SGMM-fMLLR system, a relative reduction of just over 5%.

Including the full 26 hours of non-native speech in the training and adaptation data generally resulted in higher error rates in the adapted systems than the corresponding accented-only models, as seen in Table 2. This decrease in performance approached 10% for the HMM-GMM systems. Though the SGMM-fMLLR adapted system experienced a relative reduction in performance of about 4%, the performance of the non-fMLLR SGMM increased by about the same amount. Changes in SER again correlated with the changes in WER, with the adapted speaker independent SGMM possessing a slight edge (about 1%) over its accented-only counterpart.

It is not clear from this experiment why the speaker independent SGMM system was the only one to undergo an increase in performance when adapted with the full dataset. A possible explanation is that, with enough data, the speaker adaptive techniques were simply more robust than the accent-adaptation method.

Unsurprisingly, the unadapted native-accented systems had the worst performance out of all of the models, with word error rates that were more than double than that of next best corresponding system.

The unadapted pooled models and the adapted native models were usually the second- and third-worst performing groups of models, though their ranking depended on the amount of adaptation data used. The pooled models generally gave better results when more adaptation data was provided, while the adapted native models had an advantage with less adaptation data.

Interestingly, fMLLR had relatively little effect when used with the adapted native SGMMs, regardless of the amount of adaptation data used. WER was reduced by only about 1 to 2% compared to the models' non-fMLLR counterparts. This stands in contrast with the gains that virtually every other model saw with the introduction of fMLLR. It is not clear why this was the case, though it might relate to some overlap between the SGMM adaptation method and fMLLR.

While it is possible that training the pooled model with in-domain English speech could increase performance, it seems unlikely that it would be superior to either the accented-only model or the adapted pooled model.

4   Conclusion

In this paper, we explored how non-native accent adaptation can be applied using SGMMs to yield notable improvements over the baseline model, particularly when there exists only limited in-domain data. We also demonstrated that this technique can achieve as high as a 10% relative improvement in WER in the ATC domain, where the baseline model is already highly accurate. Even with large amounts of adaptation data, speaker independent SGMMs saw a minor increase in performance when adapted, compared to when they were trained only with in-domain data.

Future avenues of research include whether the SGMM adaptation technique used here could be successfully combined with the UBM-focused adaptation method used by Juan et al. (2015) to achieve even further reductions in WER.

Furthermore, future work could explore whether smaller error rates could be achieved by training the original acoustic models on speech from the ATC domain, rather than from broadcast news, and whether the increases in perfomance found here still hold between more distantly related and phonologically dissimilar languages. It should be noted, however, that this may necesitate the creation of new corpora, as the few non-native ATC corpora that exist seem to only include European accents.

References

José Manuel Cordero, Manuel Dorado, and José Miguel de Pablo. 2012. Automated speech recognition in atc environment. In *Proceedings of ATACCS 2012, the 2nd International Conference on Application and Theory of Automation in Command and Control Systems*. IRIT Press, pages 46–53.

Jonathan Fiscus, John Garofolo, Mark Przybocki, William Fisher, and David Pallett. 1998. *1997 English Broadcast News Speech (HUB4) LDC98S71*. Linguistic Data Consortium, Philadelphia.

Claudiu-Mihai Geacăr. 2010. Reducing pilot/atc communication errors using voice recognition. In *Proceedings of ICAS 2010, the 27th Congress of the Internation Council of the Aeronautical Sciences*.

Konrad Hofbauer, Stefan Petrik, and Horst Hering. 2008. The atcosim corpus of non-prompted clean air traffic control speech. In *Proceedings of LREC 2008, the Sixth International Conference on Language Resources and Evaluation.*

Jason J. Humphries, Philip C. Woodland, and D. Pearce. 1996. Using accent-specific pronunciation modelling for robust speech recognition. In *Proceedings of ICSPL 96, Fourth International Conference on Spoken Language, 1996.* IEEE, volume 4, pages 2324–2327.

Sarah Samson Juan, Laurent Besacier, Benjamin Lecouteux, and Tien-Ping Tan. 2015. Merging of native and non-native speech for low-resource accented asr. In *Proceedings of SLSP 2015, the Third International Conference on Statistical Language and Speech Processing.* Springer, pages 255–266.

Petr Motlicek, Philip N. Garner, Namhoon Kim, and Jeongmi Cho. 2013. Accent adaptation using subspace gaussian mixture models. In *Proceedings of ICASSP 2013, IEEE International Conference on Acoustics, Speech and Signal Processing.* IEEE, pages 7170–7174.

Daniel Povey, Lukáš Burget, Mohit Agarwal, Pinar Akyazi, Feng Kai, Arnab Ghoshal, Ondřej Glembek, Nagendra Goel, Martin Karafiát, Ariya Rastrow, et al. 2011a. The subspace gaussian mixture modela structured model for speech recognition. *Computer Speech & Language* 25(2):404–439.

Daniel Povey, Arnab Ghoshal, Gilles Boulianne, Lukas Burget, Ondrej Glembek, Nagendra Goel, Mirko Hannemann, Petr Motlicek, Yanmin Qian, Petr Schwarz, et al. 2011b. The kaldi speech recognition toolkit. In *IEEE 2011 workshop on Automatic Speech Recognition and Understanding.* IEEE Signal Processing Society, EPFL-CONF-192584.

Zhirong Wang, Tanja Schultz, and Alex Waibel. 2003. Comparison of acoustic model adaptation techniques on non-native speech. In *Proceedings of ICASSP 2003, IEEE International Conference on Acoustics, Speech, and Signal Processing.* IEEE, volume 1, pages 540–543.

Silke M. Witt and Steve J. Young. 1999. Off-line acoustic modelling of non-native accents. In *Proceedings of the 6th European Conference on Speech Communication and Technology (EUROSPEECH 1999).* pages 1367–1370.

Generating Steganographic Text with LSTMs

Tina Fang
University of Waterloo
tbfang@edu.uwaterloo.ca

Martin Jaggi
École polytechnique
fédérale de Lausanne
martin.jaggi@epfl.ch

Katerina Argyraki
École polytechnique
fédérale de Lausanne
katerina.argyraki@epfl.ch

Abstract

Motivated by concerns for user privacy, we design a steganographic system ("stegosystem") that enables two users to exchange encrypted messages without an adversary detecting that such an exchange is taking place. We propose a new linguistic stegosystem based on a Long Short-Term Memory (LSTM) neural network. We demonstrate our approach on the Twitter and Enron email datasets and show that it yields high-quality steganographic text while significantly improving capacity (encrypted bits per word) relative to the state-of-the-art.

1 Introduction

The business model behind modern communication systems (email services or messaging services provided by social networks) is incompatible with end-to-end message encryption. The providers of these services can afford to offer them free of charge because most of their users agree to receive "targeted ads" (ads that are especially chosen to appeal to each user, based on the needs the user has implied through their messages). This model works as long as users communicate mostly in the clear, which enables service providers to make informed guesses about user needs.

This situation does not prevent users from encrypting a few sensitive messages, but it does take away some of the benefits of confidentiality. For instance, imagine a scenario where two users want to exchange forbidden ideas or organize forbidden events under an authoritarian regime; in a world where most communication happens in the clear, encrypting a small fraction of messages automatically makes these messages—and the users who exchange them—suspicious.

With this motivation in mind, we want to design a system that enables two users to exchange encrypted messages, such that a passive adversary that reads the messages can determine neither the original content of the messages nor the fact that the messages are encrypted.

We build on linguistic steganography, i.e., the science of encoding a secret piece of information ("payload") into a piece of text that looks like natural language ("stegotext"). We propose a novel stegosystem, based on a neural network, and demonstrate that it combines high quality of output (i.e., the stegotext indeed looks like natural language) with the highest capacity (number of bits encrypted per word) published in literature.

In the rest of the paper, we describe existing linguistic stegosystems along with ours (§2), provide details on our system (§3), present preliminary experimental results on Twitter and email messages (§4), and conclude with future directions (§5).

2 Linguistic Steganography

In this section, we summarize related work (§2.1), then present out proposal (§2.2).

2.1 Related Work

Traditional linguistic stegosystems are based on modification of an existing cover text, e.g., using synonym substitution (Topkara et al., 2006; Chang and Clark, 2014) and/or paraphrase substitution (Chang and Clark, 2010). The idea is to encode the secret information in the transformation of the cover text, ideally without affecting its meaning or grammatical correctness. Of these systems, the most closely related to ours is CoverTweet (Wilson et al., 2014), a state-of-the-art cover modification stegosystem that uses Twitter as the medium of cover; we compare to it in our preliminary evaluation (§4).

Proceedings of the 55th Annual Meeting of the Association for Computational Linguistics- Student Research Workshop, pages 100–106
Vancouver, Canada, July 30 - August 4, 2017. ©2017 Association for Computational Linguistics
https://doi.org/10.18653/v1/P17-3017

Cover modification can introduce syntactic and semantic unnaturalness (Grosvald and Orgun, 2011); to address this, Grovsald and Orgun proposed an alternative stegosystem where a human generates the stegotext manually, thus improving linguistic naturalness at the cost of human effort (Grosvald and Orgun, 2011).

Matryoshka (Safaka et al., 2016) takes this further: in step 1, it generates candidate stegotext automatically based on an n-gram model of the English language; in step 2, it presents the candidate stegotext to the human user for polishing, i.e., ideally small edits that improve linguistic naturalness. However, the cost of human effort is still high, because the (automatically generated) candidate stegotext is far from natural language, and, as a result, the human user has to spend significant time and effort manually editing and augmenting it.

Volkhonskiy et al. have applied Generative Adversarial Networks (Goodfellow et al., 2014) to image steganography (Volkhonskiy et al., 2017), but we are not aware of any text stegosystem based on neural networks.

2.2 Our Proposal: Steganographic LSTM

Motivated by the fact that LSTMs (Hochreiter and Schmidhuber, 1997) constitute the state of the art in text generation (Jozefowicz et al., 2016), we propose to automatically generate the stegotext from an LSTM (as opposed to an n-gram model). The output of the LSTM can then be used either directly as the stegotext, or Matryoshka-style, i.e., as a candidate stegotext to be polished by a human user; in this paper, we explore only the former option, i.e., we do not do any manual polishing. We describe the main components of our system in the paragraphs below; for reference, Fig. 1 outlines the building blocks of a stegosystem (Salomon, 2003).

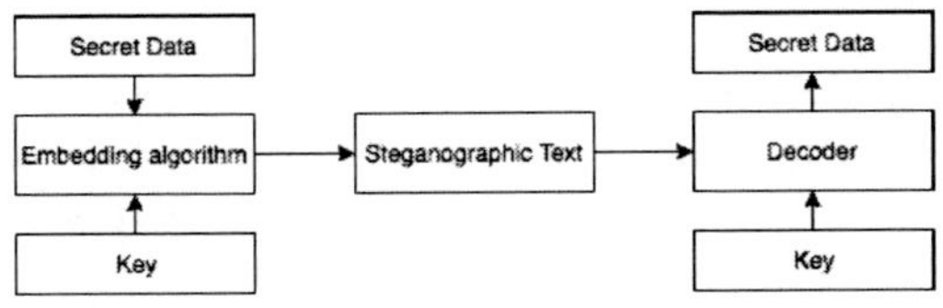

Figure 1: Stegosystem building blocks.

Secret data. The secret data is the information we want to hide. First, we compress and/or encrypt the secret data (e.g., in the simplest setting using the ASCII coding map) into a *secret-containing bit string* S. Second, we divide S into smaller *bit blocks* of length $|B|$, resulting in a total of $|S|/|B|^1$ bit blocks. For example, if $S = 100001$ and $|B| = 2$, our bit-block sequence is 10, 00, 01. Based on this bit-block sequence, our steganographic LSTM generates words.

Key. The sender and receiver share a key that maps bit blocks to token sets and is constructed as follows: We start from the *vocabulary*, which is the set of all possible tokens that may appear in the stegotext; the tokens are typically words, but may also be punctuation marks. We partition the vocabulary into $2^{|B|}$ *bins*, i.e., disjoint token sets, randomly selected from the vocabulary without replacement; each token appears in exactly one bin, and each bin contains $|V|/2^{|B|}$ tokens. We map each bit block B to a bin, denoted by W_B. This mapping constitutes the shared key.

Bit Block	Tokens
00	This, am, weather, ...
01	was, attaching, today, ...
10	I, better, an, Great, ...
11	great, than, NDA, ., ...

Table 1: Example shared key.

Embedding algorithm. The embedding algorithm uses a modified word-level LSTM for language modeling (Mikolov et al., 2010). To encode the secret-containing bit string S, we consider one bit block B at a time and have our LSTM select one token from bin W_B; hence, the candidate stegotext has as many tokens as the number of bit blocks in S. Even though we restrict the LSTM to select a token from a particular bin, each bin should offer sufficient variety of tokens, allowing the LSTM to generate text that looks natural. For example, given the bit string "1000011011" and the key in Table 1, the LSTM can form the partial sentence in Table 2. We describe our LSTM model in more detail in the next section.

Bit String	10	00	01	10	11
Token	I	am	attaching	an	NDA

Table 2: Example stegotext generation.

---

[1] If $|B| \nmid |S|$, then we leave the remainder bit string out of encryption.

Decoder. The decoder recovers the original data deterministically and in a straightforward manner: it takes as input the generated stegotext, considers one token at a time, finds the token's bin in the shared key, and recovers the original bit block.

Common-token variant. We also explore a variant where we add a set of *common tokens*, C, to all bins. These common tokens do not carry any secret information; they serve only to enhance stegotext naturalness. When the LSTM selects a common token from a bin, we have it select an extra token from the same bin, until it selects a non-common token. The decoder removes all common tokens before decoding. We discuss the choice of common tokens and its implication on our system's performance in Section 4.

3 Steganographic LSTM Model

In this section, we provide more details on our system: how we modify the LSTM (§3.1) and how we evaluate its output (§3.2).

3.1 LSTM Modification

Text generation in classic LSTM. Classic LSTMs generate words as follows (Sutskever et al., 2011): Given a word sequence $(x_1, x_2, \ldots, x_T)$, the model has hidden states $(h_1, \ldots, h_T)$, and resulting output vectors $(o_1, \ldots, o_T)$. Each output vector o_t has length $|V|$, and each output-vector element $o_t^{(j)}$ is the unnormalized probability of word j in the vocabulary. Normalized probabilities for each candidate word are obtained by the following softmax activation function:

$$softmax(o_t)_j := \exp(o_t^{(j)}) \Big/ \sum_k \exp(o_t^{(k)}).$$

The LSTM then selects the word with the highest probability $P[x_{t+1} \mid x_{\leq t}]$ as its next word.

Text generation in our LSTM. In our steganographic LSTM, word selection is restricted by the shared key. That is, given bit block B, the LSTM has to select its next word from bin W_B. We set $P[x = w_j] = 0$ for $j \notin W_B$, so that the multinomial softmax function selects the word with the highest probability within W_B.

Common tokens. In the common-token variant, we restrict $P[x = w_j] = 0$ only for $j \notin (W_B \cup C)$, where C is the set of common tokens added to all bins.

3.2 Evaluation Metrics

We use perplexity to quantify stegotext quality; and capacity (i.e., encrypted bits per output word) to quantify its efficiency in carrying secret information. In Section 4, we also discuss our stegotext quality as empirically perceived by us as human readers.

Perplexity. Perplexity is a standard metric for the quality of language models (Martin and Jurafsky, 2000), and it is defined as the average per-word log-probability on the valid data set: $\exp(-1/N \sum_i \ln p[w_i])$ (Jozefowicz et al., 2016). Lower perplexity indicates a better model.

In our steganographic LSTM, we cannot use this metric as is: since we enforce $p[w_i] = 0$ for $w_i \notin W_B$, the corresponding $\ln p[w_i]$ becomes undefined under this vocabulary.

Instead, we measure the probability of w_i by taking the average of $p[w_i]$ over all possible secret bit blocks B, under the assumption that bit blocks are distributed uniformly. By the Law of Large Numbers (Révész, 2014), if we perform many stegotext-generating trials using different random secret data as input, the probability of each word will tend to the expected value, $\sum p[w_i, B]/2^{|B|}$. Hence, we set $p[w_i] := \sum p[w_i, B]/2^{|B|}$ instead of $p[w_i] = 0$ for $w_i \notin W_B$.

Capacity. Our system's capacity is the number of encrypted bits per output word. Without common tokens, capacity is always $|B|$ bits/word (since each bit block of size $|B|$ is always mapped to one output word). In the common-token variant, capacity decreases because the output includes common tokens that do not carry any secret information; in particular, if the fraction of common tokens is p, then capacity is $(1 - p) \cdot |B|$.

4 Experiments

In this section, we present our preliminary experimental evaluation: our Twitter and email datasets (§4.1), details about the LSTMs used to produce our results (§4.2), and finally a discussion of our results (§4.3).

4.1 Datasets

Tweets and emails are among the most popular media of open communication and therefore provide very realistic environments for hiding information. We thus trained our LSTMs on those two domains, Twitter messages and Enron emails

(Klimt and Yang, 2004), which vary greatly in message length and vocabulary size.

For Twitter, we used the NLTK tokenizer to tokenize tweets (Bird, 2006) into words and punctuation marks. We normalized the content by replacing usernames and URLs with a username token (<user>) and a URL token (<url>), respectively. We used 600 thousand tweets with a total of 45 million words and a vocabulary of size 225 thousand.

For Enron, we cleaned and extracted email message bodies (Zhou et al., 2007) from the Enron dataset, and we tokenized the messages into words and punctuation marks. We took the first 100MB of the resulting messages, with 16.8 million tokens and a vocabulary size of 406 thousand.

4.2 Implementation Details

We implemented multi-layered LSTMs based on PyTorch[2] in both experiments. We did not use pre-trained word embeddings (Mikolov et al., 2013; Pennington et al., 2014), and instead trained word embeddings of dimension 200 from scratch.

We optimized with Stochastic Gradient Descent and used a batch size of 20. The initial learning rate was 20 and the decay factor per epoch was 4. The learning rate decay occurred only when the validation loss did not improve. Model training was done on an NVIDIA GeForce GTX TITAN X.

For Twitter, we used a 2-layer LSTM with 600 units, unrolled for 25 steps for back propagation. We clipped the norm of the gradients (Pascanu et al., 2013) at 0.25 and applied 20% dropout (Srivastava et al., 2014). We stopped the training after 12 epochs (10 hours) based on validation loss convergence.

For Enron, we used a 3-layer LSTM with 600 units and no regularization. We unrolled the network for 20 steps for back propagation. We stopped the training after 6 epochs (2 days).

4.3 Results and Discussion

4.3.1 Tweets

We evaluate resulting tweets generated by LSTMs of 1 (non-steganographic), 2, 4, 8 bins. Furthermore, we found empirically that adding 10 most frequent tokens from the Twitter corpus was enough to significantly improve the grammatical correctness and semantic reasonableness of

tweets. Table 3 shows the relationship between capacity (*bits per word*), and quantitative text quality (*perplexity*). It also compares models with and without adding common tokens using perplexity and bits per word.

Table 4 shows example output texts of LSTMs with and without common tokens added. To reflect the variation in the quality of the tweets, we represent tweets that are good and poor in quality[3].

We replaced <user> generated by the LSTM with mock usernames for a more realistic presentation in Table 4. In practice, we can replace the <user> tokens systematically, randomly selecting followers or followees of that tweet sender, for example.

Re-tweet messages starting with "RT" can also be problematic, because it will be easy to check whether the original message of the retweeted message exists. A simple approach to deal with this is to eliminate "RT" messages from training (or at generation). Finally, since we made all tweets lower case in the pre-processing step, we can also post-process tweets to adhere to proper English capitalization rules.

	Original		Common Tokens	
# of Bins	bpw	ppl	bpw	ppl
1	0	134.73	0	134.73
2	1	190.84	0.65	171.35
4	2	381.2	1.17	277.55
8	3	833.11	1.53	476.66

Table 3: An increase of of capacity correlates with an increase of perplexity, which implies that there is a negative correlation between capacity and text quality. After adding common tokens, there is a significant reduction in perplexity *(ppl)*, at the expense of a lower capacity *(bits per word)*.

4.3.2 Emails

We also tested email generation, and Table 5 shows sample email passages[4] from each bin. We post-processed the emails with untokenization of punctuations.

The biggest difference between emails and tweets is that emails have a much longer range for

[2]https://github.com/pytorch

[3]For each category, we manually evaluate 60 randomly generated tweets based grammatical correctness, semantic coherence, and resemblance to real tweets. We select tweets from the 25th, 50th, and 75th percentile, and call them "good", "average", and "poor" respectively. We limit to tweets that are not offensive in language.

[4]We only present passages "average" in quality to conserve space.

# of Bins	Tweets	Tweets with Common Tokens
2	**good:** i was just looking for someone that i used have. **poor:** cry and speak! rt @user421: relatable personal hygiene for body and making bad things as a best friend in life	**good:** i'm happy with you. i'll take a pic **poor:** rt: cut your hair, the smallest things get to the body.
4	**good:** @user390 looool yeah she likes me then ;). you did? **poor:** "where else were u making?... i feel fine? - e? lol" * does a voice for me & take it to walmart?	**good:** i just wanna move. collapses. **poor:** i hate being contemplating for something i want to.
8	**good:** @user239 hahah. sorry that my bf is amazing because i'm a bad influence ;). **poor:** so happy this to have been working my ass and they already took the perfect. but it's just cause you're too busy the slows out! love... * dancing on her face, holding two count out cold * (a link with a roof on punishment... - please :)	**good:** i hate the smell of my house. **poor:** a few simple i can't. i need to make my specs jump surprisingly.

Table 4: We observe that the model with common tokens produces tweets simpler in style, and uses more words from the set of common tokens. There is a large improvement in grammatical correctness and context coherence after adding common tokens, especially in the "poor" examples. For example, adding the line break token reduced the length of the tweet generated from the 8-bin LSTM.

context dependency, with context spanning sentences and paragraphs. This is challenging to model even for the non-steganographic LSTM. Once the long-range context dependency of the non-steganographic LSTM improves, the context dependency of the steganographic LSTMs should also improve.

# of Bins	Sample Email
1	——Original Message—— From: Nelson, Michelle Sent: Thursday, January 03, 2002 3:35 PM To: Maggi, Mike Subject: Hey, You are probably a list of people that are around asleep about the point of them and our wife. Rob
2	If you do like to comment on the above you will not contact me at the above time by 8:00 a.m. on Monday, March 13 and July 16 and Tuesday, May 13 and Tuesday, March 9 - Thursday, June 17, - 9:00 to 11:30 AM.
4	At a moment when my group was working for a few weeks, we were able to get more flexibility through in order that we would not be willing.

Table 5: The issue of context inconsistency is present for all bins. However, the resulting text remains syntactical even as the number of bins increases.

4.4 Comparison with Other Stegosystems

For all comparisons, we use our 4-bin model with no common tokens added.

Our model significantly improves the state-of-the-art capacity. Cover modification based stegosystems hide 1-2 bits per sentence (Chang and Clark, 2012). The state-of-the-art Twitter stegosystem hides 2.8 bits of per tweet (Wilson and Ker, 2016). Assuming 16.04 words per tweet[5], our 4-bin system hides **32 bits per tweet**, over 11 times higher than (Wilson and Ker, 2016).

We hypothesize that the subjective quality of our generated tweets will be comparable to tweets produced by CoverTweet (2014). We present some examples[6] in Table 6 to show there is potential for a comparison. This contrasts the previous conception that cover generation methods are fatally weak against human judges (Wilson et al., 2014). CoverTweet was tested to be secure against human judges. Formal experiments will be necessary to establish that our system is also secure against human judges.

CoverTweet (2014)	Steganographic LSTM
yall must have 11:11 set 1 minute early before yall tweet it, because soon as 11:11 hit yall don't wastes no time. lol	i wanna go to sleep in the gym, ny in peoples houses & i'm in the gym..! :((
you can tell when somebody hating on you!	i would rather marry a regular sunday!!
most of the people who got mouth can't beat you.	my mom is going so hard to get his jam.

Table 6: The tweets generated by the 4-bin LSTM (32 bits per tweet) are reasonably comparable in quality to tweets produced by CoverTweet (2.8 bits per tweet).

Our system also offers flexibility for the user to freely trade-off capacity and text quality. Though we chose the 4-bin model with no common tokens for comparison, user can choose to use more bins

---

[5] Based a random sample of 2 million tweets.

[6] Tweets selected for comparison are "average" in quality.

to achieve an even higher capacity, or use less bins and add common tokens to increase text quality. This is not the case with existing cover modification systems, where capacity is bounded above by the number of transformation options (Wilson et al., 2014).

5 Conclusion and Future Work

In this paper, we opened a new application of LSTMs, namely, steganographic text generation. We presented our steganographic model based on existing language modeling LSTMs, and demonstrated that our model produces realistic tweets and emails while hiding information.

In comparison to the state-of-the-art steganographic systems, our system has the advantage of encoding much more information (around 2 bits per word). This advantage makes the system more usable and scalable in practice.

In future work, we will formally evaluate our system's security against human judges and other steganography detection (steganalysis) methods (Wilson et al., 2015; Kodovsky et al., 2012). When evaluated against an automated classifier, the setup becomes that of a Generative Adversarial Network (Goodfellow et al., 2014), though with additional conditions for the generator (the secret bits) which are unknown to the discriminator, and not necessarily employing joint training. Another line of future research is to generate tweets which are personalized to a user type or interest group, instead of reflecting all twitter users. Furthermore, we plan to explore if capacity can be improved even more by using probabilistic encoders/decoders, as e.g. in Matryoshka (Safaka et al., 2016, Section 4).

Ultimately, we aim to open-source our stegosystem so that users of open communication systems (e.g. Twitter, emails) can use our stegosystem to communicate private and sensitive information.

References

Steven Bird. 2006. Nltk: the natural language toolkit. In *Proceedings of the COLING/ACL on Interactive presentation sessions*. Association for Computational Linguistics, pages 69–72.

Ching-Yun Chang and Stephen Clark. 2010. Linguistic steganography using automatically generated paraphrases. In *Human Language Technologies: The 2010 Annual Conference of the North American Chapter of the Association for Computational Linguistics*. Association for Computational Linguistics, pages 591–599.

Ching-Yun Chang and Stephen Clark. 2012. Adjective deletion for linguistic steganography and secret sharing. In *COLING*. pages 493–510.

Ching-Yun Chang and Stephen Clark. 2014. Practical linguistic steganography using contextual synonym substitution and a novel vertex coding method. *Computational Linguistics* 40(2):403–448.

Ian Goodfellow, Jean Pouget-Abadie, Mehdi Mirza, Bing Xu, David Warde-Farley, Sherjil Ozair, Aaron Courville, and Yoshua Bengio. 2014. Generative adversarial nets. In *Advances in neural information processing systems*. pages 2672–2680.

Michael Grosvald and C Orhan Orgun. 2011. Free from the cover text: a human-generated natural language approach to text-based steganography. *Journal of Information Hiding and Multimedia Signal Processing* 2(2):133–141.

Sepp Hochreiter and Jürgen Schmidhuber. 1997. Long short-term memory. *Neural computation* 9(8):1735–1780.

Rafal Jozefowicz, Oriol Vinyals, Mike Schuster, Noam Shazeer, and Yonghui Wu. 2016. Exploring the limits of language modeling. *arXiv preprint arXiv:1602.02410* .

Bryan Klimt and Yiming Yang. 2004. The enron corpus: A new dataset for email classification research. In *European Conference on Machine Learning*. Springer, pages 217–226.

Jan Kodovsky, Jessica Fridrich, and Vojtěch Holub. 2012. Ensemble classifiers for steganalysis of digital media. *IEEE Transactions on Information Forensics and Security* 7(2):432–444.

James H Martin and Daniel Jurafsky. 2000. Speech and language processing. *International Edition* 710.

Tomas Mikolov, Martin Karafiát, Lukas Burget, Jan Cernockỳ, and Sanjeev Khudanpur. 2010. Recurrent neural network based language model. In *Interspeech*. volume 2, page 3.

Tomas Mikolov, Ilya Sutskever, Kai Chen, Greg S Corrado, and Jeff Dean. 2013. Distributed representations of words and phrases and their compositionality. In *Advances in neural information processing systems*. pages 3111–3119.

Razvan Pascanu, Tomas Mikolov, and Yoshua Bengio. 2013. On the difficulty of training recurrent neural networks. *ICML (3)* 28:1310–1318.

Jeffrey Pennington, Richard Socher, and Christopher D Manning. 2014. Glove: Global vectors for word representation. In *EMNLP*. volume 14, pages 1532–1543.

Pál Révész. 2014. *The laws of large numbers*, volume 4. Academic Press.

Iris Safaka, Christina Fragouli, and Katerina Argyraki. 2016. Matryoshka: Hiding secret communication in plain sight. In *6th USENIX Workshop on Free and Open Communications on the Internet (FOCI 16)*. USENIX Association.

David Salomon. 2003. *Data privacy and security: encryption and information hiding*. Springer Science & Business Media.

Nitish Srivastava, Geoffrey E Hinton, Alex Krizhevsky, Ilya Sutskever, and Ruslan Salakhutdinov. 2014. Dropout: a simple way to prevent neural networks from overfitting. *Journal of Machine Learning Research* 15(1):1929–1958.

Ilya Sutskever, James Martens, and Geoffrey E Hinton. 2011. Generating text with recurrent neural networks. In *Proceedings of the 28th International Conference on Machine Learning (ICML-11)*. pages 1017–1024.

Umut Topkara, Mercan Topkara, and Mikhail J Atallah. 2006. The hiding virtues of ambiguity: quantifiably resilient watermarking of natural language text through synonym substitutions. In *Proceedings of the 8th workshop on Multimedia and security*. ACM, pages 164–174.

Denis Volkhonskiy, Ivan Nazarov, Boris Borisenko, and Evgeny Burnaev. 2017. Steganographic generative adversarial networks. *arXiv preprint arXiv:1703.05502* .

Alex Wilson, Phil Blunsom, and Andrew Ker. 2015. Detection of steganographic techniques on twitter. In *EMNLP*. pages 2564–2569.

Alex Wilson, Phil Blunsom, and Andrew D Ker. 2014. Linguistic steganography on twitter: hierarchical language modeling with manual interaction. In *IS&T/SPIE Electronic Imaging*. International Society for Optics and Photonics, pages 902803–902803.

Alex Wilson and Andrew D Ker. 2016. Avoiding detection on twitter: embedding strategies for linguistic steganography. *Electronic Imaging* 2016(8):1–9.

Yingjie Zhou, Mark Goldberg, Malik Magdon-Ismail, and Al Wallace. 2007. Strategies for cleaning organizational emails with an application to enron email dataset. In *5th Conf. of North American Association for Computational Social and Organizational Science*.

Predicting Depression for Japanese Blog Text

Misato Hiraga
Indiana University
mhiraga@indiana.edu

Abstract

This study aims to predict clinical depression, a prevalent mental disorder, from blog posts written in Japanese by using machine learning approaches. The study focuses on how data quality and various types of linguistic features (characters, tokens, and lemmas) affect prediction outcome. Depression prediction achieved 95.5% accuracy using selected lemmas as features.

1 Introduction

The World Health Organization (WHO) recognizes that depression is a leading cause of ill health and disability (2017). In Japan, it is also the most frequent reason for sick leave from work (Kitanaka, 2012). However, many people with depression may not be aware that their mood change and fatigue are due to depression. In order to offer help for those who need it, we first need to identify them. This study examines whether linguistic features in written texts can help predict whether the author is depressed by using a supervised machine learning approach. Specifically, we examine the effectiveness of morphological (character n-grams), syntactic (token n-grams), and (syntactic-)semantic (lemmas of selected POS categories) features. In addition, we remove the topic bias so that the methods can be used to predict depression in people who do not know they are depressed and thus do not write about depression. The results show that lemmas from verb and adverb categories improve performance in classifying authors. Additionally, the selected words include words not typically thought of as related to depression. Thus, the study suggests that feature engineering should not be constrained by our notion of what would be related to certain mental conditions or personalities as changes in people's language use may be very subtle.

Section 2 discusses previous work on author profiling and depression detection. In Section 3, we describe data acquisition, topic modeling, and classifications with different features. Section 4 summarizes the results, and Section 5 discusses the results. Finally, Section 6 concludes the paper with a summary and an outlook.

2 Related Work

Language and social media activities have been utilized for author profiling including personality prediction (Bachrach et al., 2012; Golbeck et al., 2011). Although depression is not a personality, the studies in personality prediction can be extended to predicting depression since one's mental state is often reflected in his or her language and social activities.

Character n-grams are reported to do well in gender prediction in English blog text (Sarawgi et al., 2011) and personality prediction in Dutch (Noecker et al., 2013). However, the PAN 2014 challenge (Rangel et al., 2014) reports that character n-grams are not useful in author profiling (age and gender) in English and Spanish social media, Twitter, blogs, and hotel reviews. Japanese is different from Germanic or Romance languages in terms of how much information can be encoded in one character. Japanese basic characters, *hiragana* and *katakana*, represent one mora, which is a sound unit similar to a syllable, and *kanji* (Chinese characters) can encode more than one mora. Moreover, there are many characters: 50 each for *hiragana* and *katakata*, and approximately 2000 *kanji* for everyday writing. The current study thus examines the effectiveness of character n-grams as features in Japanese text classification.

Matsumoto et al. (2012) built a classifier to

Proceedings of the 55th Annual Meeting of the Association for Computational Linguistics- Student Research Workshop, pages 107–113
Vancouver, Canada, July 30 - August 4, 2017. ©2017 Association for Computational Linguistics
https://doi.org/10.18653/v1/P17-3018

	Class	# of Author	Word/Author	# of Document	Word/Doc
All	Depressed	51	3666	842	222
	Non-Depressed	60	3692	1020	220
Topic	Depressed	49	2630	739	192
	Non-Depressed	59	2890	904	191

Table 1: Number of authors and documents and average word count before and after topic modeling

predict whether a blog text is written by a depressed author or a non-depressed author, using approximately 1800 blog texts written by 30 depressed authors and 30 non-depressed authors. They experimented with bag-of-word (BOW) features and also examined whether words that are associated with emotions from the JAppraisal dictionary (Sato, 2011) were useful in classification. Their classifier using Naive Bayes and BOW performed the best, resulting in average of 88.1% accuracy with 10-fold cross validation. One would question whether their prediction with BOW was based on topic, however. By browsing blogs written by depressed authors, we find many blogs are about depression. Therefore, texts written by depressed authors are biased towards the topic of depression. Unless Matsumoto et al. (2012) controlled topic-bias, their system may be heavily affected by topic. The goal of this study is to predict depression from topic-general texts. Thus, the current study controls topic by performing topic modeling (Section 3.2) before classification and examines its effect. As their model using emotion-related words did worse (<70%) than BOW, the current study examines various features that are not obviously related to depression.

3 Method

3.1 Data

Blog texts are collected from a blog ranking site[1] and by searching on blog provider websites (Yahoo Japan, Livedoor, Hatena, FC2, Seesaa, Nifty, Muragon, and Ameblo)[2]. The blog ranking site ranks registered blogs by the number of votes from readers who visit the blogs. The site is divided into categories which include "depression". In this category, most authors state that they are diagnosed with or have been suffering from depression. Blogs are chosen to be included in the study if the authors report that they themselves are suffering from depression and have written their

blogs for at least three months. Some authors write only a little in a month, but most write at least 10 entries within three months. Thus, for each author, three months' worth of blog posts are collected. This "depressed" group consists of 51 authors. Three months' worth of texts for 60 "non-depressed" authors are also collected. They are randomly chosen among those who have a similar profile as the depressed authors. For example, if a depressed author is a male in his 40's, a blog author who had the similar profile is chosen. Moreover, non-depressed authors with the same interest as the depressed authors are collected. Their interests include pets, food, and sports.[3] As many blogs written by depressed authors are retrieved from a blog ranking site, they include fixed phrases, such as "Please vote", to encourage their readers to vote for their blogs. These fixed phrases that appear repeatedly are removed as they do not appear in blogs written by the non-depressed authors. Moreover, a document whose file size is smaller than 100 bytes is removed as it contained very few words. The average number of words and characters per author and per document are in Table 1.

3.2 Removing Blog entries on depression

Before performing classification, topic modeling is performed to divide documents into topic classes. The purpose of topic modeling is to remove blog entries that are biased towards the topic of depression so that classification will not classify documents based on topics (see Section 2). MALLET (McCallum, 2002) is used for topic-modeling. Dividing documents into 5 topics with a hyperparameter optimization value of 50 is found to work the best by manually testing different values. Two of the five topics included topic keys that are related to depression, and thus the documents in those two topics are excluded in the study. The numbers are summarized in Table 1.

---

[1] http://mental.blogmura.com/utsu/
[2] Data by Matsumoto et al. (2012) was not available

[3] We are aware that we cannot guarantee that non-depressed authors are not depressed.

	Class	# of Author	Word/Author	# of Document	Word/Doc
Train	Depressed	39	2404	590	193
	Non-Depressed	47	2466	722	195
Test	Depressed	10	3512	149	186
	Non-Depressed	12	4233	182	177

Table 2: Number of authors and documents and average word count in training and test sets

The number of authors is reduced to 49 depressed and 59 non-depressed authors. The reason for the reduction in non-depressed authors seemed to be because documents that are related to companies or work are classified together with the topic of depression. For example, one topic class which include the topic key "depression" also includes keys, such as "company", and "investment".

3.3 Classification

We perform classification of texts into whether the author is depressed or not. Our system learns from texts written by a group of both depressed and non-depressed authors, and classifies unseen texts written by a different group of depressed and non-depressed authors. We perform classification of texts per author (henceforth, *author-level* classification) and per document (*document-level* classification). In author-level classification, one document contains all the blog entries written by one author. In document-level classification, one document contains one blog entry. For both experiments, data are divided into a training and a testing set. In document-level classification, documents written by the authors in the training set do not appear in the test set, and thus none of the authors have their documents in both training and testing sets. The number of documents are summarized in Table 2.

Classification is performed using Multinomial NaiveBayes (NB), Linear Support Vector Machines (SVM), and Logistic Regression (LR) in scikit-learn (Pedregosa et al., 2011). Multinominal NB is used with the default alpha value (alpha=1.0), and SVM and LR classifiers are both used with the default regularization value (C=1). Univariate and model-based feature selection is performed for each experiment. In univariate feature selection, features that are above the 75 percentile are chosen. For model-based feature selection, SVM and LR, both with penalty of L1 and C=1 are used to select features with non-zero coefficients.

3.4 Features

3.4.1 Character *n*-grams

The first feature set is character *n*-grams. Character n-grams worked well in other languages as discussed in Section 2, and they provide a generic cross-linguistic way of getting at morphological units. To test the effects of the writing system, two types of character *n*-grams, Japanese character *n*-grams and Romanized Japanese *n*-grams, are used. Japanese has three types symbols (hiragana, katakana, and kanji (Chinese characters)), and thus one word could be written in several ways. For example, the word *kawaii* "cute" could be written all in hiragana or katakana, or combination of hiragana and katakana, or combination of kanji and hiragana. Without Romanization, all of them would be treated differently despite their shared meaning. However, Romanization can also collapse words that are pronounced the same but written differently with different meanings. *hashi* can mean "chopsticks", "bridge", and "edge" depending on which Chinese characters are used and in what context they are used. To experiment with Romanized Japanese character *n*-grams, Japanese characters are converted to Romaji (Roman alphabets) using jConverter[4]. The value of *n* ranges between 1 and 10, and only features of one *n* value are used as features in one experiment, and features of different values of *n* are not combined together, to avoid the number of features from becoming too large. For instance, an experiment with trigrams only uses trigram features.

3.4.2 Token *n*-grams

The next feature set is token *n*-grams with varying values of n (1-10). Tokens retain inflections and conjugation, so token *n*-grams represent syntactic properties of written text. The Japanese text is tokenized with Cabocha (Kudo and Matsumoto, 2002), as Japanese does not use a space to indicate word boundaries.

---

[4]`http://jprocessing.readthedocs.io/en/latest/#id2`

	Author			Document		
Features	NB	SVM	LR	NB	SVM	LR
CharUni	68.2	54.5	54.5	65.3	63.8	67.2
CharUni+FS	63.6 (U)	68.2 (U)	68.2 (U)	65.6 (U)	65.9 (L)	67.2 (L)
CharN(n)	81.8 (3)	59.1 (5)	54.5 (3)	70.0 (3)	69.7 (10)	70.3 (7)
CharN+FS	**86.4 (U)**	59.1 (U)	72.7 (U)	**75.5 (U)**	73.4 (U)	75.2 (U)
RomUni	56.5	52.5	69.6	50.2	56.8	56.8
RomUni+FS	65.2 (L)	60.9 (S)	69.6 (L)	52.6 (L)	57.1 (L)	57.1 (S)
RomN(n)	82.6 (5)	60.9 (3)	78.3 (2)	71.6 (5)	68.3 (8)	70.4 (8)
RomN+FS	**82.6 (U)**	60.9 (L,U)	65.2 (L,S)	**71.9 (U)**	68.9 (U)	70.7 (U)

Table 3: Accuracies (%) for character n-grams. CharUni and CharN: Japanese character uni- and n-grams. RomUni and RomN: Romanized character uni- and n-grams. FS:Feature Selection. The value in parentheses indicates the best value of n for n-gram and a method for feature selection (L:Logistic Regression, S:SVM, U:Univariate)

	Author			Document		
	NB	SVM	LR	NB	SVM	LR
TokenUni	**86.4**	54.5	59.1	63.2	58.9	62.0
TokenUni+FS	**86.4 (U)**	72.7 (U)	72.7 (U)	64.8 (L)	62.6 (S)	65.1 (S)
TokenN (n)	77.3 (2)	54.5 (8)	59.1 (2)	66.0 (2)	63.2 (3)	66.7 (3)
TokenN+FS	81.8 (U)	72.7 (S)	81.8 (U)	65.7 (U)	**68.8 (U)**	67.3 (U)

Table 4: Accuracies (%) for Token and Token n-grams. The value in parentheses indicates the value of n for n-grams or model of feature selection (L:Logistic Regression, S:SVM, U:Univariate)

3.4.3 Lemmas and selected lemmas

The next feature set is lemmas. As lemmatization suppresses inflections, lemmas represent use of words regardless of their form in a sentence. Given this semantic nature and the results of token n-grams (Section 4.2), we only examine lemma unigrams. In addition, certain types of words may convey more relevant information than others, and thus in order to find whether certain categories of words are more informative in classification, POS categories are used to extract groups of words. First, words are POS-tagged with Cabocha (Kudo and Matsumoto, 2002), and words from each POS category (e.g. Noun) are used as features. Then, all possible combinations of 13 POS categories (Noun, Verb, Auxiliary, Adverb, Adjective, Particle, Symbol, Filler, Rentaishi[5], Conjunction, Affix, Interjection, Other) are created and a feature set containing words from each set of combined POS categories is evaluated.

4 Results

4.1 Character n-grams

The accuracy scores for Japanese character n-grams and Romanized character n-grams are summarized in Table 3. Selected trigrams (97,992 features) achieved an accuracy of 86.4% with NB in author-level classification. Trigrams selected by univariate feature selection (114,303 features) worked best for the document-level classification, resulting in 75.5% accuracy. Romaji n-grams achieved similar accuracies, but they were below Japanese character n-grams.

4.2 Token n-grams

Table 4 shows the results of classification with token n-grams as features. Token unigrams with the NB classifier yielded 86.4% with (14,656 features) or without feature selection (10,992 features) in author-level classification, which was the same accuracy as the model with selected character trigrams. For the document-level classification, SVM with selected token trigrams (124,528 features) worked the best (68.8%) though it was not as good as the accuracy obtained from character trigrams.

---

[5]*Rentaishi* is a category of words that are not adjectives but modify nouns.

	Author			Document		
	NB	SVM	LR	NB	SVM	LR
Lemma	81.8	50.0	59.1	66.8	57.8	60.7
Lemma+FS	81.8 (U)	68.2 (L)	77.3 (U)	68.1 (U)	63.6 (U)	64.2 (L)
POS feature	V,Adv	N,Adv, Ren	N,Adv,Ren, Sym,Fill	Adj,Aux, V,Ren	Aux,V, Ren	Aux,V, Ren,Fill
POS	**95.5**	77.3	81.8	**69.0**	64.5	63.6
POS+FS	**95.5** (U)	90.9 (L)	86.4 (S)	67.4 (U)	67.1 (L)	67.4 (L)

Table 5: Accuracies (%) for lemmas and lemmas of POS categories with the highest accuracy. The character in parentheses shows a model of feature selection (L:Logistic Regression, S:SVM, U:Univariate)

		Depressed		Non-Depressed
Verb	*iru*	"there is (someone)"	*agaru*	"go up"
	naru	"become"	*aru*	"there is (something)"
	dekiru	"can do"	*wakaru*	"understand"
	suru	"do"	*yaru*	"do"
	kangaeru	"think"	*motsu*	"have"
	tsukareru	"get tired"	*yomu*	"read"
	shinu	"die"	*yaru*	"do"
Adv	*nandaka*	"somehow"	*itsumo*	"always"
	sukoshi	"a little"	*maa*	"relatively"

Table 6: Some selected verbs and adverbs.

4.3 Lemmas and Selected Lemmas

The accuracy score for each classifier with the lemma feature set is shown in Table 5. The NB classifier resulted in the highest accuracy of 95.5% with verbs and adverbs as features (2,627 features). After feature selection within the set of verbs and adverbs (2,007 features), the accuracy stayed the same. With different set of features, the SVM achieved 90.9% accuracy after further feature selection. For document-level classification, the highest accuracy was 69.0% with selected lemmas of four POS categories (2,579 features). Even though the accuracy improved from the baseline, it did worse than the character *n*-grams. Some of the selected lemmas from the best resulting author-level classification are shown in Table 6. Words that appear more frequently in one class are listed under that class.

5 Discussion

5.1 Classification and features

In all the experiments, author-level classification is better than document-level classification. This may be because each document contains around 200 words in document-level classification, and many features may not appear in one document, leaving feature vectors sparse.

Lemmas of verb and adverb categories give the best accuracy for the author-level classification. This suggests that frequency of words, regardless of their inflection or the surrounding context, is most useful when provided with sufficient amount of text. Although some of the selected lemmas are related to symptoms of depression (fatigue, suicidal thoughts), lemmas appearing frequently in depressed authors' documents are not necessarily related to emotions or mood (e.g. somehow, always). This suggests that there are subtle differences in choice of words by depressed authors which we may not immediately associate with depression.

Morphological and syntactic information such as inflection and word order, may be useful, but they do not provide accuracies that are as good as lemmas in the author-level classification. However, the experiment with character trigrams results into having the best accuracies for the document-level classification. This is likely because within a limited amount of text, character *n*-grams appear more often than lemmas. Romanizing characters do not improve the performance. Representing Japanese language with Romaji suppresses homonyms and *kanji* that may otherwise

	Author		Document	
	Before	After	Before	After
CharUni	81.8 (NB)	68.2 (NB)	75.3 (LR)	67.2 (LR)
TokenUni	72.7 (NB)	86.4 (NB)	71.5 (LR)	63.2 (NB)
LemmaUni	72.7 (NB)	81.8 (NB)	71.5 (LR)	66.8 (NB)

Table 7: Accuracies before and after topic modeling

be informative (see Section 3.4.1).

5.2 Topic bias

We now take a closer look at the effect of topic bias, i.e., we compare the results when the entries on depression have been removed (see Section 3.2 for details) to the condition when these entries are kept in the training and the test set. The latter condition corresponds to the settings that have been used by Matsumoto et al. (2012). The classification on the document-level with the full data set does worse than the classification with the cleaned data (see Table 7). This is expected because topic bias is factored out after topic-modeling. However, on the author-level, it is a more complex picture: for word-based units (token and lemma), accuracy actually goes up once topic bias is removed. As a blog entry tends to focus on one topic, and depressed authors' documents contain more words about depression, the document-level classification seems to be affected by the topic. We will investigate why the author-level classification improves with the cleaned data in future work.

6 Conclusion and Future work

This study showed that selected lemmas can predict whether authors of written texts are depressed or not with an accuracy of 95.5%. This is higher than Matsumoto et al. (2012) though it is difficult to compare because of different data sets. The better performance of author-level classification suggests that documents should contain enough text to be classified correctly. The next step will involve finding out how much text per document is necessary to achieve such high accuracy.

As the current study only tested default parameters for SVM and LR in classification and feature selection, different parameter settings will be tested in the future work.

As the study is small-scale, it is necessary to examine how the results extend to larger data. Moreover, expanding the scope of study to other mental conditions may reveal the nature of language use in relation to mental health. Further investigation of selected lemmas in connection with clinical studies may provide us insights on why these words work well as features.

Finally, the methods of the current study can easily be adapted to other languages with different character systems if a language can be tokenized and POS-tagged. It would be worth exploring how depression can be detected from texts in different languages and performing a cross-linguistic comparison of characteristics found in depressed authors' writings.

References

Yoram Bachrach, Michal Kosinski, Thore Graepel, Pushmeet Kohli, and David Stillwell. 2012. Personality and patterns of facebook usage. In *Proceedings of the 4th Annual ACM Web Science Conference*. ACM, pages 24–32.

Jennifer Golbeck, Cristina Robles, Michon Edmondson, and Karen Turner. 2011. Predicting personality from twitter. In *Privacy, Security, Risk and Trust (PASSAT) and 2011 IEEE Third Inernational Conference on Social Computing (SocialCom), 2011 IEEE Third International Conference on*. IEEE, pages 149–156.

Junko Kitanaka. 2012. *Depression in Japan: Psychiatric cures for a society in distress*. Princeton University Press.

Taku Kudo and Yuji Matsumoto. 2002. Japanese dependency analysis using cascaded chunking. In *CoNLL 2002: Proceedings of the 6th Conference on Natural Language Learning 2002 (COLING 2002 Post-Conference Workshops)*. pages 63–69.

Kazuyuki Matsumoto, Nobuhiro Yoshioka, Kenji Kita, and Fuji Ren. 2012. Utsu key phrase to kanjo hyogen hendo ni motozuku blog kara no utsu kensyutsu syuho. *The Association for Natural Language Processing 18th Conference Proceedings* pages 1126–1129.

Andrew Kachites McCallum. 2002. Mallet: A machine learning for language toolkit. Http://mallet.cs.umass.edu.

John Noecker, Michael Ryan, and Patrick Juola. 2013. Psychological profiling through textual analysis. *Literary and Linguistic Computing* 28(3):382–387.

F. Pedregosa, G. Varoquaux, A. Gramfort, V. Michel, B. Thirion, O. Grisel, M. Blondel, P. Prettenhofer, R. Weiss, V. Dubourg, J. Vanderplas, A. Passos, D. Cournapeau, M. Brucher, M. Perrot, and E. Duchesnay. 2011. Scikit-learn: Machine learning in Python. *Journal of Machine Learning Research* 12:2825–2830.

Francisco Rangel, Paolo Rosso, Martin Potthast, Martin Trenkmann, Benno Stein, Ben Verhoeven, Walter Daeleman, et al. 2014. Overview of the 2nd author profiling task at pan 2014. In *CEUR Workshop Proceedings*. CEUR Workshop Proceedings, volume 1180, pages 898–927.

Ruchita Sarawgi, Kailash Gajulapalli, and Yejin Choi. 2011. Gender attribution: tracing stylometric evidence beyond topic and genre. In *Proceedings of the Fifteenth Conference on Computational Natural Language Learning*. Association for Computational Linguistics, pages 78–86.

Hiroki Sato. 2011. Japanese dictionary of appraisal - attitude- (jappraisal dictionary). *JAppraisal Dictionary ver1* .

World Health Organization. 2017. Depression. http://www.who.int/mediacentre/factsheets/fs369/en/.

Fast Forward through Opportunistic Incremental Meaning Representation Construction

Petr Babkin
Rensselaer Polytechnic Institute
Troy, New York
babkip@rpi.edu

Sergei Nirenburg
Rensselaer Polytechnic Institute
Troy, New York
nirens@rpi.edu

Abstract

One of the challenges semantic parsers face involves upstream errors originating from pre-processing modules such as ASR and syntactic parsers, which undermine the end result from the get go. We report the work in progress on a novel incremental semantic parsing algorithm that supports simultaneous application of independent heuristics and facilitates the construction of partial but potentially actionable meaning representations to overcome this problem. Our contribution to this point is mainly theoretical. In future work we intend to evaluate the algorithm as part of a dialogue understanding system on state of the art benchmarks.

1 Introduction

The versatility of human language comprehension overshadows countless transient failures happening under the hood. At various points during a conversation we are bound to tolerate error and uncertainty: coming either from the speech itself (e.g., disfluencies, omissions) or resulting from our own mistakes and deficiencies as a hearer (e.g., misinterpretation of an ambiguous utterance due to incomplete knowledge, etc.). The entire process is an ever recurring cycle of gap filling, error recovery and proactive re-evaluation. Better yet, some of the arising issues we choose not to resolve completely — leaving room for underspecification and residual ambiguity, or abandoning altogether. Similarly, we are highly selective with respect to material to attend to, glancing over the bits deemed of only minor relevance or redundant.

We believe incrementality and opportunism to be key to achieving this type of behavior in a computational NLU system. Incremental construction of meaning representations allows for their contin-

uous refinement and revision with gradually accumulating evidence. In addition, it gives the system an opportunity to make meta-level decisions of whether to pursue analysis of further material and/or to a greater depth; or to satisfice with a partial meaning representation built so far — thereby reducing the amount of work and avoiding potentially problematic material.

By opportunism we refer to the ability to simultaneously engage all available sources of decision making heuristics (morphological, syntactic, semantic, and pragmatic knowledge) as soon as their individual preconditions are met. On one hand, this provides a degree of independence among the knowledge sources such that a failure of any one of them does not necessarily undermine the success of the process as a whole. On the other hand, opportunistic application of heuristics facilitates the construction of partial or underspecified meaning representations when their complete versions are infeasible to obtain.

As a step towards incorporating these principles in an NLU system, we present a novel opportunistic incremental algorithm for semantic parsing. The rest of the paper is organized as follows. In the following section, we will introduce our approach while providing necessary background. Next, we will work through an example derivation, highlighting some of the features of the algorithm. Then, in the discussion section, we will position this work in the context of related work in the field, as well as within our own research agenda. Finally, we will conclude with the progress to date and plans for the evaluation.

2 Approach

2.1 Framework

Our description will be grounded within the theoretico-computational framework of Ontological Semantics (OntoSem) — a cognitively inspired

Proceedings of the 55th Annual Meeting of the Association for Computational Linguistics- Student Research Workshop, pages 114–119
Vancouver, Canada, July 30 - August 4, 2017. ©2017 Association for Computational Linguistics
https://doi.org/10.18653/v1/P17-3019

and linguistically motivated knowledge-rich account of NLU and related cognitive processes (McShane and Nirenburg, 2016).

The goal of the algorithm we are presenting in this paper is to build meaning representations of text (TMRs) in an incremental and opportunistic fashion. As a source of building blocks for the TMRs we will use the OntoSem lexicon and ontology. The lexicon provides a bridge between surface forms (e.g., word lemmas, multi-word expressions, or phrasals) and their corresponding semantic types (called concepts), while the ontology encodes the relationships among concepts, such as case roles defined on them. In addition, OntoSem provides accounts of modality, reference, temporal relations, and speech acts, which become part of the search space for our algorithm. A meaning representation in OntoSem is denoted as a collection of numbered frames with key-value entries called slots. An example of such a TMR corresponding to the natural language utterance "Apply pressure to the wound!" is shown below:

```
REQUEST-ACTION-1
    agent HUMAN-1
    theme APPLY-1
    beneficiary HUMAN-2
APPLY-1
    agent HUMAN-2
    instrument PRESSURE-1
    theme WOUND-INJURY-1
```

The root of this TMR is an instance of the REQUEST-ACTION speech act evoked by the imperative mood of the utterance. The agent (requester) of this speech act is the implied speaker of the utterance. The beneficiary (or patient, in other semantic formalisms) is the implied addressee of this message. Next, the theme of the speech act (the action being requested) is an instance of the APPLY event defined in the ontology. The agent of the action requested is specified to be the same as the addressee. The instrument is specified to be an instance of PRESSURE. Finally, the theme (or target) of the requested action references some known instance of a WOUND-INJURY, either introduced earlier in text, or contained in the common ground of the interlocutors.

2.2 Algorithm

A TMR can be represented as a (possibly rooted) graph $G = (V, E)$, where the set of vertices V represents semantic instances and the set of edges E

denotes case role linkings among them. We can thus formulate our problem generally as that of producing a pair (V, E) for an input utterance u as a sequence of tokens $\langle u_1, u_2, ..., u_n \rangle$, so as to maximize some score: $\arg\max_{(V,E)} score(V, E)$.

The algorithm operates in two phases: the forward pass generates candidate solutions and the backward pass extracts the best scoring solution. The forward pass of the algorithm proceeds iteratively: by performing a series of incremental operations: $next$ and $link$, which we define in order. The basic data structure used is an abstract set S of items p_0 through p_n.

$next$ is defined as an incremental operation consuming one or more tokens from the input utterance $\langle u_1, u_2, ..., u_n \rangle$ and returning zero or more items p to be added to the set S.

$link$ operation is defined as accepting a set S_i and returning a new set S_{i+1} and a bipartite graph defined by $(S_i, S_{i+1}, L_{i+1,i})$, where $L_{i+1,i}$ is a set of edges between the two sets-partitions.

The following snippet provides a high level description of the execution of the forward pass of the algorithm.

```
function EXPAND(⟨u₁, u₂, ..., uₙ⟩)
    Sᵢ ← ∅
    initialize lattice C with tuple ⟨Sᵢ, ∅, ∅⟩
    while NO-ACTIONABLE-TMR(C) do
        if MORE-INPUT-NEEDED(C) then
            Sᵢ ← Sᵢ∪NEXT(⟨u₁, u₂, ..., uₙ⟩)
        else
            C ← C ∪ {LINK(Sᵢ)}
            Sᵢ ← Sᵢ₊₁
            if FIXED-POINT(C) then
                return ∅
            end if
        end if
    end while
    return C
end function
```

Expand in the name of the function refers to the fact that the lattice data structure used to store the candidate solutions is repeatedly expanded by the two incremental operations we just introduced. The *next* operation expands the width of the lattice by adding new elements to the set S_i, which can be thought of as a "layer" of the lattice. The *link* operation, expands the depth of the lattice by creating a new "layer" and connecting it to the elements of the previous layer. Intuitively, the process can be visualized diagonally as alternating horizontal and vertical expansions. The entire lattice can be thought of as a metaphorical "loom", on which meaning representations are "woven". The depth of the lattice is the depth of nesting in the corresponding meaning representation tree with a linear upper bound. In practice, however, we expect it to approach $O(log|U|)$ as most of the nesting occurs in multiple-argument instances.

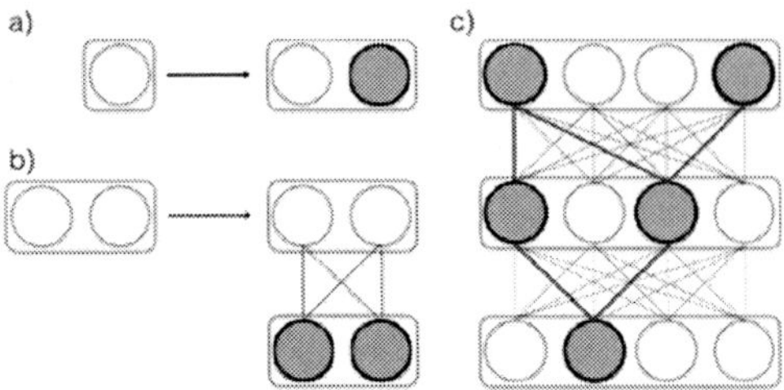

Figure 1: A schematic depiction of the incremental operations *next* (a), *link* (b), and the resulting lattice containing a solution (c).

The following conditionals are employed to control the execution flow of the main algorithm:

1. NO-ACTIONABLE-TMR captures high-level desiderata for execution continuation. In the current implementation the algorithm simply requires that the TMR is headed by an event and that its as well as its constituents' core roles (e.g., agent, theme) are filled; and that it spans all components of the input. Work is ongoing to operationalize pragmatic considerations for actionability, including whether a partial TMR is coherent with preceding discourse or is consistent with a known script, that could warrant early halting.

2. MORE-INPUT-NEEDED is triggered when there are no components to link despite the TMR being non-actionable.

3. FIXED-POINT basically means that further iteration does not produce any novel interpretations.

The subsequent solution extraction phase amounts to simply extracting TMR candidates from the lattice via depth-first traversal and ranking them by the cumulative scores of constituent nodes and edges. It should be noted that this procedure operates on a considerably reduced subset of the original search space as it effectively chooses among a limited set of viable candidates produced during the forward pass. Going a level deeper in our description, we will now turn to the implementation details of the incremental operations *next* and *link*.

The *next* operation translates the next word token (or a group of tokens) from the input utterance into corresponding semantic type that are then combined together into a TMR. It is currently realized as a basic lexical look-up by lemma, with greedy matching for multi-word expressions and non-semantically loaded tokens are skipped. For polysemous words, semantic representations for all variants are considered. While the OntoSem lexicon specifies a battery of syntactic and morphological constraints imposed on each word sense (e.g., syntactic dependencies they are expected to have — cf. McShane and Nirenburg (2016) for an in-depth overview), their application is deferred until the scoring stage as word sense disambiguation is pursued jointly, as part of meaning representation construction by the algorithm, rather than as a pre-processing stage.

The *link* operation is the core TMR-building routine of the algorithm.

---

function LINK(S_i)
    $S_{i+1} \leftarrow S_i$; $L_{i+i,i} \leftarrow \emptyset$
    for all argument taking p_j in S_{i+1} **do**
        $R_j \leftarrow$ CASE-ROLES(p_j)
        for all F in ALIGN(S_i, R_j) **do**
            $F \Leftrightarrow \{p_k \in S_i | \text{SAT}(p_k, r_{j,k} \in R_j)\}$
            yield$\langle j, k, r_{j,k}, \text{SCORE}(p_j, p_k, r_{j,k}) \rangle$
        end for
    end for
    return $(S_i, S_{i+1}, L_{i+1,i})$
end function

On each application, it considers a superposition of TMR fragments of depth 1 formed by the elements of the two adjacent partitions S_i and S_{i+i}. The set L_{i+1}^i is used to store edges connecting the elements of the two sets. For each argument-taking instance p_j in S_{i+1}, the function attempts to find alignments from roles R_j to instances $F \subset S_i$ that would satisfy their semantic constraints.

For each such alignment, the function yields the resulting edges as tuples containing the end point indices along with the corresponding case role label and link score. In addition to the already mentioned ranking of candidate meaning representations during the solution extraction phase, link scores can also be used to drive beam search during the forward pass to prune the search space on the fly. Scores are currently assigned based on a) how closely the filler matches the role's type constraint (inverse ontological distance) and b) whether the role matches the expected syntactic dependency specified for it in the lexicon. A large part of future work will involve incorporation of pragmatic heuristics including those based on coreference, coherence (e.g., prefer the role agent if a filler in question took on the that role in a series of events in preceding discourse), and knowledge of scripts, all of which we hypothesize especially crucial in situations with unreliable syntax.

The computational complexity of this operation is a little harder to estimate since it depends on variable numbers of word senses and corresponding case roles. Treating them as constant factors gives us quadratic worst-case complexity in the length of the utterance. A more accurate estimate can be obtained but the key point is that the overlapping representation of hypotheses with iterative deepening eliminates the branching factor of exhaustive permutation and results in polynomial rather than exponential order of complexity.

2.3 A Worked Example

We will now proceed with the derivation of the meaning representation for the example sentence.

Although the OntoSem lexicon specifies more fine grain senses of the words used, to keep the example simple, we will only consider a subset. Our description will follow the derivation in Table 1.

1. The algorithm initializes with the empty sets of semantic instances S and case roles links L.

2. Both NO-ACTIONABLE-TMR and MORE-INPUT-NEEDED conditions are triggered, invoking the *next* operation. The first token "Apply" has an instrumental sense e.g., "apply paint to the wall", but to introduce some degree of ambiguity we will also consider a phrasal sense as in "he needs to apply himself", having a meaning of the modality of type EFFORT.

3. At the next step, the conditions are triggered again since neither of the current head event candidates have their roles specified. The next token "pressure" instantiates two possible interpretations: literal, physical PRESSURE, and figurative i.e. "to be pressured to do something" translating into a modality of type POTENTIAL.

4. The currently disjoint TMR components (p_1, p_2, p_3, p_4) can now be connected via case

#	Op	u_z	$\Delta S_i, \Delta L^i_{i+1}$	C
1	*init*	$\emptyset$		$\emptyset$
2	*next*	Apply	p_1:APPLY, p_2:EFFORT	$p_1 \quad p_2$
3-4	*next*	pressure	p_3:PRESSURE, p_4:POTENTIAL	
	link		l^1_4, l^2_4, l^4_2:scope, l^3_1: instrument, theme	
5-6	*next*	wound	p_5:WOUND-INJURY	
	link		l^5_1:theme	
7-8	*next*	!	p_6:REQUEST-ACTION	
	link		l^1_6, l^2_6, l^4_6:theme	
9	*link*	n/a	$L^2_3 \leftarrow L^1_2 \setminus \{l^*_1\}$ $L^1_2 \leftarrow L^1_2 \setminus \{l^*_6\}$	
10	*extract*	n/a	p_6:REQUEST-ACTION — scope — p_1:APPLY, instrument — p_3:PRESSURE, theme — p_5:WOUND-INJURY	

Table 1: Example TMR derivation. The columns respectively indicate: operation performed, current token, instantiated concept or linked semantic role, and the visual representation of the solution lattice.

roles, which triggers the *link* operation, resulting in four compound TMR fragments: (APPLY instrument/theme PRESSURE), (EFFORT scope POTENTIAL), (POTENTIAL scope APPLY), (POTENTIAL scope EFFORT). The first interpretation has a role ambiguity to be resolved during the solution extraction phrase.

5. Neither of the TMR fragments are complete, still having unspecified roles, thereby triggering the *next* operation. The following token "wound" translates into p_8:WOUND-INJURY concept[1].

6. During the next iteration of linking p_8:WOUND-INJURY is employed as a theme of p_1:APPLY resulting in the (APPLY (instrument PRESSURE) (theme WOUND-INJURY)) TMR fragment.

7. The last token "!" confirms the imperative mood of the utterance, signaling the instantiation of the REQUEST-ACTION speech act.

8. The three TMR heads are then linked to the theme slot of of the REQUEST-ACTION instance.

9. Since none of the current fragments alone spans all of the components of the input despite their aggregate coverage, they need to be combined together through the creation of a new layer producing nested TMR fragments. Certain links have been pruned as not leading to novel solutions.

10. The termination condition is fulfilled as there now exists a complete TMR candidate accounting for all of the lexemes observed in the input. It is shown in the table both as a tree and as a highlighted fragment of the solution lattice.

3 Discussion & Related Work

Syntax plays a formidable role in the understanding of meaning. In a number of theories of semantics, important aspects such as case role alignment are determined primarily based on some syntactico-semantic interface such as in Lexical Functional Grammars (Ackerman, 1995), Combinatory Categorial Grammars (Steedman and Baldridge, 2011), or others. Some approaches have even gone as far as to cast the entire problem of semantic parsing as that of decorating a dependency parse (May, 2016). However, such tight coupling of semantics with syntax has its downsides. First, linguistic variation in the expression of the same meaning needs to be accounted for explicitly (e.g., by creating dedicated lexical senses

or production rules to cover all possible realizations). Second and more importantly, the feasibility of a semantic interpretation becomes conditional on the well-formedness of the language input and the correctness of the corresponding syntactic parse. This requirement seems unnecessarily strong considering a) human outstanding ability to make sense of ungrammatical and fragmented speech (Kong et al., 2014) and b) still considerably high error rates of ASR transcription and parsing (Roark et al., 2006).

The algorithm we present, by contrast, operates directly over the meaning representation space, while relying on heuristics of arbitrary provenance (syntax, reference, coherence, etc.) in its scoring mechanism for disambiguation and to steer the search process towards the promising region of the search space. This allows it to focus on exploring conceptually plausible interpretations while being less sensitive to upstream noise. The algorithm is opportunistic as the overlapping lattice representation allows it to simultaneously pursue multiple hypotheses, while the explicit evaluation of the candidates is deferred until a promising solution is found.

Incremental semantic parsing has come back to the forefront of NLU tasks (Peldszus and Schlangen, 2012), (Zhou et al., 2016). Accounting for incrementality helps to make dialogues more human-like by accommodating sporadic asynchronous feedback as well as corrections, wedged-in questions, etc. (Skantze and Schlangen, 2009). In addition, incrementality of meaning representation construction coupled with sensory grounding has been shown to help prune the search space and reduce ambiguity during semantic parsing (Kruijff et al., 2007). The presented algorithm is incremental as it proceeds via a series of operations gradually extending and deepening the lattice structure containing candidate solutions. The algorithm constantly re-evaluates its partial solutions and potentially produces an actionable TMR without exhaustive search over the entire input.

The design of the algorithm was influenced by the classical blackboard architecture (Carver and Lesser, 1992). Blackboard architectures offer significant benefits: they develop solutions incrementally by aggregating evidence; employ different sources of knowledge simultaneously; and entertain multiple competing or cooperating lines of

---

[1] Although a verbal sense is also conceivable, we will assume it has been ruled out by morphology.

reasoning concurrently. Some implementation details of our algorithm were inspired by the well-known Viterbi algorithm: e.g., forward and backward passes, solution scoring (Viterbi, 1967); as well as the relaxed planning graph heuristic from autonomous planning: namely, the lattice representation of partial solutions and the repeated simultaneous application of operators (Blum and Furst, 1995).

4 Conclusion & Future Work

The opportunistic and incremental algorithm we presented in this paper has the potential to improve the flexibility and robustness of meaning representation construction in the face of ASR noise, parsing errors, and unexpected input. This capability is essential for NLU results to approach true human capability (Peldszus and Schlangen, 2012). We implemented the algorithm and integrated it with non-trivial subsets of the current OntoSem's domain-general lexicon (9354 out of 17198 senses) and ontology (1708 concept realizations out of 9052 concepts) (McShane et al., 2016). Once fully integrated and tuned, we plan to formally evaluate the performance of the algorithm on a portion of the SemEval 2016 AMR parsing shared task dataset (May, 2016) while measuring the impact of parsing errors on the end TMR quality. In addition, it would be interesting to empirically quantify the utility of our proposed pragmatic heuristics in the domain of a task-oriented dialogue such as the Dialogue State Tracking Challenge (Williams et al., 2013).

Acknowledgements

This research was supported in part by Grant N00014-16-1-2118 from the U.S. Office of Naval Research and by the Cognitive and Immersive Systems Laboratory collaboration between Rensselaer Polytechnic Institute and IBM Research. We would also like to thank the three anonymous reviewers for their valuable feedback.

References

Farrell Ackerman. 1995. Lexical functional grammar. In Jef Verschuren, Jan-Ola Östman, and Jan Blommaert, editors, *Handbook of Pragmatics*, pages 346–350. John Benjamins, Amsterdam.

Avrim L. Blum and Merrick L. Furst. 1995: Fast planning through planning graph analysis. *Artificial Intelligence*, 90(1):1636–1642.

Norman Carver and Victor Lesser. 1992. The Evolution of Blackboard Control Architectures.

Lingpeng Kong, Nathan Schneider, Swabha Swayamdipta, Archna Bhatia, Chris Dyer, and Noah A. Smith. 2014. A Dependency Parser for Tweets.

Geert-Jan Kruijff, Pierre Lison, Trevor Benjamin, Henrik Jacobsson, and N. Hawes. 2007. Incremental, multi-level processing for comprehending situated dialogue in human-robot interaction. In *Language and Robots: Proceedings from the Symposium (LangRo'2007)*. University of Aveiro, 12.

Jonathan May. 2016. SemEval-2016 Task 8: Meaning Representation Parsing.

Marjorie McShane and Sergei Nirenburg. 2016. Decisions for semantic analysis in cognitive systems.

Marjorie McShane, Sergei Nirenburg, and Stephen Beale. 2016. Language understanding with ontological semantics.

Andreas Peldszus and David Schlangen. 2012. Incremental Construction of Robust but Deep Semantic Representations for Use in Responsive Dialogue Systems. In Eva Hajiov, editor, *Proceedings of the Coling Workshop on Advances in Discourse Analysis and its Computational Aspects*.

Brian Roark, Mary Harper, Eugene Charniak, Bonnie Dorr, Mark Johnson, Jeremy G. Kahn, Yang Liu, Mari Ostendorf, John Hale, Anna Krasnyanskaya, Matthew Lease, Izhak Shafran, Matthew Snover, Robin Stewart, and Lisa Yung. 2006. Sparseval: Evaluation metrics for parsing speech.

Gabriel Skantze and David Schlangen. 2009. Incremental dialogue processing in a micro-domain. In *Proceedings of the 12th Conference of the European Chapter of the Association for Computational Linguistics*, EACL '09, pages 745–753, Stroudsburg, PA, USA. Association for Computational Linguistics.

Mark Steedman and Jason Baldridge, 2011. *Combinatory Categorial Grammar*, pages 181–224. Wiley-Blackwell.

Andrew Viterbi. 1967. Error bounds for convolutional codes and an asymptotically optimum decoding algorithm. *IEEE Transactions on Information Theory*, 13(2):260–269, April.

Jason Williams, Antoine Raux, Deepak Ramach, and Alan Black. 2013. The dialog state tracking challenge. In *In Proceedings of the 14th Annual Meeting of the Special Interest Group on Discourse and Dialogue SIGDIAL*.

Junsheng Zhou, Feiyu Xu, Hans Uszkoreit, Weiguang Qu, Ran Li, and Yanhui Gu. 2016. AMR parsing with an incremental joint model. In *EMNLP*.

Modeling Situations in Neural Chat Bots

Shoetsu Sato
The University of Tokyo
`shoetsu@tkl.iis.u-tokyo.ac.jp`

Naoki Yoshinaga
Institute of Industrial Science,
the University of Tokyo
`ynaga@tkl.iis.u-tokyo.ac.jp`

Masashi Toyoda
Institute of Industrial Science,
the University of Tokyo
`toyoda@tkl.iis.u-tokyo.ac.jp`

Masaru Kitsuregawa
Institute of Industrial Science,
the University of Tokyo
National Institute of Informatics
`kitsure@tkl.iis.u-tokyo.ac.jp`

Abstract

Social media accumulates vast amounts
of online conversations that enable data-
driven modeling of chat dialogues. It is,
however, still hard to utilize the neural
network-based SEQ2SEQ model for dialogue modeling in spite of its acknowledged success in machine translation. The
main challenge comes from the high degrees of freedom of outputs (responses).
This paper presents neural conversational
models that have general mechanisms for
handling a variety of situations that affect
our responses. Response selection tests on
massive dialogue data we have collected
from Twitter confirmed the effectiveness
of the proposed models with situations derived from utterances, users or time.

1 Introduction

The increasing amount of dialogue data in social
media has opened the door to data-driven modeling of non-task-oriented, or chat, dialogues (Ritter et al., 2011). The data-driven models assume
a response generation as a sequence to sequence
mapping task, and recent ones are based on neural
SEQ2SEQ models (Vinyals and Le, 2015; Shang
et al., 2015; Li et al., 2016a,b; Xing et al., 2017).
However, the adequacy of responses generated by
these neural models is somewhat insufficient, in
contrast to the acknowledged success of the neural
SEQ2SEQ models in machine translation (Johnson
et al., 2016).

The contrasting outcomes in machine translation and chat dialogue modeling can be explained

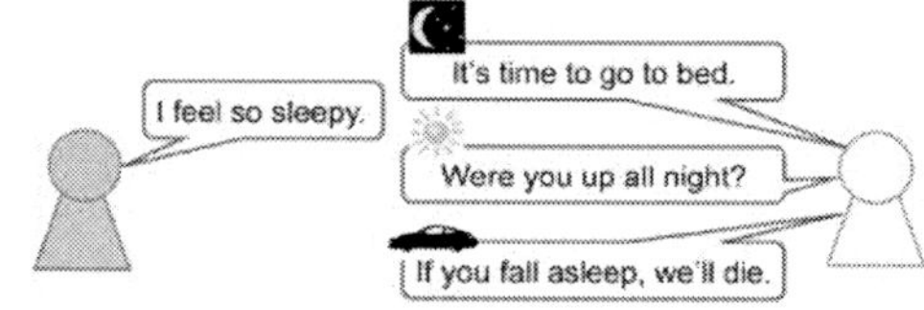

Figure 1: Conversational situations and responses.

by the difference in the degrees of freedom on output for a given input. An appropriate response
to a given utterance is not monolithic in chat dialogue. Nevertheless, since only one ground truth
response is provided in the actual dialogue data,
the supervised systems will hesitate when choosing from the vast range of possible responses.

So, how do humans decide how to respond? We
converse with others while (implicitly) considering not only the utterance but also other various
conversational situations (§ 2) such as time, place,
and the current context of conversation and even
our relationship with the addressee. For example,
when a friend says "I feel so sleepy." in the morn-
ing, a probable response could be "Were you up
all night?" (Figure 1). If the friend says the same
thing at midnight, you might say "It's time to go
to bed." Or if the friend is driving a car with you,
you might answer "If you fall asleep, we'll die."

Modeling situations behind conversations has
been an open problem in chat dialogue modeling,
and this difficulty has partly forced us to focus
on task-oriented dialogue systems (Williams and
Young, 2007), the response of which has a low degree of freedom thanks to domain and goal specificity. Although a few studies have tried to exploit
conversational situations such as speakers' emo-

Proceedings of the 55th Annual Meeting of the Association for Computational Linguistics- Student Research Workshop, pages 120–127
Vancouver, Canada, July 30 - August 4, 2017. ©2017 Association for Computational Linguistics
https://doi.org/10.18653/v1/P17-3020

tions (Hasegawa et al., 2013) or personal characteristics (Li et al., 2016b) and topics (Xing et al., 2017), the methods are specially designed for and evaluated using specific types of situations.

In this study, we explore neural conversational models that have general mechanisms to incorporate various types of situations behind chat conversations (§ 3.2). These models take into account situations on the speaker's side and the addressee's side (or those who respond) when encoding utterances and decoding its responses, respectively. To capture the conversational situations, we design two mechanisms that differ in how strong of an effect a given situation has on generating responses.

In experiments, we examined the proposed conversational models by incorporating three types of concrete conversational situations (§ 2): utterance, speaker/addressee (profiles), and time (season), respectively. Although the models are capable of generating responses, we evaluate the models with a response selection test to avoid known issues in automatic evaluation metrics of generated responses (Liu et al., 2016a). Experimental results obtained using massive dialogue data from Twitter showed that modeling conversational situations improved the relevance of responses (§ 4).

2 Conversational situations

Various types of conversational situations could affect our response (or initial utterance) to the addressee. Since neural conversational models need massive data to train a reliable model, our study investigates conversational situations that are naturally given or can be identified in an unsupervised manner to make the experimental settings feasible.

In this study, we represent conversational situations as discrete variables. That allows models to handle unseen situations in testing by classifying them into appropriate situation types via distributed representations or the like as described below, and helps to analyze the outputs. We consider the following conversational situations to each utterance and response in our dialogue dataset (§ 4), and cluster the situations to assign specific situation types to the utterances and responses in the training data of our conversational models.

Utterance The input utterance (to be responded to by the system) is a primary conversational situation and is already modeled by the encoder in the neural SEQ2SEQ model. However, we may be able to induce a different aspect of situations that

are represented in the utterance but are not captured by the SEQ2SEQ sequential encoder (Sato et al., 2016). We first represent each utterance of utterance-response pairs in our dialogue dataset by a distributed representation obtained by averaging word2vec[1] vectors (pre-trained from our dialogue datasets (§ 4.1)) for words in the utterances. The utterances are then classified by k-means clustering to identify utterance types.[2]

User (profiles) User characteristics should affect his/her responses as Li et al. (2016b) have already discussed. We classify profiles provided by each user in our dialogue dataset (§ 4.1) to acquire conversational situations specific to the speakers and addressees. The same as with the input utterance, we first construct a distributed representation of each user's profile by averaging the pre-trained word2vec vectors for verbs, nouns and adjectives in the user profiles. The users are then classified by k-means clustering to identify user types.[3]

Time (season) Our utterances can be affected by when we speak as illustrated in § 1, so we adopted time as one conversational situation. On the basis of timestamp of the utterance and the response in our dataset, we split the conversation data into four season types: namely, spring (Mar. – May.), summer (Jun. – Aug), autumn (Sep. – Nov.), and winter (Dec. – Feb.). This splitting reflects the climate in Japan since our data are in Japanese whose speakers mostly live in Japan.

In training our neural conversational models, we use each of the above conversational situation types for the speaker side and addressee (who respond) side, respectively. Note that the utterance situation is only considered for the speaker side since its response is unseen in response generation. In testing, the conversational situation types for input utterances (or speaker and addressee's profiles) are identified by finding the closest centroid obtained by the k-means clustering of the utterances (profiles) in the training data.

3 Method

Our neural conversational models are based on the SEQ2SEQ model (Sutskever et al., 2014) and integrate mechanisms to incorporate various conversa-

---

[1] https://code.google.com/p/word2vec/

[2] We set k to 10. Although the space limitations preclude results when varying k, this does not affect our conclusions.

[3] We set k to 10, and add another cluster for users whose profiles were not available (6.3% of the users in our datasets).

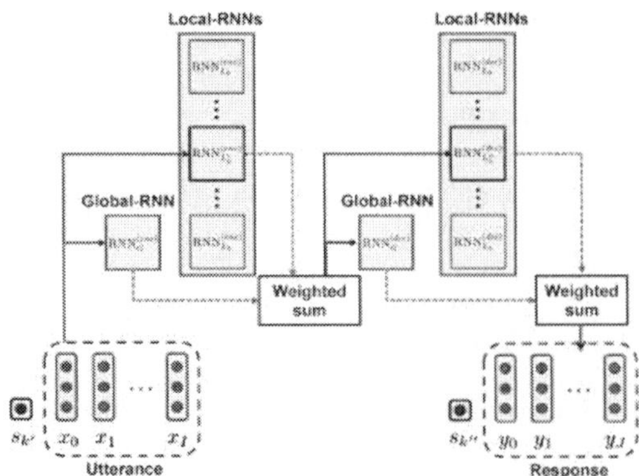

Figure 2: Local-global SEQ2SEQ.

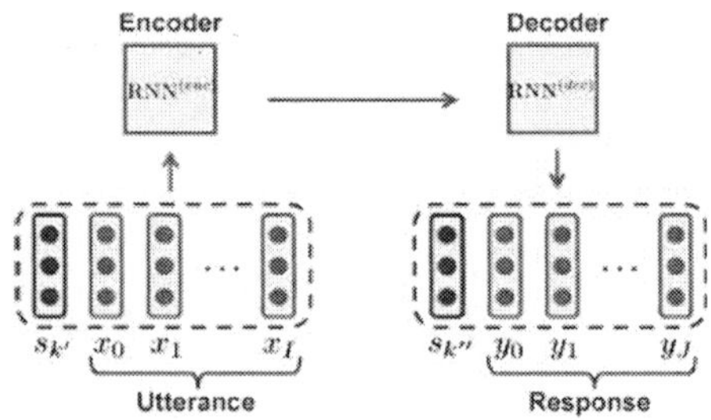

Figure 3: SEQ2SEQ with situation embeddings.

tional situations (§ 2) at speaker side and addressee side. In the following, we briefly introduce the SEQ2SEQ conversational model (Vinyals and Le, 2015) and then describe two mechanisms for incorporating conversational situations.

3.1 SEQ2SEQ conversational model

The SEQ2SEQ conversational model (Vinyals and Le, 2015) consists of two recurrent neural networks (RNNs) called an encoder and a decoder. The encoder takes each word of an utterance as input and encodes the input sequence to a real-valued vector representing the utterance. The decoder then takes the encoded vector as its initial state and continues to generate the most probable next word and to input the word to itself until it finally outputs EOS.

3.2 Situation-aware conversational models

The challenge in designing situation-aware neural conversational models is how to inject given conversational situations into RNN encoders or decoders. In this paper, we present two situation-aware neural conversational models that differ in how strong of an effect a given situation has.

3.2.1 Local-global SEQ2SEQ

Motivated by a recent success in multi-task learning for a deep neural network (Liu et al., 2016c,b; Gupta et al., 2016; Luong et al., 2016), our local-global SEQ2SEQ trains two types of RNN encoder and decoder for modeling situation-specific dialogues and universal dialogues jointly (Figure 2).

Local-RNNs are meant to model dialogues in individual conversational situations at both the speaker and addressee sides. Each local-RNN is trained (i.e., its parameters are updated) only on

dialogues under the corresponding situation. A salient disadvantage of this modeling is that the size of training data given to each local-RNN decreases as the number of situation types increases.

To address this problem, we combine another global-RNN encoder and decoder trained on all the dialogue data and take the weighted sum of the hidden states hs of the two RNNs for both the encoder and decoder to obtain the output as:

$$h_i^{(enc)} = W_G^{(enc)} \text{RNN}_G^{(enc)}(h_{i-1}^{(enc)}, x_i) + $$
$$W_L^{(enc)} \text{RNN}_{L_{k'}}^{(enc)}(h_{i-1}^{(enc)}, x_i), \quad (1)$$
$$h_j^{(dec)} = W_G^{(dec)} \text{RNN}_G^{(dec)}(h_{j-1}^{(dec)}, y_{j-1}) + $$
$$W_L^{(dec)} \text{RNN}_{L_{k''}}^{(dec)}(h_{j-1}^{(dec)}, y_{j-1}), \quad (2)$$

where $\text{RNN}_G^{(\cdot)}(\cdot)$ and $\text{RNN}_L^{(\cdot)}(\cdot)$ denote global-RNN and local-RNN, respectively, and the Ws are trainable matrices for the weighted sum. The embedding and softmax layers of the RNNs are shared.

3.2.2 SEQ2SEQ with situation embeddings

The local-global SEQ2SEQ (§ 3.2.1) assumes that dialogues with different situations involve different domains (or tasks) that are independent of each other. However, this assumption could be too strong in some cases and thus we devise another weakly situation-aware conversational model.

We represent the given situations at speaker and addressee sides, $s_{k'}$ and $s_{k''}$, as situation embeddings and then feed them to the encoder and decoder prior to processing sequences (Figure 3) as:

$$h_0^{(enc)} = \text{RNN}(h_{init}, s_{k'}), \quad (3)$$
$$h_i^{(enc)} = \text{RNN}(h_{i-1}^{(enc)}, x_{i-1}), \quad (4)$$
$$h_0^{(dec)} = \text{RNN}(h_{I+1}^{(enc)}, s_{k''}), \quad (5)$$
$$h_j^{(dec)} = \text{RNN}(h_{j-1}^{(dec)}, y_{j-1}), \quad (6)$$

where h_{init} is a vector filled with zeros and $h_{I+1}^{(enc)}$ is the last hidden state of the encoder.

Average length in words (utterances)	15.7
Average length in words (responses)	10.1
Average length in words (user profiles)	37.4
Number of users	386,078

Table 1: Statistics of our dialogue datasets (training, validation, and test portions are merged here).

Vocabulary size	100,000
Dropout rate	0.25
Mini-batch size	800
Dimension of embedding vectors	100
Dimension of hidden states	100
Learning rate	1e-4
Number of samples in sampled softmax	512

Table 2: Hyperparameters for training.

This encoding was inspired by a neural machine translation system (Johnson et al., 2016) that enables multilingual translation with a single model. Whereas it inputs the target language embedding only to the encoder to control the target language, we input the speaker-side situation to the encoder and the addressee-side one to the decoder.

4 Evaluation

In this section, we evaluate our situation-aware neural conversational models on massive dialogue data obtained from Twitter. We compare our models (§ 3.2) with SEQ2SEQ baseline (§ 3.1) using a response selection test instead of evaluating generated responses, since Liu et al. (2016a) recently pointed out several problems of existing metrics such as BLEU (Papineni et al., 2002) for evaluating generated responses.

4.1 Settings

Data We built massive dialogue datasets from our Twitter archive that have been compiled since March, 2011. In this archive, timelines of about 1.5 million users[4] have been continuously collected with the official API. It is therefore suitable for extracting users' conversations in timelines.

On Twitter, a post (tweet) and a mention to it can be considered as an utterance-response pair. We randomly extracted 23,563,865 and 1,200,000 pairs from dialogues in 2014 as training and validation datasets, and extracted 6000 pairs in 2015 as a test dataset in accordance with the following procedure. Because we want to exclude utterances that need contexts in past dialogue exchanges to respond from our evaluation dataset, we restrict ourselves to only tweets that are not mentions to other tweets (in other words, utterances without past dialogue exchanges are chosen for evaluation). For each utterance-response pair in the test dataset, we randomly chose four (in total, 24,000) responses in 2015 as false response

candidates which together constitute five response candidates for the response selection test. Each utterance and response (candidate) is tokenized by MeCab[5] with NEologd[6] dictionary to feed the sequence to the word-based encoder decoder.[7] Table 1 shows statistics on our dialogue datasets.

Models In our experiments, we compare our situation-aware neural conversational models (we refer to the model in § 3.2.1 as **L/G SEQ2SEQ** and the model in § 3.2.2 as **SEQ2SEQ emb**) with situation-unaware **baseline** (§ 3.1) for taking each type of conversational situations (§ 2) into consideration. We also evaluate the model in § 3.2.1 without global-RNNs (referred to as **L SEQ2SEQ**) to observe the impact of global-RNNs.

We used a long-short term memory (LSTM) (Zaremba et al., 2014) as the RNN encoder and decoder, sampled softmax (Jean et al., 2015) to accelerate the training, and TensorFlow[8] to implement the models. Our LSTMs have three layers and are optimized by Adam (Kingma and Ba, 2015). The hyperparameters are fixed as in Table 2.

Evaluation procedure We use the above models to rank response candidates for a given utterance in the test set. We compute the averaged cross-entropy loss for words in each response candidate (namely, its perplexity) by giving the candidate following the input utterance to each conversational model, and used the resulting values for ranking candidates to choose top-k plausible ones. We adopt **1 in t P@k** (Wu et al., 2016) as the evaluation metric, which indicates the ratio of utterances that are provided the single ground truth in top k responses chosen from t candidates. Here we use **1 in 2 P@1**,[9] **1 in 5 P@1**, and **1 in 5 P@2**.

---

[4]Our collection started from 26 popular Japanese users in March 2011, and the user set has iteratively expanded to those who are mentioned or retweeted by already targeted users.

[5]http://taku910.github.io/mecab/

[6]https://github.com/neologd/mecab-ipadic-neologd

[7]The number of words in the utterances and the response candidates in the test set is limited to equal or less than 20, since very long posts do not constitute usual conversation.

[8]https://www.tensorflow.org/

[9]We randomly selected one false response candidate from the four pre-selected ones when $t = 2$.

Model	1 in 2 P@1	1 in 5 P@1	1 in 5 P@2
Baseline	64.5%	33.9%	56.6%
Situation: utterance			
L SEQ2SEQ	67.2%	37.2%	60.6%
L/G SEQ2SEQ	**68.5%**	**38.2%**	**62.1%**
SEQ2SEQ emb	65.6%	35.4%	58.2%
Situation: speaker/addressee (profiles)			
L SEQ2SEQ	67.3%	**38.0%**	60.9%
L/G SEQ2SEQ	66.4%	36.4%	59.2%
SEQ2SEQ emb	**67.8%**	37.5%	**61.1%**
Situation: time (season)			
L SEQ2SEQ	*62.0%*	*30.8%*	*54.8%*
L/G SEQ2SEQ	65.9%	35.8%	58.1%
SEQ2SEQ emb	**67.3%**	**37.6%**	**60.7%**

Table 3: Results of the response selection test.

4.2 Results

Table 3 lists the results of the response selection test. The proposed conversational models successfully improved the relevance of selected responses by incorporating conversational situations.

The proposed model that performed best is different depending on the situation type. We found from the dataset that many of the conversations did not seem to be affected by the seasons, that is, time (season) situation is less influential than other situations. This explains the poor performance of **L SEQ2SEQ** with time (season) situations due to the data sparseness in training local-RNNs, although the sparseness is mostly addressed by global RNNs in **L/G SEQ2SEQ**.

As stated in § 3.2.2, **L/G SEQ2SEQ** is expected to capture situations more strongly than **SEQ2SEQ emb**. To confirm this, we plotted scattergrams of the utterance vectors (Figure 4) and the user profile vectors (Figure 5) in the training data by using t-SNE (Maaten and Hinton, 2008). We provide cluster descriptions by manually looking into the content of the utterances and user profiles in each cluster. The descriptions are followed by ↗ if **L/G SEQ2SEQ** performed better than **SEQ2SEQ emb** in terms of 1 in 5 P@1 for test utterances with the corresponding situation type, by ↘ if the opposite and by → if comparable (differences are within ± 1.0%). Elements of clusters were randomly sampled.

L/G SEQ2SEQ tends to perform better for utterances with densely concentrated (or coherent) speaker profile clusters (Figure 5). This is because utterances given by the speakers in these coherent clusters (and the associate responses) have similar conversations, situations of which are captured by local-RNNs in the local-global SEQ2SEQ.

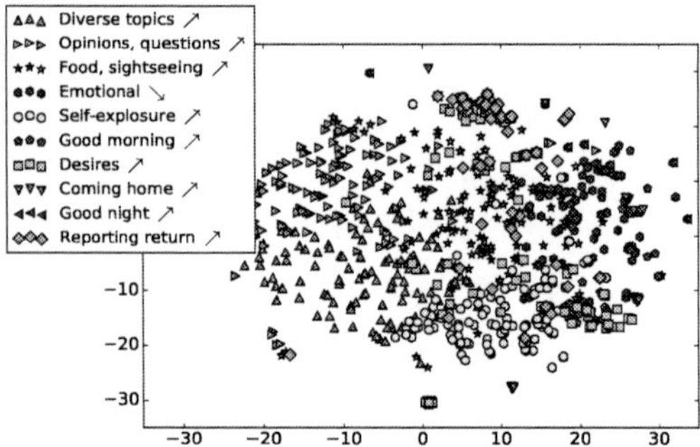

Figure 4: The scattergram of sampled utterance vectors visualized using t-SNE.

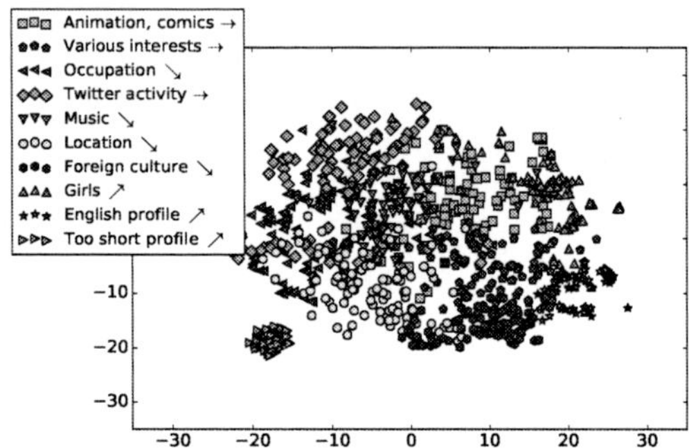

Figure 5: The scattergram of sampled user profile vectors visualized using t-SNE.

This explains the reason why **L/G SEQ2SEQ** outperformed the other situation-aware conversational models when utterance situations are considered (Figure 4). Conversations in the same clusters are naturally consistent, and conversations assigned to the same clusters form typical activities or specific tasks (*e.g.*, greetings, following other users, and questions (and answering)) in Twitter conversation. **L/G SEQ2SEQ**, designed as a kind of multi-task SEQ2SEQ, literally captures these task-specific behaviors in the conversations.

Although some utterance clusters have general conversations (*e.g.*, diverse topics), the response performances in those clusters have still improved. This is because these general clusters are free from harmful common responses that are quarantined into situation-specific clusters (*e.g.*, greetings etc.) and the corresponding local-RNNs should avoid generating those common responses. Note that this problem has been pointed out and addressed by Li et al. (2016a) in a totally different way.

Situation: utterance (opinions, questions)	
Input:	ちょっと最近BOTのフォロー多いんですけど (I've recently been followed by many bot accounts.)
Baseline	お疲れ様やで (You've gotta be tired.)
L/G SEQ2SEQ	ブロックしちゃいましょう (Let's block them.)
Situation: addressee profiles (girls)	
Input:	なに グラブル 始めてるんだ原稿しろ (Why am I starting Granblue Fantasy? I have to write the paper...)
Baseline	おい、大丈夫か？ (Hey, are you okay?)
SEQ2SEQ emb	フレンドなろ♡ (Let's be friends♡)
Situation: time (season) (summer)	
Input:	7月になって、流石にパーカーは暑くなってきた (July is too warm to wear a hoodie.)
Baseline	そうなんです! (Yes!)
SEQ2SEQ emb	まだ着てたの!? (Do you still wear one?)

Table 4: Responses selected by the systems.

Examples Table 4 lists the response candidate selected by the baseline and our models. As we had expected, the situation-aware conversational models are better at selecting ground-truth responses for situation-specific conversations.

5 Related Work

Conversational situations have been implicitly addressed by preparing datasets specific to the target situations and by solving the problem as a task-oriented conversation task (Williams and Young, 2007); examples include troubleshooting (Vinyals and Le, 2015), navigation (Wen et al., 2015), interviewing (Kobori et al., 2016), and restaurant search (Wen et al., 2017). In what follows, we introduce non-task-oriented conversational models that explicitly consider conversational situations.

Hasegawa et al. (2013) presented a conversational model that generates a response so that it elicits a certain emotion (*e.g.*, joy) in the addressee mind. Their model is based on statistical machine translation and linearly interpolates two conversational models that are trained from a small emotion-labeled dialogue corpus and a large non-labeled dialogue corpus, respectively. This model is similar to our local-global SEQ2SEQ but differs in that it has hyperparameters for the interpolation, whereas our local-global SEQ2SEQ automatically learns W_G and W_L from the training data.

Li et al. (2016b) proposed a neural conversational model that generates responses taking into consideration speakers' personalities such as gender or living place. Because they fed a specific speaker ID to their model and represent individual (known) speakers with embeddings, Their model cannot handle unknown speakers. In contrast, our model can consider any speakers with profiles because we represent each cluster of profiles with an embedding and find an appropriate profile type for the given profile by nearest-neighbor search.

Sordoni et al. (2015) encoded a given utterance and the past dialogue exchanges, and combined the resulting representations for RNN to decode a response. Zhao et al. (2017) used a conditional variational autoencoder and automatically-induced dialogue acts to handle discourse-level diversity in the encoder. While these sophisticated architectures are designed to take dialogue histories into consideration, our simple models can easily exploit various situations.

Recently, Xing et al. (2017) proposed to explicitly consider topics of utterances to generate topic-coherent responses. Although they used latent Dirichlet allocation while we use k-means clustering, both methods confirmed the importance of utterance situations. The way to obtain specific situations is still an open research problem. As demonstrated in this study, our primary contribution is the invention of neural mechanisms that can consider various conversational situations.

Our local-global SEQ2SEQ model is closely related to a many-to-many multi-task SEQ2SEQ proposed by Luong et al. (2016). The critical difference is in that their model assumes only local tasks, while our model assumes many local tasks (situation-specific dialogue modeling) and one global task (general dialogue modeling).

6 Conclusion

We proposed two situation-aware neural conversational models that have general mechanisms for handling various conversational situations represented by discrete variables: (1) local-global SEQ2SEQ that combines two SEQ2SEQ models (§ 3.2.1) to handle situation-specific dialogues and universal dialogues jointly, and (2) SEQ2SEQ with situation embeddings (§ 3.2.2) that feeds the situations directly to a SEQ2SEQ model. The response selection tests on massive Twitter datasets confirmed the effectiveness of using situations such as utterances, user (profiles), or time.

Acknowledgements This work was partially supported by JSPS KAKENHI Grant Number 16K16109 and 16H02905.

References

Pankaj Gupta, Hinrich Schütze, and Bernt Andrassy. 2016. Table filling multi-task recurrent neural network for joint entity and relation extraction. In *Proceedings of the 26th International Conference on Computational Linguistics (COLING-16)*. pages 2537–2547.

Takayuki Hasegawa, Nobuhiro Kaji, Naoki Yoshinaga, and Masashi Toyoda. 2013. Predicting and eliciting addressee's emotion in online dialogue. In *Proceedings of the 51st Annual Meeting of the Association for Computational Linguistics (ACL)*. pages 964–972.

Sébastien Jean, Kyunghyun Cho, Roland Memisevic, and Yoshua Bengio. 2015. On using very large target vocabulary for neural machine translation. In *Proceedings of the 53rd Annual Meeting of the Association for Computational Linguistics and the 7th International Joint Conference on Natural Language Processing (ACL-IJCNLP-16)*. pages 1–10.

Melvin Johnson, Mike Schuster, Quoc V Le, Maxim Krikun, Yonghui Wu, Zhifeng Chen, Nikhil Thorat, Fernanda Viégas, Martin Wattenberg, Greg Corrado, et al. 2016. Google's multilingual neural machine translation system: Enabling zero-shot translation. *arXiv preprint arXiv:1611.04558* .

Diederik Kingma and Jimmy Ba. 2015. Adam: A method for stochastic optimization. In *Proceedings of the third International Conference on Learning Representations (ICLR-15)*.

Takahiro Kobori, Mikio Nakano, and Tomoaki Nakamura. 2016. Small talk improves user impressions of interview dialogue systems. In *Proceedings of the 17th Annual Meeting of the Special Interest Group on Discourse and Dialogue (SIGDIAL-16)*. pages 370–380.

Jiwei Li, Michel Galley, Chris Brockett, Jianfeng Gao, and Bill Dolan. 2016a. A diversity-promoting objective function for neural conversation models. In *Proceedings of the 2016 Conference of the North American Chapter of the Association for Computational Linguistics: Human Language Technologies (NAACL-HLT-16)*. pages 110–119.

Jiwei Li, Michel Galley, Chris Brockett, Georgios P Spithourakis, Jianfeng Gao, and Bill Dolan. 2016b. A persona-based neural conversation model. In *Proceedings of the 54th Annual Meeting of the Association for Computational Linguistics (ACL-16)*. pages 994–1003.

Chia-Wei Liu, Ryan Lowe, Iulian Serban, Mike Noseworthy, Laurent Charlin, and Joelle Pineau. 2016a. How not to evaluate your dialogue system: An empirical study of unsupervised evaluation metrics for dialogue response generation. In *Proceedings of the 2016 Conference on Empirical Methods in Natural Language Processing (EMNLP-16)*. pages 2122–2132.

Pengfei Liu, Xipeng Qiu, and Xuanjing Huang. 2016b. Deep multi-task learning with shared memory for text classification. In *Proceedings of the 2016 Conference on Empirical Methods in Natural Language Processing (EMNLP-16)*. pages 118–127.

Pengfei Liu, Xipeng Qiu, and Xuanjing Huang. 2016c. Recurrent neural network for text classification with multi-task learning. In *Proceedings of the Twenty-Fifth International Joint Conference on Artificial Intelligence (IJCAI-16)*. pages 2873–2879.

Minh-Thang Luong, Quoc V. Le, Ilya Sutskever, Oriol Vinyals, and Lukasz Kaiser. 2016. Multi-task sequence to sequence learning. In *Proceedings of the fifth International Conference on Learning Representations (ICLR-16)*.

Laurens van der Maaten and Geoffrey Hinton. 2008. Visualizing data using t-sne. *Journal of Machine Learning Research* 9(Nov):2579–2605.

Kishore Papineni, Salim Roukos, Todd Ward, and Wei-Jing Zhu. 2002. Bleu: a method for automatic evaluation of machine translation. In *Proceedings of 40th Annual Meeting of the Association for Computational Linguistics (ACL-02)*. pages 311–318.

Alan Ritter, Colin Cherry, and William B Dolan. 2011. Data-driven response generation in social media. In *Proceedings of the 2011 Conference on Empirical Methods in Natural Language Processing (EMNLP-11)*. pages 583–593.

Shoetsu Sato, Naoki Yoshinaga Shonosuke Ishiwatari, Masashi Toyoda, and Masaru Kitsuregawa. 2016. UT dialogue system at NTCIR-12 STC. In *Proceedings of the 12th NTCIR Conference on Evaluation of Information Access Technologies*. pages 518–522.

Lifeng Shang, Zhengdong Lu, and Hang Li. 2015. Neural responding machine for short-text conversation. In *Proceedings of the 53rd Annual Meeting of the Association for Computational Linguistics and the 7th International Joint Conference on Natural Language Processing (ACL-IJCNLP-15)*. pages 1577–1586.

Alessandro Sordoni, Michel Galley, Michael Auli, Chris Brockett, Yangfeng Ji, Margaret Mitchell, Jian-Yun Nie, Jianfeng Gao, and Bill Dolan. 2015. A neural network approach to context-sensitive generation of conversational responses. In *Proceedings of the 2015 Conference of the North American Chapter of the Association for Computational Linguistics: Human Language Technologies (NAACL-HLT-15)*. pages 196–205.

Ilya Sutskever, Oriol Vinyals, and Quoc V. Le. 2014. Sequence to sequence learning with neural networks. In *Proceedings of the 27th International Conference on Neural Information Processing Systems (NIPS-14)*. pages 3104–3112.

Oriol Vinyals and Quoc V. Le. 2015. A neural conversational model. In *Proceedings of Deep Learning Workshop held at the 31st International Conference on Machine Learning (ICML-15)*.

Tsung-Hsien Wen, Milica Gasic, Nikola Mrkšić, Pei-Hao Su, David Vandyke, and Steve Young. 2015. Semantically conditioned lstm-based natural language generation for spoken dialogue systems. In *Proceedings of the 2015 Conference on Empirical Methods in Natural Language Processing (EMNLP-15)*. pages 1711–1721.

Tsung-Hsien Wen, David Vandyke, Nikola Mrkšić, Milica Gasic, Lina M. Rojas Barahona, Pei-Hao Su, Stefan Ultes, and Steve Young. 2017. A network-based end-to-end trainable task-oriented dialogue system. In *Proceedings of the 15th Conference of the European Chapter of the Association for Computational Linguistics (EACL-17)*. pages 438–449.

Jason D. Williams and Steve Young. 2007. Partially observable markov decision processes for spoken dialog systems. *Computer Speech and Language* 21(2):393–422.

Bowen Wu, Baoxun Wang, and Hui Xue. 2016. Ranking responses oriented to conversational relevance in chat-bots. In *Proceedings of the 26th International Conference on Computational Linguistics (COLING-16)*. pages 652–662.

Chen Xing, Wei Wu, Yu Wu, Jie Liu, Yalou Huang, Ming Zhou, and Wei-Ying Ma. 2017. Topic aware neural response generation. In *Proceedings of the 31st AAAI Conference on Artificial Intelligence (AAAI-17)*. pages 3351–3357.

Wojciech Zaremba, Ilya Sutskever, and Oriol Vinyals. 2014. Recurrent neural network regularization. In *Proceedings of the third International Conference on Learning Representations (ICLR-14)*.

Tiancheng Zhao, Ran Zhao, and Maxine Eskenazi. 2017. Learning discourse-level diversity for neural dialog models using conditional variational autoencoders. In *Proceedings of the 55th Annual Meeting of the Association for Computational Linguistics (ACL-17)*.

An Empirical Study on End-to-End Sentence Modelling

Kurt Junshean Espinosa

National Centre for Text Mining, School of Computer Science, University of Manchester, UK
Department of Computer Science, University of the Philippines Cebu, Philippines
kurtjunshean.espinosa@postgrad.manchester.ac.uk
kpespinosa@up.edu.ph

Abstract

Accurately representing the meaning of a piece of text, otherwise known as sentence modelling, is an important component in many natural language inference tasks. We survey the spectrum of these methods, which lie along two dimensions: input representation granularity and composition model complexity. Using this framework, we reveal in our quantitative and qualitative experiments the limitations of the current state-of-the-art model in the context of sentence similarity tasks.

1 Introduction

Accurately representing the meaning of a piece of text remains an open problem. To illustrate why it is difficult, consider the pair of sentences A and B below in the context of a sentence similarity task.

```
A:The shares of the company dropped.
B:The organisation's stocks slumped.
```

If we use a very naïve model such as bag-of-words to represent a sentence and use discrete counting of common words between the two sentences to determine their similarity, the score would be very low although they are highly similar. How then do we represent the meaning of sentences?

Firstly, we must be able to represent them in ways that computers can understand. Based on the Principle of Compositionality (Frege, 1892), we define the meaning of a sentence as a function of the meaning of its constituents (i.e., words, phrases, morphemes). Generally, there are two main approaches to representing constituents: localist and distributed representations. With the localist representation[1], we represent each constituent with a unique representation usually taken from its position in a vocabulary V. However, this kind of representation suffers from the curse of dimensionality and does not consider the syntactic relationship of a constituent with other constituents. These two shortcomings are addressed by the distributed representation (Hinton, 1984) which encodes a constituent based on its co-occurrence with other constituents appearing within its context, into a dense n-dimensional vector where $n \ll |V|$. Estimating the distributed representation has been an active research topic in itself. Baroni et al. (2014) conducted a systematic comparative evaluation of context-counting and context-predicting models for generating distributed representations and concluded that the latter outperforms the former, but Levy et al. (2015) later have shown that simple pointwise mutual information (PMI) methods also perform similarly if they are properly tuned. To date, the most popular architectures to efficiently estimate these distributed representations are *word2vec* (Mikolov et al., 2013a) and *GloVe* (Pennington et al., 2014). Subsequent developments estimate distributed representations at other levels of granularity (see Section 2.1).

While much research has been directed into constructing representations for constituents, there has been far less consensus regarding the representation of larger semantic structures such as phrases and sentences (Blacoe and Lapata, 2012). A simple approach is based on looking up the vector representation of the constituents (i.e., embeddings) and taking their sum or average which yields a single vector of the same dimension. This strategy is effective in simple tasks but loses word order information and syntactic relations in the process (Mitchell and Lapata, 2008; Turney et al., 2010). Most modern neural network models have a sentence encoder that learns the representation of sentences more efficiently while preserving word or-

---

[1] The best example of this sparse representation is the "one-hot" representation (see Appendix A for details)

Proceedings of the 55th Annual Meeting of the Association for Computational Linguistics- Student Research Workshop, pages 128–135
Vancouver, Canada, July 30 - August 4, 2017. ©2017 Association for Computational Linguistics
https://doi.org/10.18653/v1/P17-3021

der and compositionality (see Section 2.1).

In this work, we present a generalised framework for sentence modelling based on a survey of state-of-the-art methods. Using the framework as a guide, we conducted preliminary experiments by implementing an end-to-end version of the state-of-the-art model in which we reveal its limitations after evaluation on sentence similarity tasks.

2 Related Work

The best way to evaluate sentence models is to assess how they perform on actual natural language inference (NLI) tasks. In this work, we examine three related tasks which are central to natural language understanding: paraphrase detection (Dolan et al., 2004; Xu et al., 2015), semantic similarity measurement (Marelli et al., 2014; Xu et al., 2015; Agirre et al., 2016a) and interpretable semantic similarity measurement (Agirre et al., 2016b). (We refer the reader to the respective papers for the task description and dataset details).

Among the four broad types of methods we have identified in the literature (see Appendix C.1), we focus in this paper on deep learning (DL) methods because they support end-to-end learning, i.e., they use few hand-crafted features—or none at all, making them easier to adapt to new domains. More importantly, these methods have obtained comparable performance relative to other top-ranking methods.

2.1 Sentence Modelling Framework

As a contribution of this work, we survey the spectrum of DL methods, which lie on two dimensions: input representation granularity and composition model complexity, which are both central to sentence modelling (see Appendix Figure C.2 for a graphical illustration).

The first dimension (see horizontal axis of Appendix Figure C.2) is the granularity of input representation. This dimension characterises a trade-off between syntactic dependencies captured in the representation and data sparsity. On the one hand, character-based methods (Vosoughi et al., 2016; dos Santos and Zadrozny, 2014; Wieting et al., 2016) are not faced with the data sparsity problem; however, it is not straightforward to determine whether composing sentences based on individual character representations would represent the originally intended semantics. On the other

hand, while sentence embeddings (Kiros et al., 2015), which are learned by predicting the previous and next sentences given the current sentence, could intuitively represent the actual semantics, it suffers from data sparsity.

The second dimension (see vertical axis of Appendix Figure C.2) is the spectrum of composition models ranging from bag-of-items-driven[2] architectures to compositionality-driven ones to account for the morphological, lexical, syntactic, and compositional aspects of a sentence. Some of the popular methods are based on Bag-of-Item models, which represent a sentence by performing algebraic operations (e.g., addition or averaging) over the vector representations of individual constituents (Blacoe and Lapata, 2012). However, these models have received criticism as they use linear bag-of-words context and thus do not take into account syntax. *Spatial neural networks*, e.g., Convolutional Neural Networks or ConvNets (LeCun et al., 1998), have been shown to capture morphological variations in short subsequences (dos Santos and Zadrozny, 2014; Chiu and Nichols, 2016). However, this architecture still does not capture the overall syntactic information. Thus Sutskever et al. (2014) proposed the use of *sequence-based neural networks*, e.g., Recurrent Neural Networks, Long Short Term Memory models (Hochreiter and Schmidhuber, 1997), because they can capture long-range temporal dependencies. Tai et al. (2015) introduced Tree-LSTM, a generalisation of LSTMs to *tree-structured network* topologies, e.g., Recursive Neural Networks (Socher et al., 2011). However, this type of network requires input from an external resource (i.e., dependency/constituency parser).

More complex models involved stacked architectures of the three basic forms above (He and Lin, 2016; Yin et al., 2015; Cheng and Kartsaklis, 2015; Zhang et al., 2015; He et al., 2015) which capture the syntactic and semantic structure of a language. However, in addition to being computationally intensive, most of these architectures model sentences as vectors with a fixed size, they risk losing information especially when input sentence vectors are of varying lengths. Recently, Bahdanau et al. (2014) introduced the concept of attention, originally in the context of machine translation, where the network learns to align parts

---

[2]We use *items* instead of *words* to generalise amongst various representations.

of the source sentence that match the constituents of the target sentence, without having to explicitly form these parts as hard segments. This enables phrase-alignments between sentences as described by Yin and Schütze (2016) in the context of a textual entailment recognition task.

3 Preliminary Experiments

In this section, we describe the preliminary experiments we conducted in order to gain deeper understanding on the limitations of the state-of-the-art model.

Firstly, we define sentence similarity as a supervised learning task where each training example consists of a pair of sentences $(x_1^a, ..., x_{T_a}^a)$, $(x_1^b, ..., x_{T_b}^b)$ of fixed-sized vectors (where $x_i^a, x_j^b \in \mathbb{R}^{d_{input}}$ denoting constituent vectors from each sentence, respectively, which may be of different lengths $T_a \neq T_b$) along with a single real-valued label y for the pair. We evaluated the performance of the state-of-the-art model on this task.

3.1 Model Overview

Since we focus on end-to-end sentence modelling, we implement a simplified (see Table 1) version of MaLSTM (Mueller and Thyagarajan, 2016), i.e., the state-of-the-art model on this task (see Appendix Figure C.1). The model uses a siamese architecture of Long-Short Term Memory (LSTM) to read word vectors representing each input sentence. Each LSTM cell has four components: input gate i_t, forget gate f_t, memory state c_t, and output gate o_t; which decides the information to retain or forget in a sequence of inputs. Equations 1-6 are the updates performed at each LSTM cell for a sequence of input $(x_1, ..., x_T)$ at each timestep $t \in \{1, ..., T\}$, parameterised by weight matrices $W_i, W_f, W_c, W_o, U_i, U_f, U_c, U_o$ and bias vectors b_i, b_f, b_c, b_o.

$$i_t = \sigma(W_i x_t + U_i h_{t-1} + b_i) \tag{1}$$
$$f_t = \sigma(W_f x_t + U_f h_{t-1} + b_f) \tag{2}$$
$$\tilde{c}_t = \tanh(W_c x_t + U_c h_{t-1} + b_c) \tag{3}$$
$$c_t = i_t \odot \tilde{c}_t + f_t \odot c_{t-1} \tag{4}$$
$$o_t = \sigma(W_o x_t + U_o h_{t-1} + b_o) \tag{5}$$
$$h_t = o_t \odot \tanh(c_t) \tag{6}$$

This model computes the sentence similarity based on the Manhattan distance between the final hidden state representations for each sentence:
$$g(h_{T_a}^a, h_{T_b}^b) = exp(-\|h_{T_a}^a - h_{T_b}^b\|_1) \in [0, 1],$$
which was found to perform better empirically

Model Feature	MaLSTM	Ours
pre-training	yes	no
synonym augmentation	yes	no
prediction calibration	yes	no
optimisation method	Adadelta	Adam

Table 1: Model comparison between MaLSTM and our implementation

than other simple similarity functions such as cosine similarity (Mueller and Thyagarajan, 2016).

3.2 Training Details

We use the 300-dimensional pre-trained *word2vec*[3](Mikolov et al., 2013b) word embeddings and compare the performance with that of *GloVe*[4] (Pennington et al., 2014) embeddings. Out-of-embedding-vocabulary (OOEV) words are replaced with an <unk> token. We retain the word cases and keep the digits. For character representation, we *fine-tune* the 50-dimensional initial embeddings, modifying them during gradient updates of the neural network model by back-propagating gradients. The chosen size of the embeddings was found to perform best after initial experiments with different sizes.

Our model uses 50-dimensional hidden representations h_t and memory cells c_t. Optimisation of the parameters is done using the SGD-based Adam method (Kingma and Ba, 2014) and we perform gradient clipping to prevent exploding gradients. We tune the hyper-parameters on the validation set by random search since it is infeasible to do a random search across the full hyper-parameter space due to time constraints. After conducting initial experiments, we found the optimal training parameters to be the following: batch size = 30, learning rate = 0.01, learning rate decay = 0.98, dropout = 0.5, number of LSTM layers = 1, maximum epochs = 10, patience = 5 epochs. Patience is the early stopping condition based on performance on validation sets. We used the Tensorflow[5] library to implement and train the model.

3.3 Dataset and Evaluation

We measure the model's performance on three benchmark datasets, i.e., SICK 2014 (Marelli et al., 2014), STS 2016 (Agirre et al., 2016a) and

---

[3]code.google.com/p/word2vec
[4]https://nlp.stanford.edu/projects/glove/
[5]https://www.tensorflow.org/

Dataset	Baseline	LSTM			Vector Sum		
		GloVe	word2vec	char	GloVe	word2vec	char
SICK 2014	0.5675	0.7430	0.7355	0.3487	0.4903	0.5099	0.0178
PIT 2015	0.4001	0.1187	0.0581	0.0086	0.1263	0.0845	0.0000
STS 2016	0.4757	0.3768	0.2592	0.1067	0.5052	0.4865	-0.0100

Table 2: Pearson Correlation. Performance comparison across input representations and composition models. Baseline method uses cosine similarity measure to predict similarity between sentences.

Dataset	Vocab Size	% OOEV	
		word2vec	GloVe
SICK 2014	2,423	1.4	1.1
PIT 2015	15,156	16.5	9.6
STS 2016	18,061	11.1	7.3

Table 3: Percentage of Out-of-Embedding-Vocabulary (OOEV) words

PIT 2015 (Xu et al., 2015), using Pearson correlation. We assert that a robust model should perform consistently well in these three datasets.

Furthermore, using the framework described in Section 2.1, we chose to compare the model performance at two levels of input representation (i.e., character-level vs word-level) and composition models (i.e., LSTM vs vector sum) in order to eliminate the need for external tools such as parsers.

4 Results and Discussion

Table 2 shows the performance across input representations and composition models. As expected, our simplified model performs relatively worse (Pearson correlation = 0.7355) when compared to what was reported in the original MaLSTM paper (Pearson correlation = 0.8822) on the SICK dataset (using *word2vec*). This performance difference (around 15%) could be attributed to the additional features (see Table 1) that the state-of-the-art model added to their system.

With respect to input representation, the word-based one yields better performance in all datasets over character-level representation for the obvious reason that it carries more semantic information. Furthermore, the character-level representation using LSTM performs better than using *Vector Sum (VS)* because it is able to retain sequential information. Regarding word embeddings, *GloVe* resulted in higher performance com-

pared to *word2vec* in all datasets and models except with VS on the SICK dataset where *word2vec* is slightly better. Table 3 shows the percentage of OOEV words in each dataset with respect to its vocabulary size. Upon closer inspection, we found out that *word2vec* does not have embeddings for stopwords (e.g., *a, to, of, and*). With respect to token-based statistics, these OOEVs comprised 95% (SICK), 67% (PIT) and 44% (STS) respectively in each dataset. Although further work is needed to ascertain the effect of this type of OOEVs, we hypothesise that GloVe's superior performance could be attributed to it, if not to its word vector quality as claimed by Pennington et al. (2014).

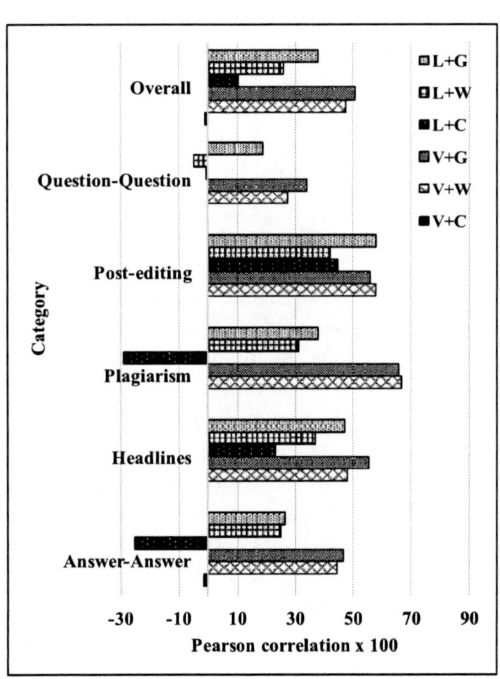

Figure 1: Pearson correlation in STS 2016 evaluation sets (*Key: L=LSTM, V=Vector Sum, C=char, W=word2vec, G=GloVe*)

Dataset	Sentence Pair	Gold Label	Vector Sum	MaLSTM
SICK	A person is scrubbing a zucchini The woman is cutting cooked octopus	0.046	0.523	0.694
STS Question-Question	What kind of socket is this ? What kind of bug is this ?	0.000	0.668	0.778
STS Answer-Answer	You should do it You should never do it	0.200	0.818	0.900
PIT	That s what were watching in Europe If only England was in Europe	0.000	0.566	0.519

Table 4: Examples of difficult sentence pairs. Compositional models use GloVe embeddings.

With respect to the composition model, LSTM performs better than VS but only in the SICK dataset while VS dominates in both the PIT and STS datasets. Specifically, Figure 1 shows the overall and the per-category performance of the model on the STS dataset. Overall, we can clearly see that VS outperforms LSTM by a considerable margin and also in each category except in *Post-editing* and *Headlines*. On the one hand, this suggests that simple compositional models can perform competitively on clean and noisy datasets (e.g., less OOEVs). On the other hand, this shows the ability of LSTM models to capture long term dependencies especially on clean datasets (e.g., SICK dataset) because they contain sufficient semantic information while their performance decreases dramatically on noisy data or on datasets with high proportion of OOEVs (e.g., PIT and STS datasets).

The worst performance was obtained on the PIT dataset in both the baseline[6] and composition models. Aside from PIT dataset's comparatively higher percentage of OOEV words (see Table 3), its diverse, short and noisy user-generated text (Strauss et al., 2016)—typical of social media text—make it a very challenging dataset.

To better understand the reason behind the performance drop of the model, we extracted the 100 most difficult sentence pairs in each dataset by ranking all of the pairs in the test set according to the absolute difference between the gold standard and predicted similarity scores.

We observed that around 60% of the difficult sentence pairs share many similar words (except for a word or two) or contain OOEV words that led to a complete change in meaning. Meanwhile the

rest are sentence pairs which are topically similar but completely mean different.

In Table 4, we show examples from each dataset and their corresponding scores (i.e., Pearson correlation) from the gold standard and the composition models. The two sentences come from an actual pair in the dataset.

Example 1 (from SICK dataset) shows a pair of sentences which, although can be interpreted to come from the same domain *food preparation*, are semantically different in their *verb*, *subject*, and *direct object*, for which, presumably, they were labelled in the gold standard as highly dissimilar. However, both of the word-based models predicted them to be highly similar (in varying degrees). This limitation can be attributed to the relatedness of their words (e.g., *person* vs *woman*, *cutting* vs *scrubbing*). Under the *distributional hypothesis assumption* (Harris, 1940; Firth, 1957), two words will have high similarity if they occur in similar contexts even if they neither have the same nor similar meanings. Since word embeddings are typically generated based on this assumption, the relatedness aspect is captured more than genuine similarity. Furthermore, the higher similarity obtained by the LSTM model over Vector Sum can be attributed to its ability to capture syntactic structure in sequences such as sentences.

Examples 2 and 3 (from STS dataset) show sentence pairs which were labelled as completely dissimilar but were predicted with high similarity in both models. This shows the inability of the models to put more weight on semantically rich words which change the overall meaning of a sentence when compared with another.

Example 4 (from PIT dataset) shows a sentence pair which was labelled as completely dissimi-

---

[6]We represent each sentence with term-frequency vectors.

lar, presumably because it lacks sufficient context for meaningful interpretation. However, they were predicted to some degree as similar possibly because some words are common to both sentences and some are likely related by virtue of co-occurrence in the same context (e.g., *England, Europe)*. See Appendix B for more examples.

5 Future Work

This work is intended to serve as an initial study on end-to-end sentence modelling to identify the limitations associated with it. The models and representations compared, while typical of current sentence modelling methods, are not an exhaustive set and some variations exist. A natural extension to this study is to explore other input granularity representations and composition models presented in the framework. For example, in this study we did not go beyond word representations; however, multi-word expressions are common occurrences in the English language. This could be addressed by modelling sentence constituents using recursive tree structures (Tai et al., 2015) or by learning phrase representations (Wieting et al., 2015).

The limitations of the current word embeddings as revealed in this paper has been studied in the context of word similarity tasks (Levy and Goldberg, 2014; Hill et al., 2016) but to our knowledge had never been investigated explicitly in the context of sentence similarity tasks. For example, Kiela et al. (2015) have shown that specialising semantic spaces to downstream tasks and applications requiring similarity or relatedness can improve performance. Furthermore, some studies (Faruqui et al., 2014; Yu and Dredze, 2014; Ono et al., 2015; Ettinger et al., 2016) have proposed to learn word embeddings by going beyond the distributional hypothesis assumption either through a retrofitting or joint-learning process with some using semantic resources such as ontologies and entity relation databases. Thus, we will explore this direction as this will be particularly important in semantic processing since entities encode much of the semantic information in a language.

Furthermore, the inability of the state-of-the-art model to encode semantically rich words (e.g., *socket*, *bug* in Example 2) with higher weights relative to other words, supports the assertion of Blacoe and Lapata (2012) that distributive semantic representation and composition must be mutually learned. Wieting et al. (2015) have showed that this kind of weighting for semantic importance can be learned automatically when training on a paraphrase database. Recent models (Hashimoto et al., 2016) proposed end-to-end joint modelling at different linguistic levels of a sentence (i.e. morphology, syntax, semantics) on a hierarchy of tasks (i.e., POS tagging, dependency parsing, semantic role labelling)—often done separately—with the assumption that higher-level tasks benefit from lower-level ones.

References

Naveed Afzal, Yanshan Wang, and Hongfang Liu. 2016. Mayonlp at semeval-2016 task 1: Semantic textual similarity based on lexical semantic net and deep learning semantic model. *Proceedings of SemEval* pages 674–679.

Eneko Agirre, Carmen Banea, Daniel Cer, Mona Diab, Aitor Gonzalez-Agirre, Rada Mihalcea, and Janyce Wiebe. 2016a. Semeval-2016 task 1: Semantic textual similarity, monolingual and cross-lingual evaluation. In *Proceedings of the 10th International Workshop on Semantic Evaluation.* pages 509–523.

Eneko Agirre, Aitor Gonzalez-Agirre, Inigo Lopez-Gazpio, Montse Maritxalar, German Rigau, and Larraitz Uria. 2016b. Semeval-2016 task 2: Interpretable semantic textual similarity. *Proceedings of SemEval* pages 512–524.

Dzmitry Bahdanau, Kyunghyun Cho, and Yoshua Bengio. 2014. Neural machine translation by jointly learning to align and translate. *arXiv preprint arXiv:1409.0473* .

Rajendra Banjade, Nabin Maharjan, Nobal B Niraula, and Vasile Rus. 2016. Dtsim at semeval-2016 task 2: Interpreting similarity of texts based on automated chunking, chunk alignment and semantic relation prediction. *Proceedings of SemEval* pages 809–813.

Marco Baroni, Georgiana Dinu, and Germán Kruszewski. 2014. Don't count, predict! a systematic comparison of context-counting vs. context-predicting semantic vectors. In *ACL (1)*. pages 238–247.

Dario Bertero and Pascale Fung. 2015. Hltc-hkust: A neural network paraphrase classifier using translation metrics, semantic roles and lexical similarity features. *Proceedings of SemEval* .

Ergun Biçici. 2015. Rtm-dcu: Predicting semantic similarity with referential translation machines. *SemEval-2015* page 56.

William Blacoe and Mirella Lapata. 2012. A comparison of vector-based representations for semantic composition. In *Proceedings of the 2012 Joint Conference on Empirical Methods in Natural Language*

Processing and Computational Natural Language Learning. Association for Computational Linguistics, pages 546–556.

Tomáš Brychcın and Lukáš Svoboda. 2016. Uwb at semeval-2016 task 1: Semantic textual similarity using lexical, syntactic, and semantic information. *Proceedings of SemEval* pages 588–594.

Jianpeng Cheng and Dimitri Kartsaklis. 2015. Syntax-aware multi-sense word embeddings for deep compositional models of meaning. *arXiv preprint arXiv:1508.02354* http://arxiv.org/abs/1508.02354.

Jason PC Chiu and Eric Nichols. 2016. Named entity recognition with bidirectional LSTM-CNNs. *Transactions of the Association for Computational Linguistics* 4:357–370. https://transacl.org/ojs/index.php/tacl/article/view/792.

Bill Dolan, Chris Quirk, and Chris Brockett. 2004. Unsupervised construction of large paraphrase corpora: Exploiting massively parallel news sources. In *Proceedings of the 20th international conference on Computational Linguistics*. Association for Computational Linguistics, page 350.

Cícero Nogueira dos Santos and Bianca Zadrozny. 2014. Learning character-level representations for part-of-speech tagging. In *ICML*. pages 1818–1826.

Allyson Ettinger, Philip Resnik, and Marine Carpuat. 2016. Retrofitting sense-specific word vectors using parallel text. In *Proceedings of NAACL-HLT*. pages 1378–1383.

Asli Eyecioglu and Bill Keller. 2015. ASOBEK: Twitter paraphrase identification with simple overlap features and SVMs. *Proceedings of SemEval* .

Manaal Faruqui, Jesse Dodge, Sujay K Jauhar, Chris Dyer, Eduard Hovy, and Noah A Smith. 2014. Retrofitting word vectors to semantic lexicons. *arXiv preprint arXiv:1411.4166* .

John Rupert Firth. 1957. *Papers in linguistics, 1934-1951*. Oxford University Press.

Gottlob Frege. 1892. Ubersicht und bedeutung. *Journal of Philosophy and Philosophical Criticism* 100:25–50.

Z. S. Harris. 1940. Review of Louis H. Gray, Foundations of Language (New York: Macmillan, 1939). *Language* 16(3):216–231.

Kazuma Hashimoto, Caiming Xiong, Yoshimasa Tsuruoka, and Richard Socher. 2016. A Joint Many-Task Model: Growing a Neural Network for Multiple NLP Tasks. *arXiv preprint arXiv:1611.01587* https://arxiv.org/abs/1611.01587.

Hua He, Kevin Gimpel, and Jimmy Lin. 2015. Multi-perspective sentence similarity modeling with convolutional neural networks. In *Proceedings of the 2015 Conference on Empirical Methods in Natural Language Processing*. pages 1576–1586.

Hua He and Jimmy Lin. 2016. Pairwise word interaction modeling with deep neural networks for semantic similarity measurement. In *Proceedings of NAACL-HLT*. pages 937–948.

Hua He, John Wieting, Kevin Gimpel, Jinfeng Rao, and Jimmy Lin. 2016. Umd-ttic-uw at semeval-2016 task 1: Attention-based multi-perspective convolutional neural networks for textual similarity measurement .

Felix Hill, Roi Reichart, and Anna Korhonen. 2016. Simlex-999: Evaluating semantic models with (genuine) similarity estimation. *Computational Linguistics* .

Geoffrey E Hinton. 1984. Distributed representations .

Sepp Hochreiter and Jürgen Schmidhuber. 1997. Long short-term memory. *Neural computation* 9(8):1735–1780.

Yangfeng Ji and Jacob Eisenstein. 2013. Discriminative Improvements to Distributional Sentence Similarity. In *EMNLP*. pages 891–896. http://jiyfeng.github.io/papers/ji-emnlp-2013.pdf.

Douwe Kiela, Felix Hill, and Stephen Clark. 2015. Specializing word embeddings for similarity or relatedness. In *EMNLP*. pages 2044–2048.

Diederik Kingma and Jimmy Ba. 2014. Adam: A method for stochastic optimization. *arXiv preprint arXiv:1412.6980* .

Ryan Kiros, Yukun Zhu, Ruslan R Salakhutdinov, Richard Zemel, Raquel Urtasun, Antonio Torralba, and Sanja Fidler. 2015. Skip-thought vectors. In *Advances in neural information processing systems*. pages 3294–3302.

Yann LeCun, Léon Bottou, Yoshua Bengio, and Patrick Haffner. 1998. Gradient-based learning applied to document recognition. *Proceedings of the IEEE* 86(11):2278–2324.

Omer Levy and Yoav Goldberg. 2014. Dependency-based word embeddings. In *ACL (2)*. pages 302–308.

Omer Levy, Yoav Goldberg, and Ido Dagan. 2015. Improving distributional similarity with lessons learned from word embeddings. *Transactions of the Association for Computational Linguistics* 3:211–225.

Simone Magnolini, Anna Feltracco, and Bernardo Magnini. 2016. Fbk-hlt-nlp at semeval-2016 task 2: A multitask, deep learning approach for interpretable semantic textual similarity. *Proceedings of SemEval* pages 783–789.

Marco Marelli, Stefano Menini, Marco Baroni, Luisa Bentivogli, Raffaella Bernardi, and Roberto Zamparelli. 2014. A sick cure for the evaluation of compositional distributional semantic models. In *LREC*. pages 216–223.

Tomas Mikolov, Kai Chen, Greg Corrado, and Jeffrey Dean. 2013a. Efficient estimation of word representations in vector space. *arXiv preprint arXiv:1301.3781* .

Tomas Mikolov, Ilya Sutskever, Kai Chen, Greg S Corrado, and Jeff Dean. 2013b. Distributed representations of words and phrases and their compositionality. In *Advances in neural information processing systems*. pages 3111–3119.

Jeff Mitchell and Mirella Lapata. 2008. Vector-based models of semantic composition. In *ACL*. pages 236–244.

Jonas Mueller and Aditya Thyagarajan. 2016. Siamese recurrent architectures for learning sentence similarity. In *AAAI*. pages 2786–2792.

Masataka Ono, Makoto Miwa, and Yutaka Sasaki. 2015. Word embedding-based antonym detection using thesauri and distributional information. In *HLT-NAACL*. pages 984–989.

Jeffrey Pennington, Richard Socher, and Christopher D Manning. 2014. Glove: Global vectors for word representation. In *EMNLP*. volume 14, pages 1532–43.

Piotr Przybyła, Nhung TH Nguyen, Matthew Shardlow, Georgios Kontonatsios, and Sophia Ananiadou. 2016. Nactem at semeval-2016 task 1: Inferring sentence-level semantic similarity from an ensemble of complementary lexical and sentence-level features. *Proceedings of SemEval* pages 614–620.

Barbara Rychalska, Katarzyna Pakulska, Krystyna Chodorowska, Wojciech Walczak, and Piotr Andruszkiewicz. 2016. Samsung poland nlp team at semeval-2016 task 1: Necessity for diversity; combining recursive autoencoders, wordnet and ensemble methods to measure semantic similarity. *Proceedings of SemEval* pages 602–608.

Richard Socher, Eric H Huang, Jeffrey Pennin, Christopher D Manning, and Andrew Y Ng. 2011. Dynamic pooling and unfolding recursive autoencoders for paraphrase detection. In *Advances in Neural Information Processing Systems*. pages 801–809.

Benjamin Strauss, Bethany E Toma, Alan Ritter, Marie-Catherine de Marneffe, and Wei Xu. 2016. Results of the wnut16 named entity recognition shared task. In *Proceedings of the 2nd Workshop on Noisy User-generated Text*. pages 138–144.

Ilya Sutskever, Oriol Vinyals, and Quoc V Le. 2014. Sequence to sequence learning with neural networks. In *Advances in neural information processing systems*. pages 3104–3112.

Kai Sheng Tai, Richard Socher, and Christopher D Manning. 2015. Improved semantic representations from tree-structured long short-term memory networks. *arXiv preprint arXiv:1503.00075* .

Peter D Turney, Patrick Pantel, et al. 2010. From frequency to meaning: Vector space models of semantics. *Journal of artificial intelligence research* 37(1):141–188.

Soroush Vosoughi, Prashanth Vijayaraghavan, and Deb Roy. 2016. Tweet2vec: Learning Tweet Embeddings Using Character-level CNN-LSTM Encoder-Decoder. ACM Press, pages 1041–1044. https://doi.org/10.1145/2911451.2914762.

John Wieting, Mohit Bansal, Kevin Gimpel, and Karen Livescu. 2015. Towards universal paraphrastic sentence embeddings. *arXiv preprint arXiv:1511.08198* .

John Wieting, Mohit Bansal, Kevin Gimpel, and Karen Livescu. 2016. Charagram: Embedding words and sentences via character n-grams. *arXiv preprint arXiv:1607.02789* .

Wei Xu, Chris Callison-Burch, and William B Dolan. 2015. Semeval-2015 task 1: Paraphrase and semantic similarity in twitter (pit). *Proceedings of SemEval* .

Wenpeng Yin and Hinrich Schutze. 2016. Discriminative Phrase Embedding for Paraphrase Identification. *arXiv preprint arXiv:1604.00503* http://arxiv.org/abs/1604.00503.

Wenpeng Yin and Hinrich Schütze. 2016. Why and how to pay different attention to phrase alignments of different intensities. *arXiv preprint arXiv:1604.06896* .

Wenpeng Yin, Hinrich Schütze, Bing Xiang, and Bowen Zhou. 2015. Abcnn: Attention-based convolutional neural network for modeling sentence pairs. *arXiv preprint arXiv:1512.05193* .

Mo Yu and Mark Dredze. 2014. Improving lexical embeddings with semantic knowledge. In *ACL (2)*. pages 545–550.

Guido Zarrella, John Henderson, Elizabeth M. Merkhofer, and Laura Strickhart. 2015. MITRE: Seven systems for semantic similarity in tweets. *Proceedings of SemEval* .

Xiang Zhang, Junbo Zhao, and Yann LeCun. 2015. Character-level convolutional networks for text classification. In *Advances in Neural Information Processing Systems*. pages 649–657.

Jiang Zhao, Tian Tian Zhu, and Man Lan. 2014. Ecnu: One stone two birds: Ensemble of heterogenous measures for semantic relatedness and textual entailment. *Proceedings of the SemEval* pages 271–277.

Yao Zhou, Cong Liu, and Yan Pan. 2016. Modelling Sentence Pairs with Tree-structured Attentive Encoder. *arXiv preprint arXiv:1610.02806* https://arxiv.org/abs/1610.02806.

MojiSem:
Varying linguistic purposes of emoji in (Twitter) context

Noa Na'aman, Hannah Provenza, Orion Montoya
Brandeis University
{nnaaman,hprovenza,obm}@brandeis.edu

Abstract

Early research into emoji in textual communication has focused largely on high-frequency usages and ambiguity of interpretations. Investigation of a wide range of emoji usage shows these glyphs serving at least two very different purposes: as content and function words, or as multimodal affective markers. Identifying where an emoji is replacing textual content allows NLP tools the possibility of parsing them as any other word or phrase. Recognizing the import of non-content emoji can be a a significant part of understanding a message as well.

We report on an annotation task on English Twitter data with the goal of classifying emoji uses by these categories, and on the effectiveness of a classifier trained on these annotations. We find that it is possible to train a classifier to tell the difference between those emoji used as linguistic content words and those used as paralinguistic or affective multimodal markers even with a small amount of training data, but that accurate sub-classification of these multimodal emoji into specific classes like attitude, topic, or gesture will require more data and more feature engineering.

1 Background

Emoji characters were first offered on Japanese mobile phones around the turn of the 21st century. These pictographic elements reached global language communities after being added to Unicode 6.0 in 2010, and then being offered within software keyboards on smartphones. In the ensuing half-decade, digitally-mediated language users have evolved diverse and novel linguistic uses for emoji.

The expressive richness of emoji communication would, on its own, be sufficient reason to seek a nuanced understanding of its usage. But our initial survey of emoji on Twitter reveals many cases where emoji serve direct semantic functions in a tweet or where they are used as a grammatical function such as a preposition or punctuation. Early work on Twitter emoticons (Schnoebelen, 2012) pre-dated the wide spread of Unicode emoji on mobile and desktop devices. Recent work (Miller et al., 2016) has explored the cross-platform ambiguity of emoji renderings; (Eisner et al., 2016) created word embeddings that performed competitively on emoji analogy tasks; (Ljubešic and Fišer, 2016) mapped global emoji distributions by frequency; (Barbieri et al., 2017) used LSTMs to predict them in context.

We feel that a lexical semantics of emoji characters is implied in these studies without being directly addressed. Words are not used randomly, and neither are emoji. But even when they replace a word, emoji are used for different purposes than words. We believe that work on emoji would be better informed if there were an explicit typology of the linguistic functions that emoji can serve in expressive text. The current project offered annotators a framework and heuristics to classify uses of emoji by linguistic and discursive function. We then used a model based on this corpus to predict the grammatical function of emoji characters in novel contexts.

2 Annotation task

Although recognizing the presence of emoji characters is trivial, the linguistic distinctions we sought to annotate were ambiguous and seemed prone to disagreement. Therefore in our annotation guidelines we structured the process to minimize cognitive load and lead the annotators to in-

Proceedings of the 55th Annual Meeting of the Association for Computational Linguistics- Student Research Workshop, pages 136–141
Vancouver, Canada, July 30 - August 4, 2017. ©2017 Association for Computational Linguistics
https://doi.org/10.18653/v1/P17-3022

tuitive decisions. This was aided somewhat by the observation that emoji are often used in contexts that make them graphical replacements for existing lexical units, and that such uses are therefore straightforward to interpret. Taking advantage of such uses, our flow presented annotators with a few simple questions at each step, to determine whether to assign a label or to move on to the next category.

2.1 Categories and subtypes

The high-level labels we defined for emoji uses were:

- **Function** (`func`): stand-ins for a function word in an utterance. These had a `type` attribute with values `prep`, `aux`, `conj`, `dt`, `punc`, `other`. An example from our data: "I 🌎 like u".
- **Content** (`cont`): stand-ins for lexical words or phrases that are part of the main informative content of the sentence. These have natural parts of speech, which annotators could subtype as: `noun`, `verb`, `adj`, `adv`, `other`. "The 🔑 to success is 📖"
- **Multimodal** (`mm`): characters that enrich a grammatically-complete text with markers of affect or stance, whether to express an attitude ("Let my work disrespect me one more time... 😌"), to echo the topic with an iconic repetition ("Mean girls 🎬", or to express a gesture that might have accompanied the utterance in face-to-face speech ("Omg why is my mom screaming so early 😫"). Subtypes: `attitude`, `topic`, `gesture`, `other`.

The POS tags we chose were deliberately coarse-grained and did not include distinctions such as noun sub-types. We wanted to capture important differences while knowing that we would have fewer instances for the function and content labels. For all three labels, annotators were asked to provide a `replacement`: a word or phrase that could replace the emoji. For `func` and `cont`, replacements were a criterion for choosing the label; for `mm` there was room for interpretation.

2.2 Data Collection

Tweets were pulled from the public Twitter streaming API using the `tweepy` Python package. The collected tweets were automatically filtered to include: only tweets with characters from the Emoji Unicode ranges (i.e. generally `U+1FXXX`, `U+26XX–U+27BF`); only tweets labeled as being in English. We excluded tweets with embedded images or links. Redundant/duplicate tweets were filtered by comparing tweet texts after removal of hashtags and @mentions; this left only a small number of cloned duplicates. After that, tweets were hand-selected to get a wide variety of emojis and context in a small sample size — therefore, our corpus does not reflect the true distribution of emoji uses or context types.

2.3 Guidelines

Our guidelines gave annotators cursory background about emoji and their uses in social media, assuming no particular familiarity with the range of creative uses of emoji. In hindsight we noticed our assumption that annotators would have a fair degree of familiarity with modes of discourse on Twitter. The short-message social platform has many distinctive cultural and communicative codes of its own, not to mention subcultures, and continuously evolving trends combined with a long memory. As two of the authors are active and engaged users of Twitter, we unfortunately took it for granted that our annotators would be able to decipher emoji in contexts that required nuanced knowledge of InterNet language and Twitter norms. This left annotators occasionally bewildered: by random users begging celebrities to follow them, by dialogue-formatted tweets, and by other epigrammatic subgenres of the short-text form.

The analytical steps we prescribed were:

- Identifying each emoji in the tweet
- Deciding whether multiple contiguous emoji should be considered separately or as a group
- Choosing the best tag for the emoji (or sequence)
- Providing a translation or interpretation for each tagged span.

Eliciting an interpretation serves two goals: first, as a coercive prompt for the user to bias them toward a linguistic interpretation. A replaceable phrase that fits with the grammar of the sentence is a different proposition than a marker that amounts to a standalone utterance such as "I am laughing" or "I am sad". Secondly, one of the eventual applications of annotated corpus may be emoji-sense disambiguation (ESD), and mapping to a lexicalized expression would be useful grounding for future ESD tasks. The `text` field was very helpful during the adjudication process, clarifying the annotators' judgments and understanding of the task.

For each tweet, annotators first read without annotating anything, to get a sense of the general message of the tweet and to think about the relationship between the emoji and the text. On subsequent readings, they are asked to determine whether the emoji is serving as punctuation or a function word; then if it is a content word; and if it is neither of those, then to examine it as a multimodal emoji. A key test, in our opinion, was asking annotators to simulate reading the message of the tweet aloud to another person. If a listener's comprehension of the core message seemed to require a word or phrase to be spoken in place of an emoji, then that would be a compelling sign that it should be tagged as function or content.

For each step we provided examples of tweets and emoji uses that clearly belong in each category. These examples were not included in the data set. Uses that failed the first two tests were assigned the multimodal category. We provided guidance and examples for deciding between 'topic', 'attitude' or 'gesture' as subtypes of the multimodal category.

2.4   Inter-annotator agreement

Four annotators, all computational linguistics grad students, were given 567 tweets with 878 total occurrences of emoji characters; in the gold standard these amounted to 775 tagged emoji spans. For the first 200 tweets annotated ('Set 1' and 'Set 2' in Table 1), each was marked by four annotators. After establishing some facility with the task we divided annotators into two groups and had only two annotators per tweet for the remaining 367.

There are two separate aspects of annotation for which IAA was relevant; the first, and less interesting, was the marking of the extent of emoji spans. Since emoji are unambiguously visible, we anticipated strong agreement. The one confounding aspect was that annotators were encouraged to group multiple emoji in a single span if they were a semantic/functional unit. The overall Krippendorff's α for extent markings was around 0.9.

The more significant place to look at IAA is the labeling of the emoji's functions. Because we were categorizing tokens, and because these categories are not ordered and we presented more than two labels, we used Fleiss's κ. But Fleiss's κ requires that annotators have annotated the same things, and in some cases annotators did not complete the dataset or missed an individual emoji character in a tweet. In order to calculate the statistics on actual agreement, rather than impute disagreement in the case of an 'abstention', we removed from our IAA-calculation counts any spans that were not marked by all annotators. There are many of these in the first dataset, and progressively fewer in each subsequent dataset as the annotators become more experienced. A total of 150 spans were excluded from Fleiss' kappa calculations for this reason.

2.5   Agreement/disagreement analysis

Content words. Part-of-speech identification is a skill familiar to most of our annotators, so we were not surprised to see excellent levels of agreement among words tagged for part of speech. These content words, however, were a very small proportion of the data (51 out of 775 emoji spans) which may be problematically small. For datasets 3B and 4B, annotators were in perfect agreement.

Multimodal. Agreement on multimodal sublabels was much lower, and did not improve as annotation progressed. Multimodal emoji may be inherently ambiguous, and we need a labeling system that can account for this. A smiley face ☺ might be interpreted as a `gesture` (a smile), an `attitude` (joy), or a `topic` (for example, if the tweet is about what a good day the author is having) — and any of these would be a valid interpretation of a single tweet. A clearer typology of multimodal emojis, and, if possible, a more deterministic procedure for labeling emoji with these subtypes, may be one approach.

Worst overall cross-label agreement scores were for week one, but all following datasets improved on that baseline after the annotation guidelines were refined.

3   Tag prediction experiment

We trained a sequence tagger to assign the correct linguistic-function label to an emoji character. Our annotators had assigned labels and subtypes, but due to the low agreement on multimodal (mm) labels, and the small number of cont and func la-

Dataset	# taters	span rem	total	mm	content
Set 1	4	78	0.2071	0.4251	0.1311
Set 2	4	49	0.8743	0.7158	0.8531
Set 3A	2	11	0.9096	0.4616	0.792
Set 3B	2	6	0.7436	0.3905	1.0
Set 4A	2	3	0.8789	0.4838	0.7435
Set 4B	2	1	0.3954	0.5078	1.0
Total/mean	4	150	0.6681	0.4974	0.7533

Table 1: Fleiss's κ scores and other annotation/agreement variables

Label	count
Multi-modal (mm)	total 686
attitude	407
topic	184
gesture	93
other	2
Content (cont)	total 51
noun	40
adj	6
verb	4
adv	1
Functional (func)	total 38
punct	34
aux	2
dt	1
other	1
emoji spans	total 775
words	6174
punctuation	668

Table 2: Label counts and subtypes in gold-standard data

bels assigned, we narrowed the focus of our classification task to simply categorizing things correctly as either mm or cont / func. After one iteration, we saw that the low number of func tokens was preventing us from finding any func emoji, so we combined the cont and func tokens into a single label of cont. Therefore our sequence tagger needed simply to decide whether a token was serving as a substitute for a textual word, or was a multimodal marker.

3.1 Feature engineering

For reasons described above, we had a small and arbitrary sample of emoji usage available to study. After annotating 775 spans in 567 tweets, we had tagged 300 distinct emoji, 135 of which occurred only once. Given that our task is sequence tagging and our features are complex and independent, Conditional Random Fields seemed a good choice for our task. We used CRFSuite (Okazaki, 2007) and, after experimenting with the training algorithms available, found that training with av-

eraged perceptron (Collins, 2002) yielded the best predictive results. Results for several iterations of features are given in Table 3, generally in order of increasing improvement until "prev +emo_class".

- The emoji span itself, here called 'character' although it may span multiple characters.

- 'emo?' is a binary feature indicating whether the token contains emoji characters (emo), or is purely word characters (txt).

- 'POS', a part-of-speech tag assigned by nltk.pos_tag, which did apply part-of-speech labels to some emoji characters, and sometimes even correct ones.

- 'position' was a set of three positional features: an integer 0–9 indicating a token's position in tenths of the way through the tweet; a three-class BEGIN/MID/END to indicate tokens at the beginning or end of a tweet (different from the 0–9 feature in that multiple tokens may get 0 or 9, but only one token will get BEGIN or END); and the number of characters in the token.

- The 'contexty' feature is another set of three features, this time related to context: A boolean preceded_by_determiner aimed at catching noun emoji; and two features to record the pairing of the preceding and following part of speech with the present token type (i.e. emo/txt);

- Unicode blocks, which inhere in the ordering of emoji characters. Thus far, emoji have been added in semantically-related groups that tend to be contiguous. So there is a block of smiley faces and other 'emoticons'; a block of transport images; blocks of food, sports, animals, clothing; a whole block of hearts of different colors and elaborations; office-related, clocks, weather, hands, plants, and celebratory characters. These provide

feature	F1 `word`	F1 `mm`	P `cont`	R `cont`	F1 `cont`	Macro-avg F1
character	0.9721	0.7481	0.3571	0.3333	0.3448	0.8441
prev +emo?	0.9914	0.8649	0.4286	0.4000	0.4000	0.8783
prev +POS	0.9914	0.8784	0.5000	0.4667	0.4828	0.8921
prev +position	0.9914	0.8844	0.4667	0.4667	0.4667	0.9028
prev +contexty	0.9914	0.8831	0.6250	0.3333	0.4348	0.8848
prev +emo_class (best)	0.9914	**0.8933**	**0.7273**	0.5333	0.6154	**0.9168**
best − character	0.9906	0.8514	0.6429	**0.6000**	**0.6207**	0.9090
best − contexty	0.9922	0.8750	0.4706	0.5333	0.5000	0.8945
emo?+POS+emo_class	0.9914	0.8421	0.6000	0.4000	0.4800	0.8855

Table 3: Performance of feature iterations. Only the F1 score is given for `word` and `mm` labels because precision and recall were pretty consistent. `cont` labels are broken down by precision, recall and F1 because they varied in interesting ways.

a very inexpensive proxy to semantics, and the 'emo_class' feature yielded a marked improvement in both precision and recall on content words, although the small number of cases in the test data make it hard to be sure of their true contribution.

We did a few other experiments to explore our features. 'best − character' showed that ignoring the character actually improved recall on content words, at the expense of precision. 'best − contexty' removed the 'contexty' feature, since it had actually slightly worsened several metrics, but removing it from the final '(best)' feature set also worsened several metrics.

3.2 Full-feature performance

The results in Table 3 show what we could reliably label with coarse-grained labels given the small size of our data set: 511 training tweets, 56 test tweets. But given that we annotated with finer-grained labels as well, it is worth looking at the performance on that task so far; results are shown in Table 3. Our test set had only two of each of the verbal content words — `content_verb` and `func_aux` — and didn't catch either of them, nor label anything else with either label. In fact, the only two `func_aux` in our dataset were in the test set, so they never actually got trained on. We saw fairly reasonable recall on the `mm_topic` and `mm_attitude` labels, but given that those are the most frequent labels in the entire data set, it is more relevant that our precision was low.

4 Future directions

89 examples of content and functional uses of emoji is not enough to reliably model the behav-ior of these categories. More annotation may yield much richer models of the variety of purposes of emoji, and will help get a better handle on the range of emoji polysemy. Clustering of contexts based on observed features may induce more empirically valid subtypes than the ones defined by our specification.

Anglophone Twitter users use emoji in their tweets for a wide range of purposes, and a given emoji character means different things in different contexts. Every emoji linguist notes the fascinating range of pragmatic and multimodal effects that emoji can have in electronic communication. If these effects are to be given lexicographical treatment and categorization, they must also be organized into functional and pragmatic categories that are not part of the typical range of classes used to talk about printed words.

We have mentioned the notion of emoji-sense disambiguation (ESD). ESD in the model of traditional WSD would seem to require an empirical inventory of emoji senses. Even our small sample has shown a number of characters that are used both as content words and as topical or gestural cues. Our data included "Mean girls ", i.e. 'I am watching the movie Mean Girls', which has no propositional content in common with (unattested in our data set) "Mean girls ", i.e. 'girls who are mean upset me'. There are a number of flower emoji: sometimes they are used to decorate a message about flowers themselves, and sometimes they add sentiment to a message—and, just as in culture away from keyboards, a rose is always marked as conveying a message of 'love', while a cherry blossom is consistently associated with 'beauty'.

feature	TP	labeled	true	precision	recall	F1
mm_topic	38	53	44	0.7170	0.8636	0.7835
mm_attitude	11	26	16	0.4231	0.6875	0.5238
content_noun	6	11	11	0.5455	0.5455	0.5455
mm_gesture	2	2	8	1.0000	0.2500	0.4000
content_verb	0	0	2	0.0000	0.0000	0.0000
func_aux	0	0	2	0.0000	0.0000	0.0000

Table 4: performance of best model on subtype labels

There can be little question that individuals use emoji differently, and this will certainly confound the study of emoji semantics in the immediate term. The study of community dialects will be essential to emoji semantics, and there is certain also to be strong variation on the level of idiolect. The categorizations may need refinement, but the phenomenon is undeniably worthy of further study.

References

Francesco Barbieri, Miguel Ballesteros, and Horacio Saggion. 2017. Are emojis predictable? *EACL 2017*, page 105.

Michael Collins. 2002. Discriminative training methods for Hidden Markov Models: Theory and experiments with perceptron algorithms. In *Proceedings of the ACL-02 Conference on Empirical Methods in Natural Language Processing - Volume 10*, EMNLP '02, pages 1–8, Stroudsburg, PA, USA. Association for Computational Linguistics.

Ben Eisner, Tim Rocktäschel, Isabelle Augenstein, Matko Bošnjak, and Sebastian Riedel. 2016. emoji2vec: Learning emoji representations from their description. In *Conference on Empirical Methods in Natural Language Processing*, page 48.

Nikola Ljubešic and Darja Fišer. 2016. A global analysis of emoji usage. *ACL 2016*, page 82.

Hannah Miller, Jacob Thebault-Spieker, Shuo Chang, Isaac Johnson, Loren Terveen, and Brent Hecht. 2016. "Blissfully happy" or "ready to fight": Varying interpretations of emoji. In *Proceedings of the Tenth International Conference on Web and Social Media, ICWSM 2016, Cologne, Germany, May 17–20, 2016*. Association for the Advancement of Artificial Intelligence, May.

Naoaki Okazaki. 2007. CRFsuite: a fast implementation of Conditional Random Fields (CRFs).

Tyler Schnoebelen. 2012. Do you smile with your nose? Stylistic variation in Twitter emoticons. In *University of Pennsylvania Working Papers in Linguistics*, volume 18, pages 117–125. University of Pennsylvania.

Negotiation of Antibiotic Treatment in Medical Consultations:
A Corpus based Study

Nan Wang
University of California, Los Angeles
nwang3@ucla.edu

Abstract

Doctor-patient conversation is considered a contributing factor to antibiotic over-prescription. Some language practices have been identified as parent pressuring doctors for prescribing; other practices are considered as likely to engender parent resistance to non-antibiotic treatment recommendations. In social science studies, approaches such as conversation analysis have been applied to identify those language practices. Current research for dialogue systems offer an alternative approach. Past research proved that corpus-based approaches have been effectively used for research involving modeling dialogue acts and sequential relations. In this proposal, we propose a corpus-based study of doctor-patient conversations of antibiotic treatment negotiation in pediatric consultations. Based on findings from conversation analysis studies, we use a computational linguistic approach to assist annotating and modeling of doctor-patient language practices, and analyzing their influence on antibiotic over-prescribing.

1 Introduction

"How to do things with words" has long been a topic interested to researchers from various disciplines, such as pragmatics (Austin, 1962; Levinson, 1983), conversation analysis (CA) (Drew and Heritage, 1992; Heritage and Maynard, 2006), and computational linguistics (Stolcke et al., 2000; Williams et al., 2013; Schlöder and Fernandez, 2015). Although computational methods have been widely used to conduct text mining tasks such as detecting reader bias and predicting mood shift in vast populations (Flaounas et al., 2013;

Lansdall-Welfare et al., 2012; Ritter et al., 2011), studies on computational modeling of human natural conversational acts are rare, especially for investigating associations with social behavioral outcomes.

Doctor-patient conversations have been proved highly consequential on a lot of worldwide public health problems and population health outcomes (Zolnierek and DiMatteo., 2009; Mangione-Smith et al., 2015). Over-prescription of antibiotics is often related to interaction-generated problems arising from doctor-patient conversations, which has little to do with rational medical judgments (Macfarlane et al., 1997). For example, some parent language practices are frequently understood by physicians as advocating antibiotics, resulting in significantly higher likelihood of inappropriate prescriptions (Mangione-Smith et al., 1999; Stivers, 2002, 2007).

This antibiotic resistance and over-prescription phenomenon also has its presence in China. Prescription rates of antibiotics is high (Li et al., 2012; Wang et al., 2014; Xiao et al., 2012); multiple types of antibiotic resistant pathogens have been discovered nationwide. However, determinants of the over-prescription problem in China have not been well studied, especially the impact of doctor-patient conversation in medical consultations.

In this proposal, we propose a corpus based study to examine doctor-patient conversation of antibiotic treatment negotiation in Chinese pediatric settings, using a mixed methodology of conversation analysis and computational linguistics. Particularly, we aim to discover (1) how parent requests of antibiotic prescriptions are made in doctor-patient conversations and their effects on prescribing decision outcomes; (2) how physicians' non-antibiotic treatment recommendations are delivered and responded by parents; In conducting this study, our findings about doctor-

Proceedings of the 55th Annual Meeting of the Association for Computational Linguistics- Student Research Workshop, pages 142–149
Vancouver, Canada, July 30 - August 4, 2017. ©2017 Association for Computational Linguistics
https://doi.org/10.18653/v1/P17-3023

patient conversation are expected to be extended beyond medical setting to natural human conversations. These findings include:

- How actions are formulated with various forms of language practice in conversations;

- How meaning of language practices is understood by speakers as performing a certain action;

- How choice of one form of language practices in performing an action is associated with its response of various kinds.

In conducting this study, we attempt to bridge the gap between social scientific methods and computational methods in researching the aforementioned questions.

In the following sections, we will introduce our corpus, preliminary findings from CA, and related computational approaches. This is followed by a discussion of contributions of the proposed study.

2 Data

The corpus of this study is constructed from natural human conversations. In order to obtain the conversations, 318 video-recorded doctor-patient conversations were collected in 6 Chinese hospitals between September and December in 2013. Each conversation is around 5 minutes in length, resulting in 30 hours of video-recordings in total. The conversations were mostly between doctors and patients' caregivers regarding patients' health conditions and lifestyle-related issues that are commonly discussed in pediatrics.

Video-recordings were then transcribed manually. Six researchers were employed to transcribe the data, including one manager and five annotators. All of them are native speakers of Chinese. The five annotators received basic training in CA and its transcribing conventions before they started transcribing. The manager is a specialist in CA, who controlled the work flow and troubleshot during the transcribing process.

Following the Jeffersonian transcribing conventions (Jefferson, 2004), the video-recorded conversational data were transcribed with considerable details with respect to speech production, including the speech text verbatim and other paralinguistic features such as intonations, overlaps, visible non-verbal activities and noticeable timed silence (Auer et al., 1992).

TID	SID	RID	UID	Speech text
1	1	0	M	您好. 就是咳嗽. Hello. He's just coughing.
2	2	0	D	((处理病历文件)) ((Processing medical document))
3	3	0	D	来看过的, 是啊? You have visited us for this, have you?
4	3	3	M	嗯, 那天晚上来挂了急诊室,= Yeah, we came to the emergency room that night.
5	4	4	D	=嗯, 嗯. Yeah, yeah.

Table 1: An example of annotated conversation.

To answer our research questions, we developed an annotation schema, capturing the following aspects of the conversations, including (1) turn-taking and speakership (TID, UID), (2) multi-turn dependency relations, such as adjacency pair[1] (SID) and rhetorical relations[2] (RID). In addition, the speech text was also word segmented corresponding to Chinese Penn Tree Bank segmentation guideline (Xia et al., 2000). An example of the corpus is shown in Table 1.

The current annotated corpus contains 318 conversations with nearly 40K turns and 470K Chinese characters. It has on average 123 turns and 81 adjacency pairs in each conversation. The average number of participants is 3 in each conversation, with a minimum of 2 speakers and a maximum of 8 speakers.

3 Conversation Analysis

Conversation analysis (CA) is used to identify the dialogue acts in the corpus. CA views sequence organization a core feature of conversation that is important for understanding the meaning of an utterance and its significance as an action in conversation (Schegloff, 1968). The idea is that the action which some talk is doing can be grounded in its position, not just its composition. Therefore, some talk (e.g. "It's raining.") can be heard as an answer to a question (e.g. "Are we going to the game?"), even they are apparently semantically unrelated. The relationship of adjacency between turns is central to the ways in which talk in conversation is organized and understood (Schegloff,

---

[1] A basic sequential relationship defined in conventional conversation analysis literature, to be explained in the next section.

[2] RID: Information reflecting topical relevances across turns.

2007). The adjacency relationship most powerfully operates in two ways: (1) backwards - next turns are understood by co-participants to display their speaker's understanding of the prior turn and to embody an action responsive to the prior turn so understood; (2) prospective - a first pair part in an adjacency pair projects some prospective relevance rules for the second pair part. Specifically, it makes relevant a limited set of possible second pair parts, and thereby sets some terms by which a next turn will be understood (Schegloff, 2007).

The methodology of CA relies on audio or video-recordings of naturally occurring conversations, which are then transcribed in details for analyses of turns and sequences in the conversation (Sidnell et al., 2013) and the embodied actions that speakers use to accomplish their goals in social interactions (Drew and Heritage, 1992; Drew et al., 2001). In general, CA looks for patterns in the conversation which form evidence of systematic usage that can be identified as a 'practice' through which people accomplish a social action. To be identified as a practice, a particular communication behavior must be seen to be recurrent and to be routinely treated by recipients in a way such that it can be discriminated from related or similar practices (Heritage, 1984; Stivers, 2005).

Utilizing CA, we identify parent practices of making requests and physician practices making treatment recommendations in our corpus. These findings are then used for developing an annotation schema for computational modeling of these dialogue acts and the associations with their responses or action outcomes.

4 Preliminary Results

Based on conversation analytical study, we find that four parent language practices are recurrently treated by physicians as requesting antibiotic treatment:

- Explicit requests of an antibiotic treatment;

- Desire statements of an antibiotic treatment;

- Inquiries about an antibiotic treatment;

- Evaluations of a past treatment.

Among the four language practices, only the first practice takes a canonical form of request (e.g., *"Can you prescribe me some antibiotics?"*), while the other three practices take less explicit language

formats, putting varying degree of impositions on physicians' responsive acts.

For example, an explicit request of antibiotic treatment is the strongest form of request as it puts the highest degree of impositions on physicians' responsive action, by making physicians' grant or rejection of the request relevant in the next turn. In contrast, a statement of desire for antibiotic treatment does not put physicians under any constraint for granting an antibiotic prescription, but it generates an understanding that prescribing antibiotics is a desirable act under this circumstance. Similarly, an inquiry about antibiotics raises antibiotic treatment as a topic for discussion and implicates a preference for the treatment, yet it does not put physicians under the constraint as an explicit request does. Moreover, a positive evaluation of past experience with antibiotics may be subject to physicians' understanding as desiring for antibiotics for the current condition, yet it does not even require any response physicians as an inquiry about antibiotics does.

The CA study of the requesting practices enables us to identify the utterances that are recurrently understood or subject to speakers' understanding as doing the act of requesting. In addition, we find that explicit requests are least frequently used by parents, while less explicit forms of requests occur more frequently. Table 2 describes the frequency (number of cases) and percentage of the requesting practices out of total number of cases in the corpus.

In order to quantitatively investigate the correlation between the presence of the requesting practices and the prescribing decision outcomes, we conduct a Pearson's χ^2 test between the two variables X and Y, where X is whether parents use at least one of the four requesting practices, and Y is whether they receive an antibiotic treatment by the end of the consultation. The χ^2 test suggests that parents using at least one of the four requesting practices is significantly associated with that they receive an antibiotic treatment (χ^2=5.625, $df = 1$[3], $p = 0.018$[4]). It is worth noting that this is an approximation of the correlation between parent use of the requesting practices and the prescribing outcomes. Investigation of correlations between individual parent requesting practices and the prescribing outcomes will be carried out in our ongo-

---

[3]Degrees of freedom.
[4]At the 0.05 significance level.

Request	Frequency	Percentage
Explicit requests	23	7.23%
Desire statements	38	11.94%
Inquiries	90	28.30%
Evaluations	69	21.70%
Total	220	69.17%

Table 2: Distribution of requesting practices in the corpus. Each cell reports the number of cases (and percentage) containing the practice.

Recommendation	Frequency	Percentage
Assertions	128	51.00%
Proposals	87	34.66%
Offers	31	12.35%
Total	246	98.01%

Table 3: Distribution of recommending practices in the corpus. Each cell reports the number of cases (and percentage) containing the corresponding practice.

ing work. Moreover, computational methods will also be introduced to examine the correlations.

In examining what kind of treatment recommendations are more likely to be resisted by parents, we investigate the association between physicians' non-antibiotic treatment recommendations and parents' responses in the next turn.

One way to distinguish the delivery format of a non-antibiotic treatment recommendation is whether it is negative-format or positive-format (Stivers, 2005). A negative-format recommendation is to recommend against a particular treatment (e.g., *"She doesn't need any antibiotics."*); while a positive-format one is to recommend for a particular treatment (e.g., *"I'm gonna give her some cough medicine."*). Findings from the American pediatric settings show that physicians' positive-format recommendations are less likely to engender parent resistant response to a non-antibiotic treatment recommendation than negative-format recommendations, and thus suggests that recommendations delivered in an affirmative, specific form are most receptive to parents for non-antibiotic treatment (Stivers, 2005).

Beyond distinguishing the recommendations into positive-format and negative-format, there are many other features which could be taken into consideration regarding to their consequences on parents' responses (e.g. epistemic stances[5] and deontic stances[6] that are embodied in the recommending practices). For example, physicians' treatment recommendations can be produced with the following types, including assertions, proposals and offers. The assertions are recommen-

dations such as *"You have to take some fever medicine."*. Proposals are such as *"Why don't you take some cough syrup?"*. Offers are mostly recommendations that are offered following parent indication of their treatment preference or desires, e.g. *"I'll give you some fever medicine if you want."*. The assertions index higher physician epistemic and deontic rights in terms of who knows the best about the treatment and who determines what the patient needs to do respectively. Compared to assertions, physicians claim less epistemic and deontic authority by using the proposal format; and offers embody the least amount epistemic and deontic primacy. Table 3 describes the distribution of physicians' practices of making treatment recommendations across the corpus.

We also conduct a Pearson's χ^2 test between physicians' choice of recommending practice and parent response. The test shows that we cannot reject the null hypothesis that physicians' choices of recommending practice type are independent of parent response types (χ^2=0.327, $df = 2$, $p = 0.849$). Thus our ongoing work is to examine other complexities of treatment recommending practices and their effect on parents' response.

5 Computational Approach

Conversation analysis allows us to manually identify language practices that are recurrently understood and subject to speaker understanding of doing a particular act; while computational approach is used to assist tasks such as entity type recognition, dialogue act classification, and analyses of interested correlations in a more scalable way.

Early research (Jurafsky et al., 1998; Stolcke et al., 2000) on computational modeling of conversational language has demonstrated that automatic modeling based on manually transcribed conversational data by including features such as speakership, dependency relations have achieved supe-

---

[5]The epistemic stance refers to speakers' orientation toward the relative primacy/subordination in terms of their knowledge access. See (Heritage and Raymond, 2005) for more details.

[6]The deontic stance refers to speakers' orientation toward their relative primacy/subordination in terms of their rights to decide future events. See (Stevanovic and Peräkylä, 2014) for more details.

rior performance results compared to datasets otherwise. In using the computational approach in our study, several techniques will be used. In general, we can divide our computational tasks into two categories, fundamental and dialogue specific tasks.

5.1 Fundamental Tasks

Fundamental tasks mainly involve solving general problems that are across all language processing tasks, e.g. named entity recognition and coreference resolution. This part of work lays foundations for more advanced dialogue specific tasks to be discussed in the next section.

5.1.1 Named Entity Recognition

Entities are very important in spoken language understanding, as it conveys key information in determining task objectives, intents, etc. In the medical domain, entity recognition is particularly crucial in identifying information such as treatment or prescriptions. As a fundamental natural language processing (NLP) technique for various tasks, e.g. machine translation (Babych and Hartley, 2003), information retrieval (Guo et al., 2009), named entity recognition (NER) (Nadeau and Sekine, 2007) is also used in our study. Using NER in our study has several challenges. For example, utterances in dialogues are shorter compared to other types of texts. Also, NER is conducted on Chinese. Thus, domain specific word segmentation (Song and Xia, 2012) is a prerequisite if we extend our work to larger datasets in a more scalable way. However, using NER in our study has the advantage that utterances in dialogues are not isolated. The sequential relations between the utterances thus potentially provides us with more information to build a better model. Previous work (Weston et al., 2015) proved that information extraction which takes into account information from previous utterances with recurrent neural networks was more effective. NER in our study can provide more in-depth annotations to the corpus, allowing models trained on the corpus to incorporate more information. To accelerate the annotation process, semi-supervised methods are used for dialogue acts recognition and classification. Specifically, we annotate some seed data, use the trained model to automatically annotate the rest, and finally check the automatically generated annotations manually.

5.1.2 Coreference Resolution

In natural language, reference is used widely for communication efficiency. In dialogue environments, person reference and even omissions are very common. Therefore, coreference resolution can help us add useful semantic information into our language models (Recasens et al., 2013; Clark and Manning, 2015). General coreference resolution is usually performed on multiple sentences in a document; however, the relations of these sentences are vague. Based on our multi-turn rhetorical relation annotations, information that are absent or abstract in a turn can be extracted from turns that are rhetorically related. This could effectively enhance the performance of coreference resolution and provide more accurate information about the referent. For example, the pronoun *that* may not be clear about what it refers to in one utterance; however, the co-reference resolution technique links it to previous turns which contain the information of its referent.

5.2 Dialogue Specific Tasks

Our research is closely related to the studies on dialogue systems (Henderson, 2015), in which models are built to structure conversations. To achieve our research goals, models are built to track states in a dialogue and to build connections between utterances and action outcomes.

5.2.1 Dialogue State Modeling

One important task is to classify types of an utterance and types of the action required. For example, to judge whether an utterance is a question, answer, or other dialogue act, classification can be performed, taking into account turns in previous context. Previous work (Henderson et al., 2013; Ren et al., 2014) demonstrated that using a classifier was effective for modeling user intents and utterance types. In our research, we will use this approach to classify utterances into different types such as dialogue acts, parent responses and treatment decisions. In order to perform such classification, further annotations are conducted based on the findings of conversation analyses, including:

- Dialogue act - parent requests for antibiotic treatment, physician treatment recommendations;

- Treatment type - antibiotic or non-antibiotic treatment;

- Response type - grant or rejection to recommendation.

By using these classifiers, it allows us to investigate the features that are most important for classifying the utterances, and then align them with the qualitative findings from CA studies.

Another way to model dialogue states is treating dialogues as a sequence of observations and then build models (e.g., CRF (Lafferty et al., 2001), LSTM (Hochreiter and Schmidhuber, 1997)) to perform labeling or classification based on that. This is a natural way of modeling dialogues in terms of the problem proximity. Current state-of-the-art studies suggest that LSTM is a good choice for modeling not only sequences of turns, but also sequences of words (or other basic units) within a turn (Zilka and Jurcícek, 2015). Using our corpus, an LSTM model can be trained to achieve the same goal as static classifiers for practice type classification, and to model the sequential relationship between turns in real conversations.

Previous studies (Lee and Eskenazi, 2013; Williams, 2014; Henderson et al., 2014) found that systems combining the classifier approach and the sequence model approach showed competitive results. In doing so, one can train several different models with different sets of parameters and join their results accordingly (Henderson et al., 2014). For the aforementioned classification and sequence modeling tasks, the combined model is expected to outperform individual models.

5.2.2 Domain Adaptation

Since our data is of the particular domain of medicine, domain adaptation is another task involved in our research. Almost all of the aforementioned tasks can be affected by domain specific variance. Besides, conversational data in medical domain is also lacking. Therefore, acquiring more data from other or general domain can be useful in completing the tasks in the medical domain, and improving the capability of conversational understanding, Training data selection/acquisition (Axelrod et al., 2011; Song et al., 2012) could be the first step to solve the problem of domain variance, without the need to modify the existing models to fit our domain. Moreover, when this work has to be extended to other domains, e.g., law, education, etc., domain adaptation is required to transfer the knowledge from this domain to another.

6 Discussion

In this proposal, we propose a study on doctor-patient conversations based on a corpus of naturally occurring medical conversation that are transcribed and annotated manually. With the combination of the social science research method of conversation analysis and computational methods for language modeling, we aim to discover how language practices in doctor-patient conversation influence antibiotic over-prescribing.

Although previous studies (Macfarlane et al., 1997; Mangione-Smith et al., 1999; Stivers, 2007) proved that doctor-patient conversation were consequential on medical decision-making and population health outcomes, findings from the extant social science research are still limited in answering the question *"in what way the language practices that doctors and patients use in medical consultations influence the decision outcomes"*.

Based on our preliminary findings from the CA studies, we propose to use the computational approach to help answer our research questions. In doing so, language patterns that are interested in CA studies can be automatically modeled and predicted with classifier or sequence models, leading us to more interesting findings. Also, by using the computational approach, we can also build a dialogue system based on our corpus. This system can be useful for analyzing doctor-patient conversation and assisting decision-making process in medical consultations.

In addition, we constructed a manually transcribed and annotated corpus. Our ongoing work involves formalizing and adding additional annotations to the corpus. We will release the corpus to the community in near future. It will be a unique resource for both social scientific and computational linguistic studies of conversations in the medical domain.

References

Peter Auer, Frank Muller, and Elizabeth Couper-Kuhlen. 1992. *Language in Time: The Rhythm and Tempo of Spoken Interaction*. Oxford University Press, New York.

John Langshaw Austin. 1962. *How to do things with words*. William James Lectures. Oxford University Press.

Amittai Axelrod, Xiaodong He, and Jianfeng Gao. 2011. Domain adaptation via pseudo in-domain data selection. In *Proceedings of the 2011 Conference on Empirical Methods in Natural Language Processing (EMNLP-2011)*. pages 355–362.

Bogdan Babych and Anthony Hartley. 2003. Improving machine translation quality with automatic named entity recognition. In *Proceedings of the 7th International EAMT Workshop on MT and Other Language Technology Tools, Improving MT Through Other Language Technology Tools: Resources and Tools for Building MT*. Association for Computational Linguistics, Stroudsburg, PA, USA, EAMT '03, pages 1–8.

Kevin Clark and Christopher D. Manning. 2015. Entity-centric coreference resolution with model stacking. In *Association for Computational Linguistics (ACL)*.

Paul Drew, John Chatwin, and Sarah Collins. 2001. Conversation Analysis: A Aethod for Research into Interactions between Patients and Health-care Professionals. *Health Expectations* 4:58–70.

Paul Drew and John Heritage. 1992. Analyzing talk at work: an introduction. In Paul Drew and John Heritage, editors, *Talk at work: interaction in institutional settings*, Cambridge University Press, Cambridge, pages 3–65.

Ilias Flaounas, Omar Ali, Thomas Lansdall-Welfare, Tijl De Bie, Nick Mosdell, Justin Lewis, and Nello Cristianini. 2013. Research methods in the age of digital journalism. *Digital Journalism* 1(1):102–116.

Jiafeng Guo, Gu Xu, Xueqi Cheng, and Hang Li. 2009. Named entity recognition in query. In *Proceedings of the 32Nd International ACM SIGIR Conference on Research and Development in Information Retrieval*. ACM, New York, NY, USA, SIGIR '09, pages 267–274.

Matthew Henderson. 2015. Machine learning for dialog state tracking: A review. In *Proceedings of The First International Workshop on Machine Learning in Spoken Language Processing*.

Matthew Henderson, Blaise Thomson, and Steve Young. 2013. Deep neural network approach for the dialog state tracking challenge. In *Proceedings of the SIGDIAL 2013 Conference*. Metz, France, pages 467–471.

Matthew Henderson, Blaise Thomson, and Steve Young. 2014. Word-based dialog state tracking with recurrent neural networks. In *Proceedings of the 15th Annual Meeting of the Special Interest Group on Discourse and Dialogue (SIGDIAL)*. Philadelphia, PA, U.S.A., pages 292–299.

John Heritage. 1984. *Garfinkel and Ethnomethodology*. Polity Press, Cambridge.

John Heritage and Douglas W. Maynard. 2006. *Communication in Medical Care: Interaction between Primary Care Physicians and Patients*. Number 20 in Studies in Interactional Sociolinguistics. Cambridge University Press, Cambridge.

John Heritage and Geoffrey Raymond. 2005. The terms of agreement: Indexing epistemic authority and subordination in assessment sequences. *Social Psychology Quarterly* 68:15–38.

Sepp Hochreiter and Jürgen Schmidhuber. 1997. Long short-term memory. *Neural Comput.* 9(8):1735–1780.

Gail Jefferson. 2004. Glossary of transcript symbols with an introduction. In Gene H. Lerner, editor, *Conversation Analysis: Studies from the First Generation*. John Benjamins, Amsterdam / Philadelphia, chapter 2, pages 13–31.

Daniel Jurafsky, Rebecca Bates, Noah Coccaro, Rachel Martin, Marie Meteer, Klaus Ries, Elizabeth Shriberg, Andreas Stolcke, Paul Taylor, and Carol Van Ess-Dykema. 1998. Switchboard discourse language modeling project report. *Center for Speech and Language Processing, Johns Hopkins University, Baltimore, MD* .

John D. Lafferty, Andrew McCallum, and Fernando C. N. Pereira. 2001. Conditional random fields: Probabilistic models for segmenting and labeling sequence data. In *Proceedings of the Eighteenth International Conference on Machine Learning*. Morgan Kaufmann Publishers Inc., San Francisco, CA, USA, ICML '01, pages 282–289.

Thomas Lansdall-Welfare, Vasileios Lampos, and Nello Cristianini. 2012. Effects of the recession on public mood in the uk. In *Proceedings of the 21st International Conference on World Wide Web*. ACM, New York, NY, USA, pages 1221–1226.

Sungjin Lee and Maxine Eskenazi. 2013. Recipe for building robust spoken dialog state trackers: Dialog state tracking challenge system description. In *Proceedings of the SIGDIAL 2013 Conference*. Association for Computational Linguistics, Metz, France, pages 414–422.

Stephen C. Levinson. 1983. *Pragmatics*. Cambridge University Press.

Yongbin Li, Jing Xu, Fang Wang, Bin Wang, Liqun Liu, Wanli Hou, Hong Fan, Yeqing Tong, Juan Zhang, and Zuxun Lu. 2012. Overprescribing in china, driven by financial incentives, results in very high use of antibiotics, injections, and corticosteroids. *Health Affairs (Project Hope)* 31(5):1075–1082.

J. Macfarlane, W. Holmes, R. Macfarlane, and N. Britten. 1997. Influence of patients' expectations on antibiotic management of acute lower respiratory tract illness in general practice: questionnaire study. *BMJ* 315(7117):1211–1214.

R. Mangione-Smith, E. A. McGlynn, M. N. Elliott, P. Krogstad, and R. H. Brook. 1999. The relationship between perceived parental expectations and pediatrician antimicrobial prescribing behavior. *Pediatrics* 103(4):711–718.

R. Mangione-Smith, C. Zhou, J. D. Robinson, J. A. Taylor, M. N. Elliott, and J. Heritage. 2015. Communication practices and antibiotic use for acute respiratory tract infections in children. *Annals of Family Medicine* 13(3):221–227.

David Nadeau and Satoshi Sekine. 2007. A survey of named entity recognition and classification. *Linguisticae Investigationes* 30(1):3–26.

Marta Recasens, Matthew Can, and Dan Jurafsky. 2013. Same referent, different words: Unsupervised mining of opaque coreferent mentions. In *North American Association for Computational Linguistics (NAACL)*.

Hang Ren, Weiqun Xu, and Yonghong Yan. 2014. Markovian discriminative modeling for dialog state tracking. In *Proceedings of the 15th Annual Meeting of the Special Interest Group on Discourse and Dialogue (SIGDIAL)*. Philadelphia, PA, U.S.A., pages 327–331.

Alan Ritter, Colin Cherry, and William B. Dolan. 2011. Data-driven Response Generation in Social Media. In *Proceedings of the Conference on Empirical Methods in Natural Language Processing*. Stroudsburg, PA, USA, EMNLP '11, pages 583–593.

Emanuel Schegloff. 2007. *Sequence organization in interaction: Volume 1: A primer in conversation analysis*. Cambridge University Press.

Emanuel A. Schegloff. 1968. Sequencing in Conversational Openings. *American Anthropologist* 70(6):1075–1095.

Julian J. Schlöder and Raquel Fernandez. 2015. Clarifying Intentions in Dialogue: A Corpus Study. In *Proceedings of the 11th International Conference on Computational Semantics*. London, UK, pages 46–51.

Jack Sidnell, Tanya Stivers, and Eds. 2013. *The Handbook of Conversation Analysis*. Wiley-Blackwell.

Yan Song, Prescott Klassen, Fei Xia, and Chunyu Kit. 2012. Entropy-based Training Data Selection for Domain Adaptation. In *Proceedings of COLING-2012*. Mumbai, India, pages 1191–1200.

Yan Song and Fei Xia. 2012. Using a Goodness Measurement for Domain Adaptation: A Case Study on Chinese Word Segmentation. In *Proceedings of LREC-2012*. Istanbul, Turkey, pages 3853–3860.

Melisa Stevanovic and Anssi Peräkylä. 2014. Three Orders in the Organization of Human Action: On the Interface between Knowledge, Power, and Emotion in interaction and social relations. *Language in Society* 43(2):185–207.

Tanya Stivers. 2002. Participating in Decisions about Treatment: Overt Parent Pressure for Antibiotic Medication in Pediatric Encounters. *Social Science and Medicine* 54(7):1111–1130.

Tanya Stivers. 2005. Non-antibiotic treatment recommendations: Delivery formats and implications for parent resistance. *Social Science & Medicine* 5(60):949–964.

Tanya Stivers. 2007. *Prescribing under Pressure: Parent-physician Conversations and Antibiotics*. Oxford University Press, London.

Andreas Stolcke, Noah Coccaro, Rebecca Bates, Paul Taylor, Carol Van Ess-Dykema, Klaus Ries, Elizabeth Shriberg, Daniel Jurafsky, Rachel Martin, and Marie Meteer. 2000. Dialogue act modeling for automatic tagging and recognition of conversational speech. *Computational Linguistics* 26(3):339–373.

Jin Wang, Pan Wang, Xinghe Wang, Yingdong Zheng, and Yonghong Xiao. 2014. Use and prescription of antibiotics in primary health care settings in china. *JAMA Internal Medicine* 174(12):1914–1920.

Jason Weston, Antoine Bordes, Sumit Chopra, and Tomas Mikolov. 2015. Towards ai-complete question answering: A set of prerequisite toy tasks. *ArXiv pre-prints* abs/1502.05698.

Jason Williams, Antoine Raux, Deepak Ramachandran, and Alan Black. 2013. The Dialog State Tracking Challenge. In *Proceedings of the SIGDIAL 2013 Conference*. Metz, France, pages 404–413.

Jason D Williams. 2014. Web-style ranking and slu combination for dialog state tracking. In *Proceedings of the 15th Annual Meeting of the Special Interest Group on Discourse and Dialogue (SIGDIAL)*. Philadelphia, PA, U.S.A., pages 282–291.

Fei Xia, Martha Palmer, Nianwen Xue, Mary Ellen Okurowski, John Kovarik, Fudong Chiou, Shizhe Huang, Tony Kroch, and Mitch Marcus. 2000. Developing Guidelines and Ensuring Consistency for Chinese Text Annotation. In *Proceedings of the Second Language Resources and Evaluation Conference (LREC)*.

YH Xiao, P Shen, ZQ Wei, YB Chen, and HS Kong. 2012. Mohnarin report of 2011, monitoring of bacterial resistance in China. *Chinese Journal of Nosocomiology* 22:4946–4952.

Lukás Zilka and Filip Jurcícek. 2015. Incremental lstm-based dialog state tracker. *ArXiv pre-prints* abs/1507.03471.

Kelly B. Haskard Zolnierek and M. Robin DiMatteo. 2009. Physician communication and patient adherence to treatment: A meta-analysis. *Medical care* 47(8):826–834.

Author Index

Aggarwal, Srishti, 69
Argyraki, Katerina, 100

Babkin, Petr, 114
Bishnu, Ankita, 43

Carrillo, Facundo, 1
Chinchore, Tanmay, 24
Choi, Jinho D., 49

Deshmukh, Pranay, 17
Dupoux, Emmanuel, 62

Espinosa, Kurt Junshean, 128

Fang, Tina, 100

Garber, Matthew, 89, 95
Grover, Jeenu, 11

Hanumanth Rao, Aishwarya, 24
Haribhakta, Yashodhara, 17
Hiraga, Misato, 107

Jaggi, Martin, 100
Jamadagni, H. S., 24
Jawahar, Ganesh, 4

Kajiwara, Tomoyuki, 36
Kamble, Vibhavari, 17
Kitsuregawa, Masaru, 120
Komachi, Mamoru, 36

Li, Hang, 56
Lingaraju, G. M., 24
Litman, Diane, 75

Ma, Kaixin, 49
Maharnawar, Sanket, 17
Mamidi, Radhika, 69
Martin, Shane Michael, 24
Michel, Paul, 62
Mitra, Pabitra, 11
Montoya, Orion, 136

Naaman, Noa, 136
Nayak, Nihal V., 24

Nirenburg, Sergei, 114

Odagaki, Masato, 56

Patel, Labhesh, 43
Provenza, Hannah, 136

Ramirez, Jose, 89
Rao, Sudha, 30
Räsänen, Okko, 62

Sato, Shoetsu, 120
Sharma, Vasu, 43
Simha, Sagar Nagaraj, 24
Singer, Meital, 95
Soleymanzadeh, Katira, 82
Sukthankar, Nandan, 17
Suzuki, Yui, 36

Thiolliere, Roland, 62
Toyoda, Masashi, 120

Wang, Haozheng, 56
Wang, Nan, 142
Wang, Xinhao, 89
Ward, Christopher, 95

Xiao, Catherine, 49

Yang, Zhenglu, 56
Yoshinaga, Naoki, 120

Zhang, Haoran, 75

Association for Computational Linguistics
209 N. Eighth Street
Stroudsburg, Pennsylvania 18360

ISBN 978-1-5108-4569-5